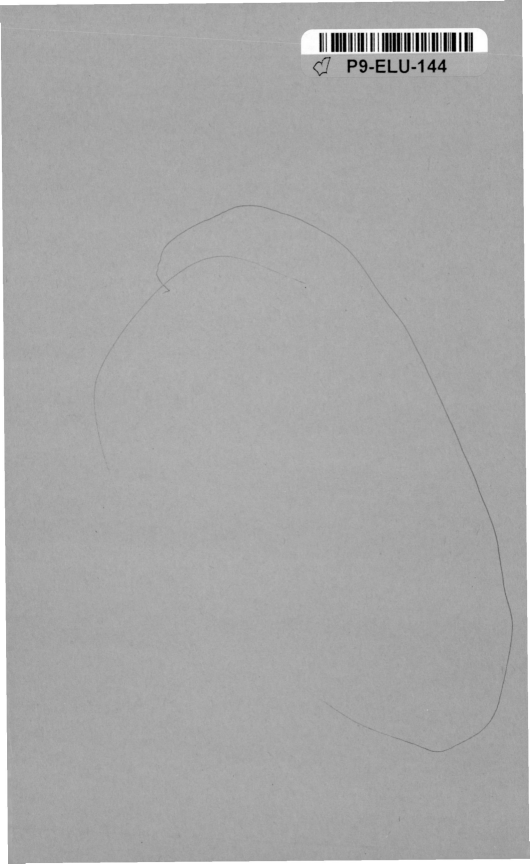

HUMAN INTERACTION
IN THE
SMALL GROUP SETTING

Lawrence B. Rosenfeld

The University of New Mexico

Charles E. Merrill Publishing Company
A Bell & Howell Company
Columbus, Ohio

Published by
Charles E. Merrill Publishing Company
A Bell & Howell Company
Columbus, Ohio 43216

ISBN: 0-675-08997-2

Library of Congress Catalog Card Number: 72-92860

3 4 5 6 7 8 / 78 77 76 75 74

Printed in the United States of America

To
My Grandparents,
Abe and Katie

CONTENTS

PREFACE

Small group communication is of interest to the fields of speech communication, social psychology, and sociology. It is the intent of this book to bring together the research from these areas in an effort to explain small group interaction. Although the emphasis is upon the findings from empirical research, theoretical approaches which lack empirical support at this time have also been considered as sources from which to draw explanations of the phenomena under investigation. Small group interaction involves a great many complex relationships among a variety of variables; therefore, no single approach to the area is sufficient in explaining small group phenomena.

Traditional textbooks on small group behavior have been either psychology or discussion textbooks. Neither type has proven satisfactory: the social psychological approach has spawned textbooks which, though well-researched and interesting, have failed in many instances to provide both evidence of the practical implications and experiences for the student to help him better understand his own behavior in the small group setting. Traditional discussion textbooks have been too narrow in their approach, focusing almost exclusively on the kinds of group behavior that exist only in the classroom.

This book, written for the junior-community college, college, and university levels, offers both theory and practice. While a theoretical perspective is developed and related to the empirical research in a given area, experiences are provided to generate data for analysis. The experiences have all been tested by several teachers, including myself, during the past few years. Although they have proven effective under a wide variety of classroom circumstances, it may be necessary to adapt them to the peculiar circumstances of your setting.

To help emphasize the practical implications of the research findings discussed in each chapter, entries from diaries kept by students engaged in group projects are provided. The entries, which provide insights into group process, have not been altered; they stand as they did in the completed diaries.

Acknowledgments are not only customary, but for this book they are mandatory. Gerry Phillips and Ted Grove helped guide me through the small group literature; they also stimulated my own interest in the area. Arlene has been so damned patient that it's scary. Mary Jensen helped rewrite and rewrite and rewrite the manuscript. It is impossible to assess the influence she has had. Of course, a final acknowledgment must be made to long hair, beautiful eyes, skinny bodies, and whatever else turns us on.

CHAPTER 1

INTRODUCTION

Every organism requires an environment of friends, partly to shield it from violent changes, and partly to supply it with its wants. . . . You may obtain individual specimens of fine trees either in exceptional circumstances, or where human cultivation has intervened. But in nature the normal way in which trees flourish is by their association in a forest. Each tree may lose something of its individual perfection of growth, but they mutually assist each other in preserving the conditions for survival. . . . A forest is the triumph of the organization of mutually dependent species.

Alfred North Whitehead, *Science and the Modern World*

Experience 1-1. Without talking, form groups with no more than four members. Once your group is formed, discuss the following questions:

    1. What is a group?
    2. What effect does the classroom environment have on the group?
    3. What cues did the members give each other to indicate that they were part of the group that was formed?
    4. What effect does the lack of oral verbal communication have on interaction?
    5. Have you attained a group identity?
    6. Can you describe the personalities of each of the members?
    7. Can you differentiate among the roles that are being enacted? Who is the leader?
    8. What problems are encountered, and how are they handled?

1

Human existence is dependent upon society; without social life no human life would be possible. Society is sustained by communication; communication makes human life possible. Social life and communication are two words which imply sharing and participating, but the 1970s is witnessing the rise of existential loneliness, the increased use of the word alienation. As interaction decreases, as we find ourselves farther and farther apart, we become less than social, and human life becomes less than what it could be.

One reason for decreased human contact may be the increased technological sophistication of our generation. Why take the time to walk to a friend's house when it is so much easier to call on the telephone? But the telephone is not real human contact. Human contact is replaced by the telephone voice. Similarly, radio, television, and the movies have separated us from each other, formed barriers between us, eliminated the necessity for human contact. Without human contact communication is curtailed, aborted. We sit and listen, or sit and watch, and realize that we cannot affect the course of action in what we observe. In a sense, communication has not taken place, if, indeed, communication is a form of exchange through which people can come into contact with each other's minds (Newcomb, Turner, and Converse 1965).

Our age, though, may be coming to realize the necessity for human contact. The rise of sensitivity groups, training groups, group marathons, human relations workshops, and the increased use of groups in academic and business settings, all provide evidence that the most efficient means for insuring "survival" is in human contact, face-to-face interaction: interpersonal communication.

Generally, groups provide a variety of experiences. Whether the specific purpose is to provide companionship, share information, solve a particular problem, or provide the group members with therapy, all groups are valuable because they serve the following purposes:

1. Encourage meaningful interaction. Meaningful interaction can best take place when there is face-to-face contact, when individuals acknowledge and adjust to each other's presence. What constitutes meaningful interaction varies from group to group. For example, *casual groups* are not established to solve a particular problem, but rather to provide members with friendship, interesting conversation, and companionship. To the extent that these things are provided, the interaction is meaningful.

2. Facilitate the learning of problem-solving procedures. Working in groups provides individuals with the opportunity to better

understand a variety of views as members present and defend opposing views. During idea development members learn to critically evaluate the ideas of others. Problem solving also entails learning how to deal with conflicts, and how to affect a compromise. Individuals in *problem-solving groups* discover alternatives which are not possible under circumstances where directives and orders are the usual methods for solving problems. Although all groups are problem-solving groups to some extent, the main characteristic of the problem-solving group is that a group goal is established which centers on a problem, goal, or task, and interaction results in a group-generated solution.

3. Facilitate the development of commitments. Individuals in a group normally develop commitments to both the group and its decisions. Group members feel a sense of responsibility and loyalty to one another; as a consequence, group-generated decisions have a higher probability of being enacted than decisions derived from authority figures. *Consciousness-raising groups,* which concentrate on creating an intense group identity, develop strong commitments in group members for each other, as well as for the group's decision to end oppression. Woman's Liberation is an example of a consciousness-raising group (Chesebro, Cragan, and McCullough 1971).

4. Provide a background for understanding the impact of communication, and developing awareness to other people. We affect one another by communicating, and in the small group setting we have the opportunity to learn what our impact as communicators is on others. The small group can provide a means whereby we observe our own behavior, and where we can see how different forms of behavior elicit different responses.

The information flow in the small group setting is intense: not only is factual information presented, but each participant also is bombarded with his own and others' feelings, wishes, commands, desires, and needs. This information may be imparted verbally, nonverbally, intentionally, or unintentionally. The more directly individuals work with others, the better opportunity they will have to become aware of and sensitive to the feelings and emotions of others. *Therapy groups,* such as sensitivity training groups, function with the expressed intent of helping individuals by increasing their awareness. This awareness helps group members to build an individual identity which will facilitate social interaction (Rogers 1970).

A short diary entry written for a five-minute meeting, the fifth of fifteen, reveals the complexity of the small group setting, and the different ways group members experienced the meeting.

November 3: The five-minute meeting.   This was a quickie emergency meeting with a single purpose: what to do with a new member, Jim. I was more upset than the others about having to re-organize, possibly because I already was set on what I wanted to do in the group. The others were more flexible.

The final result: no problem. No new division of labor (or change in idea) was necessary because Jim, the new member, was amenable to anything. I wonder what would have happened if he would have come in with a specific notion of what he wanted the group to do. Would we have been able to accommodate him? Or would he have been able to accommodate us? This was only our fifth meeting, but I believe we had, by now, become a group. We felt responsible to each other and our topic. If he hadn't been so amenable to our plans, I believe there would have been some real conflict.

At any rate, Rosemary jumped in with a request for Jim to work with her. (She was careful to state this as, "Let's work together," rather than, "Let him work with me.") No one seemed to mind. So, Jim was integrated into the group very easily; he fit into what already existed.

The game again: "Leader, leader, who's trying to be leader." The same crap! We all commented on power seats, that is, who was sitting where, and the power of the seat in relation to the others available. Sherri, stating that she wanted to be in a good position, sat down on the coffee table in the middle of the group! That broke things up. When I finally suggested that we get down to business, Paul asked if this was a plea for me to be leader for the meeting. The whole scene became funny. The problem may have been small.

Although the word group already has been used many times, no definition has been offered. How the word group is defined depends on a number of factors, but primarily on the perspective of the individual offering the definition.

Groups may be defined according to certain attributes. Homans's (1950) definition focuses exclusively on *interaction*: "A group is defined by the interaction of its members. [Each member of the group] interacts more often with [the other members] than he does with outsiders" (p. 84). A group may be defined in terms of the *patterns* of its interaction. The definition offered by Merton (1957) specifies that there is patterned interaction which can be identified, and that members have expectations of each other in terms of adherence to the patterns of interaction. These patterns of interaction are usually the result of established norms. Other definitions focus upon *perceptions:* a group is a group if individuals outside the group perceive it to be a group, and if group members themselves perceive the group. Smith (1945) offers such a definition when he writes that a group consists of individuals "who have a collective perception of their unity and who have the ability or tendency to act and/or are acting in a unitary manner toward the environment" (p. 227).

Cartwright and Zander's (1968) definition of "group," the one used to guide this study of small group behavior, is broad enough to encompass the many diverse definitions already presented, yet specific enough to help focus our attention. They define a group as "a collection of individuals who have relations to one another that make them interdependent to some significant degree" (p. 46). This definition provides parameters for group size (as the size increases the opportunity to influence other members decreases), group interaction (it is the result of the interdependency among members), and perceptions (members perceive themselves as part of a group because of the mutual interdependency and influence). The point Cartwright and Zander make about interdependency is worth repeating—individuals in a group influence and are influenced by the other members.

Even with this definition, there is still disagreement about groups. One question related to this problem is, "How real are groups?" From a psychological perspective, the only objective reality is the individual. The social psychological perspective also focuses on the individual, but emphasizes the individual in society. The sociological perspective views the group as a conceptual reality, i e., it may be described without reference to the individual members. The group must be analyzed at the group, not the individual, level. Anthropologists view groups in terms of cultural forces, and developmental stages common to all primates. The writings of Levi-Strauss (1964) and Ardrey (1970) are examples of this approach to the group.

There is difficulty in working from extreme positions. Viewing the group as *only* the sum of its individuals, or as meaningful *only* when studied as a conceptual entity, or as *only* the result of cultural forces, greatly reduces our understanding of the group as an individual and social phenomenon. Campbell (1958) has taken a middle-of-the-road position by admitting that groups vary in the degree to which they have a real existence. One of his most important considerations is the degree to which all the components (individuals) of the entity (group) share a *common fate,* that is, the extent to which they experience similar outcomes. If individuals are perceived as constituting a group, and they appear to be bound together in a relationship where each person shares a position relative to each other person, then the group is seen as a viable entity, something capable of independent existence. A second factor Campbell notes is *similarity.* Perceived member similarity affects whether they will be perceived as a group. Motorcycle gangs may be perceived as a group because members possess the same type of motorcycles and they dress similarly (leather jackets, emblems, or hats). The last consideration, less important than the other two, is *proximity.* The degree to which the members of a unity occupy a common space, or are in close proximity, affects the degree to which they are perceived as a viable entity. It is easier to attribute "groupness" to individuals who share physical environments than to individuals who are physically separated. Whether or not a group is perceived as an entity varies with the strength of these three perceptions. When common fate, similarity, and proximity are perceived, the individuals will be perceived as a group. When none of these are perceived, a group will not be perceived. Between these two points lies a range of responses.

A group is a highly complex structure. It consists of individuals, with all their personal characteristics, interacting with one another in a given environment on a particular task. McGrath and Altman (1966), synthesizing and critiquing small group research, found that the research is concerned with three levels of reference: the *individual,* the *group,* and the *environment.* On the level of the individual, the concern has been with the personality characteristics, abilities, attitudes, and group position of each of the group members. On the group level, group abilities, training, experience, interpersonal relations, and structure have been studied. On the environmental level, the concern focuses upon conditions imposed upon the group, such as the task, operating conditions, and, possibly, the social conditions.

Information provided on the level of the individual is insufficient to predict the level of group performance; information provided on the level of the group alone also is insufficient to predict the level of group performance. Group capabilities may serve to set an upper limit on a group's performance potential. Likewise, information about the environment is insufficient to predict group performance, although it obviously affects it. Therefore, it is necessary to see the combined perspectives of all three approaches to help us better understand small group phenomena.

The component parts of small group interaction are interdependent; they share a relationship in which change in one part produces changes in the others. Studying the *parts,* such as members' personality characteristics and interpersonal relations, without some picture of how these parts fit into a *whole,* is a sure way to develop a false picture of group interaction. Figure 1-1 depicts the relationships among the component parts of small group interaction. Group process takes place over *time,* and with the passage of time change occurs. Group interaction, then, is dynamic—the relationships among component parts are in constant flux.

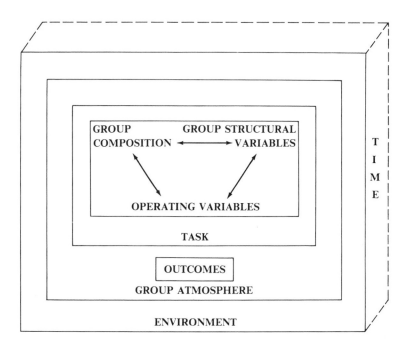

Figure 1-1. *A graphic model of small group interaction*

Group composition includes a host of variables pertaining both to individual group members and how they interact with each other. Individual characteristics include each member's personality, attitudes, beliefs, self-concept, and perceptions of the other members. Interactive variables include group size, combined problem-solving skills, and how well different members can work together. Although it seems that group composition is a "given," such is not necessarily the case. For instance, group procedures which maximize individual usefulness may serve to increase friendly attitudes.

Two group *structural variables* are of concern: the communication network and the attraction network. Communication networks can differ according to type of structure, tightness (how flexible that structure is), and effectiveness (the relationship between the structure and task requirements). The attraction network includes not only who likes whom, but also the formation of cliques and subgroups, and their effects on social-emotional and task development.

Operating variables include the kinds of procedures the group uses in its deliberations, the roles enacted, and the norms and standards set under which the group functions. Deliberation procedures are highly varied. A group may decide to research a problem before discussing it, to divide the problem into small parts which individuals may attack separately, or any one of an infinite number of other procedures. The roles enacted in a group also affect its operation. The number of roles and the willingness and abilities of members to assume necessary roles constitute only three aspects of role enactment which affect the group's behavior. Because norms prescribe the limits of acceptable behavior, they too must be considered in an analysis of group interaction. Group standards are another aspect of interaction. The extent to which members agree on norms and other evaluative criteria (of task solutions, for instance) will affect the degree to which value conflicts are avoidable.

The *task* provides the general framework within which the group operates. It is the prime reason, the rationale, for the group's existence. Aspects of the task which affect the other components of group interaction are critical task demands, that is, those aspects of the task which make certain abilities and procedures crucial to task solution; the complexity of the task; its difficulty; and the goals.

The *outcomes* of group interaction may be analyzed in terms of the quality, quantity, appropriateness, and efficiency of the solution or decision, and member satisfaction with the outcomes. It is important to note that a group's outcomes affect its subsequent interaction; outcomes are not simply the result of group interaction. A solution, for example, does not develop during the last minutes of discussion. The last minutes of discussion result from a decision to accept a certain solution. Last minute interaction is aimed at reinforcing the decision, and insuring that the members are in agreement. According to Collins and Guetzkow (1964), member satisfaction is a function of task success, success in solving interpersonal problems, and member position in the group. Both high power and a position of centrality produce member satisfaction.

The *group atmosphere* is the emotional framework within which the group operates. The group atmosphere or climate may be hostile, it may be conducive to work, and it may be affected by the task, the environment (which can create pressures under which the group must operate), and group composition.

Group interaction, structural and operating variables, atmosphere, task, and outcomes take place within a given *environment.* The environment places limitations on the group, and may serve as a facilitative or debilitative agent for task accomplishemnt. The environment includes such things as the physical area in which the group meets, the materials it either does or does not have, and other groups with which the group may or may not be in competition. Time limits are also an environmental restriction.

Proficiency in small group interaction is enhanced by experience and knowledge. The aim of this book is to provide you with both. Knowledge of the various dimensions and perspectives of small group phenomena, combined with both supervised and unsupervised experiences, should increase your effectiveness and satisfaction as a group member. If this were the only rationale for studying small group behavior, it would be sufficient, given the increasing use of groups in our society. But another, possibly more important, rationale is that the small group can, and usually does, function as a microcosm of the larger society. Consequently, the study of small group dynamics will help group members view and, hopefully, understand their social behavior better. Such understanding is crucial if

> what we are saying here to the human being is, "You are mainly responsible for your life situation. You have created your own world. Your own inter-personal behavior has, more than any other factor, determined the reception you get from others. Your slowly developing pattern of reflexes has trained others and yourself to accept you as this sort of person—to be treated in this sort of way. You are the manager of your own destiny." (Leary 1957, pp. 116-17)

Each chapter in this book was written with three goals in mind: (1) to provide the theoretical perspective or background for a given area, (2) to explain or encourage the exploration of the practical implications of the theory, and (3) to direct you in experiences that will provide data for your own analysis of small group interaction. Often, data collection precedes discussion, so it will be necessary to do first, and read about it afterwards. Finally, a fairly comprehensive bibliography is provided at the end of each chapter to facilitate and encourage your reading in each area.

Chapters 2 and 3 provide several broad theoretical perspectives that have guided most of the current thinking about small group dynamics. Chapter 2 presents several conceptual approaches underlying small group formation and operation, and so is concerned with *all* the component parts of small group interaction. Chapter 3 focuses on the *time* component of interaction. Several theoretical approaches to the phase development of groups or the developmental sequences groups go through are presented.

Chapter 4, in exploring the nature of group influence, focuses on the *task, environment, time,* and *operating variables* components of interaction. This chapter considers conformity behavior from the standpoint that it is both necessary and desirable for social interaction. A comparison of individual and group effectiveness is based on the assumption that groups are not always necessary and that they sometimes prove wasteful of time and effort.

Chapters 5 and 6 focus exclusively on *operating variables.* Chapter 5 is concerned with role behavior as it affects both the individual and the group. Chapter 6 focuses on leadership, a specific form of role behavior.

Chapter 7 focuses on a single aspect of *group composition*: member personality characteristics, more specifically with self-concept and how it relates to the small group setting. How we see ourselves, and how we think others see us form the basis for how we interact.

Chapter 8 focuses on *group structural variables* and *group composition.* The effects of various communication networks, differing in the degree to which members are dependent upon and have access to each other, and the effects of various attraction networks, differing in the degree to which members accept and reject each other, are discussed in this chapter. Also of concern is how these variables affect group interaction, which is an aspect of group composition.

Chapter 9 is mainly concerned with *group composition* and *environment,* although with the focus of this chapter on nonverbal behavior, all of the various components of interaction are affected. Whereas verbal behavior is best suited for expressing ideas and thoughts, nonverbal behavior is best suited for expressing emotions and feelings. Since group processes may be thought of as both affective and cognitive, an understanding of nonverbal behavior will increase our ability to react and interact effectively with group members.

Chapter 10 considers *all* the component parts of small group interaction as it focuses on problems and breakdowns that occur when individuals interact to achieve some goal. Some suggestions for coping with these situations are also offered.

A Final Note

Chapters 2 and 3 will require close reading, as theoretical chapters often do. By chapter 4 it should be clear sailing.

Bibliography

Ardrey, R. *The Social Contract.* New York: Atheneum, 1970.

Ayer, A. J. "What Is Communication?" In *Studies in Communication,* pp. 11-28. London: Secker and Warburg, 1955.

Barnlund, D. C., ed. *Interpersonal Communication: Survey and Studies.* Boston: Houghton Mifflin, 1968.

Bass, B. M. *Leadership, Psychology, and Organizational Behavior.* New York: Harper, 1960.

Brown, R. *Social Psychology.* New York: Free Press, 1965.

Campbell, D. T. "Common Fate, Similarity, and Other Indices of the Status of Aggregates of Persons as Social Entities." *Behavioral Science* 3 (1958): 14-25.

Cartwright, D., and Zander, A., eds. *Group Dynamics: Research and Theory.* New York: Harper and Row, 1968.

Chesebro, J., Cragan, J., and McCullough, P. "The Small Group Technique of the Radical-Revolutionary: A Synthetic Study of Consciousness Raising." Paper presented at the Speech Communication Association annual convention, December 1971.

Collins, B. E., and Guetzkow, H. *A Social Psychology of Group Processes for Decision-Making.* New York: Wiley, 1964.

Doll, H. "The Closer We Come the Further We Get: Some Thoughts on Empathic and Psychic Distance." Paper presented at the Speech Communication Association annual convention, December 1971.

Foulkes, S. H. *Therapeutic Group Analysis.* New York: International Universities Press, 1965.

Golembiewski, R. T. *The Small Group: An Analysis of Research Concepts and Operations.* Chicago: University of Chicago Press, 1962.

Hare, A. P., Borgotta, E., and Bales, R. F. *Small Groups: Studies in Social Interaction.* New York: Knopf, 1966.

Homans, G. C. *The Human Group.* New York: Harcourt, Brace, 1950.

Hymes, D. "The Anthropology of Communication." In *Human Communication Theory—Original Essays,* edited by F. E. X. Dance. New York: Holt, Rinehart and Winston, 1967.

Klein, J. *The Study of Groups.* London: Routledge and Kegan Paul, 1956.

Leary, T. *Interpersonal Diagnosis of Personality.* New York: Ronald Press, 1957.

Levi-Strauss, C. *Social Structure: Structural Anthropology.* New York: Basic Books, 1964, pp. 277-323.

McGrath, J. E., and Altman, I. *Small Group Research: A Synthesis and Critique of the Field.* New York: Holt, Rinehart and Winston, 1966.

Merton, R. K. *Social Theory and Social Structure.* Rev. ed. Glencoe, Illinois: Free Press, 1957.

Mowrer, O. H. *The New Group Therapy.* Princeton: Van Nostrand, 1964.

Newcomb, T. M., Turner, R. H. and Converse, P. E. *Social Psychology.* New York: Holt, Rinehart and Winston, 1965.

Phillips, G. M. *Communication and the Small Group.* Indianapolis: Bobbs-Merrill, 1966.

Phillips, G. M., and Erickson, E. C. *Interpersonal Dynamics in the Small Group.* New York: Random House, 1970.

Rogers, C. *On Becoming a Person.* Boston: Houghton Mifflin, 1961.

———. *On Encounter Groups.* New York: Harper and Row, 1970.

Ruitenbeek, H. *Group Therapy Today.* New York: Atherton, 1969.

Smith, M. "Social Situation, Social Behavior, Social Group." *Psychological Review* 52 (1945):224-29.

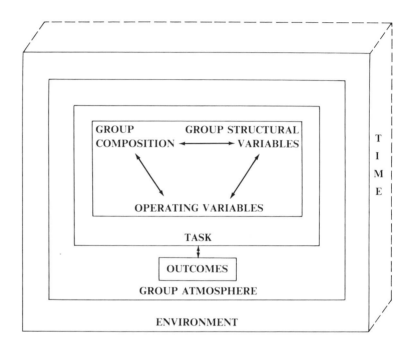

CHAPTER 2

CONCEPTUAL ORIENTATIONS

A line in a contemporary song suggests that "what you see is what you get." Underlying this notion is the idea that what you *expect* to see determines to a large extent what you *do* see. If several people observe the same group interacting, each observer will probably make a unique analysis of the behavior that occurred, as in the case of the blind men trying to describe the elephant. Similarly, how you conceive small group behavior helps determine what things you focus upon when observing or participating in small group interaction.

Accepting one conceptualization which explains the behavior we observe may blind us to other explanations. But, because of the complexity of small group interaction, analyzing a group without some expectations about what is going to take place would be a frustrating experience. For example, if you conceive of small group interaction as a process in which an equilibrium between social and task forces is sought so task work can be accomplished, then you would focus on the group's social and task behavior, note the interaction between these two, and try to understand the problems which exist as one or the other becomes the group's predominant concern.

This chapter outlines several ways to look at small group interaction which have guided the investigation of questions such as the following. Why do groups form at all? What is the basis for interaction? What generalizations can we make about interaction which will apply to all people engaged in small group behavior?

Interpersonal Needs: William Schutz

Why do we join groups? Why do we want other people to join our groups? Why is it that groups are such an integral and important part of our lives? William Schutz, in *FIRO: A Three Dimensional Theory of Interpersonal Behavior,* answers these and related questions by explaining that individuals have *interpersonal needs* which parallel biological needs in importance. Not satisfying interpersonal needs results in insanity.

Schutz states that every individual has three interpersonal needs: inclusion, control, and affection. An analysis of these three needs is sufficient to explain and predict interpersonal phenomena. An interpersonal need is one which can only be satisfied through an interpersonal relationship (a relationship in which A takes account of B when making decision D).

Inclusion is defined as each individual's need to establish and maintain satisfactory relations with others in respect to interaction and association. A satisfactory relation includes a "comfortable relation" with others both in terms of initiating interaction and of eliciting behavior. Terms that connote positive inclusion are "associate," "mingle," "belong," and "togetherness." Terms that connote negative inclusion are "outcast," "lonely," "detached," and "ignored."

Control is the need to establish and maintain satisfactory relations with people with respect to control and power. Terms that connote positive control are "power," "authority," and "leader." Terms that connote negative control are "rebellion," "resistance," "henpecked," and "anarchy."

Affection is the need to establish and maintain satisfactory relations with people with respect to love and affection. Terms connoting positive affection are "love," "like," "emotionally close," and "personal." Terms connoting negative affection are "hate," "dislike," and "cool."

Schutz distinguishes the three interpersonal needs as follows: inclusion is concerned primarily with the formation or existence of an interpersonal relationship, whereas control and affection are concerned with relations already formed. Within existing relations, control is concerned with who gives orders and makes decisions for whom. Affection is concerned with how emotionally close or distant the relation becomes. Thus, inclusion is concerned with the problem of *in* or *out,* control is concerned with *top or bottom,* and affection with *close or far* (p. 24).

Two aspects of each interpersonal need are *expressed* and *wanted.* Expressed is the behavior the individual reports that he expresses. Wanted is the behavior he *wants others* to express toward him. Measuring each individual's expressed and wanted inclusion, control, and affection provides us with information concerning the individual's characteristic attitude or posture which he applies to interpersonal relations. This characteristic attitude or posture is called an individual's *f*undamental *i*nterpersonal *r*elations *o*rientation (FIRO), and provides the necessary information for determining the probability of individuals satisfying each other's interpersonal needs.

Group harmony depends upon the mutual satisfaction of interpersonal needs, or *compatibility.* Three forms of compatibility are *reciprocal, originator,* and *interchange.* Reciprocal compatibility is based upon reciprocal need satisfaction: A gives B what B wants, and B gives A what A wants. This is most apparent in the area of control, as when A has a high expressed need for control and a low wanted control, and B has the reverse.

The second form of compatibility is originator compatibility. Originator compatibility is based upon differences in tendencies to originate or initiate behavior. Since Schutz's theory is applicable to interacting individuals, a measure of the tendency of members to interact is crucial. If, for example, A and B have high control compatibility, as in the example above, but neither has a tendency to initiate behavior, the fact that they are reciprocally compatible in the control area is irrelevant since neither would initiate interaction. A similar case occurs when both individuals are initiators and not receivers. Either situation leads to incompatibility and mutual dissatisfaction.

Interchange compatibility is based upon the desired amount of interchange between the self and others. An example should help clarify this point. Consider the student who, just before knocking on his date's front door, says to himself: "I'll wait three dates. If I can't seduce her by then, I'll forget her! If I do, I'll make it three more." Meanwhile, his date is saying to herself, "He seems like a nice person, one that my parents will approve of. I could consider spending a lifetime with him." One is looking for immediate satisfaction through little interchange, the other is looking for satisfaction through a possible extended interchange of behavior. The situation lacks interchange compatibility.

Knowing the area (inclusion, control, or affection), type (reciprocal, originator, or interchange), and level (high or low) of compatibility for members of a group leads to predictions of their behaviors and satisfactions, as well as predictions concerning the group's operation as a whole. Group interaction appears to be facilitated by compatibility: compatible groups exhibit a higher rate of verbal exchange designed to facilitate interaction than incompatible groups. Members of compatible dyads and small groups tend to prefer each other for continued personal interchange; compatible groups operate at a higher level of performance than incompatible groups; and compatible groups appear more cohesive.

Use Schutz's measuring instrument FIRO-B (*F*undamental *I*nterpersonal *R*elations *O*rientation—*B*ehavior) in a group in which you are currently a member. Determine which members are most compatible and which are least compatible in each of the three need areas. Such an analysis should provide insights into the operation of your own group, some of its strengths and some of its weaknesses, as well as potential problems. Used with other techniques, such as Laing's Interpersonal Perception Method (see pp. 31-34), Schutz's theory of group interaction should make group dynamics more meaningful.

Economic Balance: John Thibaut and Harold Kelley, and George C. Homans

---

Schutz provides us with an explanation for why people join groups. But once a relationship has formed, what will determine whether it is maintained? Groups which are incompatible may still function. How often have you been a member of a group which you disliked, yet failed to leave?

October 1.   The first meeting—and we're off! . . .

Conflict was immediately evident. Paul, noticing a side conversation between Sherri and Rosemary, made sarcastic remarks which were designed to bring them back into the general conversation. The result was negative: they indicated that they perceived everything that was happening as a power struggle between Lawrence and Paul.

Everyone seemed frustrated. Jilda wanted more leadership functions, but didn't have the background. Sherri and

Rosemary felt pushed into a project that they were unsure of. Doug was more concerned with work in other courses.

If this group project wasn't mandatory, I don't believe any of us would return for a second meeting. But the alternatives were grim: failure in the course or, less grim, drop the course.

Thibaut and Kelley

The questions to which Thibaut and Kelley address themselves are, "What standards do we use when deciding to remain in a group?" and, "What effect does interdependency in the group have on the decisions a member makes?"

The essence of any interpersonal relationship is interaction, and interaction can be described in terms of participant costs and rewards. To evaluate the acceptability of the outcomes of interaction, members of a group need some criteria. The standard against which they evaluate the attractiveness of the relationship, or how satisfactory it is, is called the *Comparison Level* (CL). The standard used to decide whether to remain in the group is called the Comparison Level for Alternatives (CL_{alt}). CL_{alt} is usually the smallest reward a member will accept to stay in the group.

CL and CL_{alt} do not work proportionately, nor do they have to correlate highly. There are circumstances when a member's outcomes (his rewards minus costs) will fall below his CL, but he will remain in the group because the alternatives offered him are not below his CL_{alt}. Consider when a teacher puts you in a group with several other students you prefer *not* to work with and then tells you that half your term grade depends upon your group product. The alternative to working with the assigned group is failure on the project. Although the outcomes of the interaction fall well below your CL, you remain in the group because they do not fall below your CL_{alt}.

The best relationship available to individuals in a group is one in which each member produces, with a minimum of cost, behavior rewarding to the other members. Problems exist when group members persistently make the costs of interpersonal action greater than the rewards. Rewards are increased by close proximity, similarity of attitudes and values, and similarity of social status. Costs are increased by interference, which exists when incompatible behaviors interact. Interference increases the costs of performing the behavior and, usually, decreases the reward value of the behavior. For interaction to continue, excessive interferences must be avoided. Behaviors must be formulated to increase rewards and decrease costs.

The degree to which a relationship is found to be satisfactory (above CL), and the degree to which it is willingly extended (above CL_{alt}), is dependent on a number of other aspects of the relationship, including power, status, norms, tasks, and two other factors which Thibaut and Kelley claim are necessary for group survival: fate and behavior control.

The effect that member A has on member B, regardless of B's behavior, is A's *fate control.* Fate control depends on A's ability to supply high rewards to B at low cost to himself. A has *behavior control* over B when A behaves in a manner that makes it desirable for B to change his behavior. A's behavior control also rests on his ability to reduce or enhance B's outcomes by interacting with B and adjusting to B's behavior. The greater the behavior control members exert over each other, the greater they tend toward similarity of values and attitudes. Taken together, behavior control and fate control constitute an important part of the power relationships within the group.

In addition to the power relationship, a status relationship also exists in each group. There are basically two kinds of status: subjective status and social status. *Subjective status* is an individual member's own evaluations of his outcomes as compared to his evaluations of the outcomes of other members in the group. *Social status* is the group's general evaluation of an individual member's outcomes compared to the outcomes of the other members in the group. CL is, to varying extents, dependent on the relationship between subjective status and social status. If subjective status and social status are high, the CL is probably exceeded. If either subjective status or social status is low, CL may not be met.

Regardless of the amount of power or status a member possesses, norms are important to him. Norms are relatively stable group-generated rules which govern behavior. They act to produce homogeneity of values and behavior, and provide for control of behavior by serving as standards against which behavior can be evaluated. This control is exercised without recourse to direct interpersonal application of power, although sanctions can be brought against members who violate norms. The more dependent a member is upon a group, or the more it satisfies his needs, the more important norms become to that member.

The relationships already discussed are not independent of the group's particular task. The task will direct or limit the activities of a group's members. If it demands behaviors which cost a great deal and offer little reward, the outcomes will fall below CL for the members. The degree to which the members must coordinate their behavior to perform a certain task, and the degree to which they are interdependent, affect rewards and costs.

> *March 28.   Official. Working in this group has just gone below both my CL and CL_{alt}. The costs in terms of anger, frustration, and hurt are greater than the rewards of remaining with the group and completing a group project for the class. Martha was incapable of supporting me; Joan was in the hospital; Janice didn't seem to care one way or the other about anything; Chuck was deliberately being antagonistic; and Laing, for whatever reasons, was lying.*
>
> *Martha needs a grade that only a project can give her. She is above her CL_{alt}, although below her CL.*
>
> *Someone suggested that two subgroups form. Chuck and Laing wanted to form a dyad, which indicated that the large group was below the CL and CL_{alt} for both of them. Joan, Janice, Martha, and I formed the other subgroup.*

> *April 5.   A week went by since the split, and only half-hearted attempts at two projects have been made. The costs to me in terms of time, energy, emotional stress, and money (for film for our project), minus the rewards of a good project, were too negative to withstand.*
>
> *I did not attend the next meeting. My "reward-cost economic balance" was bankrupt.*

In order to keep each member's position above CL_{alt} the group must serve two functions: *task functions* and *maintenance functions*. Task functions provide rewards to members by virtue of the group's ability to operate in its given environment. Although an individual may be unable to solve a complex problem, the group may be able to. The group's ability to solve the problem will be rewarding to the individual. Maintenance functions provide compensations to insure that each member is kept above his CL_{alt}. The allocation of rewards such as social status or material remuneration serve as maintenance functions for members.

To summarize, Thibaut and Kelley's perspective includes looking at the CL and CL_{alt} of each member and the rewards and costs that result from his group's interaction. Examining the means that a group uses to perform its task (including its norms, status hierarchies, power allocations, and maintenance functions) in light of each member's CL and CL_{alt} provides a picture of total group functioning. Thibaut and Kelley present the group as a dynamic structure in which individual members struggle to maintain high rewards and low costs, i.e., try to achieve "economic" balance.

George C. Homans

Like Thibaut and Kelley, Homans also develops a theory for why people stay in groups based on the reward minus cost equation. Unlike Thibaut and Kelley, who focus primarily on the *individual* as part of a group and from this try to conceptualize the group, Homans focuses on the group as a whole, the group as a social system.

According to Homans, when several individuals form a group, the behavior observed is a result of the unique social system which exists within the group. A group's behavior is best viewed as a system in which changes in one area cause changes in another area. Focusing on discrete individual acts or members does not allow for a conception of the whole. Any group constitutes a social system in which the three primary elements of social behavior are activities, interaction, and sentiments. *Activities* refer to those things which are done with non-human objects, such as recording the minutes of a meeting. *Interaction,* on the other hand, refers to people doing things together, such as performing a skit, eating lunch, or trying to arrive at an equitable solution to a problem. *Sentiments* refer to the feelings each group member has about both the human and nonhuman events or objects with which the group deals.

Homans suggests that activities, interaction, and sentiments have an interdependent relationship; changes in any one element will cause changes in the others. For example, if the group typist (who initially liked his job) decides that typing is boring, dull, and fruitless, a change in his sentiment has occurred. What effect will this have on his activities and interaction? Probably he will try to avoid sitting down in front of the typewriter (a change in his activity), and he will avoid the group members who are most likely to ask him to type (a change in his interaction).

Every group has two systems in operation: an external system and an internal system. The *external system* consists of behavior designed to help the group survive in the environment. Normative expectations from the external environment are one source of influence with which groups must deal in order to survive. For example, one normative expectation derived from the external environment is that men should avoid cursing in front of women. Therefore, when meeting in the presence of women, a group of men will avoid the usual cursing that occurs when they are alone. Their adherence to external expectations helps them avoid conflict in the environment. Any effect of the external environment on the group will be reflected in the group by the adoption of behaviors dealing with the external force. These behaviors constitute a group's external system.

The *internal system* of a group is the elaboration, differentiation, and standardization of behavior beyond that required to help it survive within the external environment. For example, one student group I was in developed an interesting norm (standardization of behavior): we began each meeting with fifteen or more minutes of small talk and wine tasting. Although this ritual was relaxing and we claimed that it would help us solve our assignment, I believe we fully realized that we persisted in these activities simply because we enjoyed them. Any effect on our ability to cope with the external environment, in the form of the directed task, was accidental. Our behavior was primarily an adaptation reflecting the internal system of the group.

What determines changes in a group member's activities, interaction, and sentiment? Homans has developed a theory of group equilibrium similar in many respects to the economic theory of Thibaut and Kelley. An individual's behavior stabilizes at that point when he is doing the best he can do for himself under the circumstances. "Best" is, of course, a personal matter—what is best for one person might appear as "second best" to another. Regardless, if we view "best" as high profit and define profit as "reward less cost," it is easy to visualize a situation in which the greatest change in behavior is the result of low, or no, profits. The behavior of each group member has cost and reward values. Equilibrium is established when profits are highest and, therefore, few changes in behavior occur.

One of the conditions of group equilibrium may be what Homans calls *distributive justice.* As mentioned before, what is perceived as "best" is a matter of individual judgment, but this does not suggest that profits among members are necessarily different. The excess of reward over cost should tend toward equality for each member of the group. When equality is reached, a state of distributive justice exists, and the group is more than likely in a state of equilibrium. To put this into Thibaut and Kelley's language, my CL and CL_{alt} are not the same as your CL and CL_{alt}, but the degree to which my two comparison levels are surpassed should tend to equal the degree to which your two levels are surpassed.

Homans's perspective of group interaction centers around the activities, interaction, and sentiments of the group as exhibited in the group's external and internal systems. Changes in behavior result from changes in the reward/cost equation for profit. An understanding of what constitutes rewards and costs for different members is essential for the determination of changes in behavior.

Task Versus Social Functions: W. R. Bion and Robert F. Bales

As already mentioned, groups have both task and maintenance (social) functions. According to Bion and Bales, group interaction may be conceptualized as a battle between opposing forces, task and social, which have to balance each other to insure both task accomplishment and member satisfaction. While each group member has personal needs which may conflict with the group's task accomplishment, individuals also have task needs which can disrupt the development of social relationships which, in turn, could further disrupt work on the task.

> *October 23.   We met in my house. This meeting was more social than anything else. There was work to be done, but it appeared obvious (to me) that the social aspect of our development was, at this time, more important. And it was worth it! Everyone seemed to relax and, while talking about things unrelated to our topic, raised questions of pertinence to the task. We did not solve any task problems, but we solved some social ones. I believe we developed a better sense of "groupness" during this meeting.*
>
> *At the beginning of the meeting I tried to get us back into task work, but the attempts failed. I even stopped trying when Rosemary commented on my "paper rattling," which she called "an obvious attempt to get us to work on the task at hand." We all laughed, and that ended that!*

W. R. Bion

According to Bion, a group can be thought of as a series of emotional states, or *basic assumption cultures,* and individuals either acquiesce or react against these basic assumption cultures. There are three emotional states in groups: (1) work—dependency, (2) work—pairing, and (3) fight—flight. *Work—dependency* is characterized by a group working as if its function is to find support and direction from outside itself. The basic assumption is that an external object exists which has the function of providing security for the immature organism. One person, a leader, is always felt to be in a position to supply the needs of the group; the rest are in a position to have their needs satisfied.

Work—pairing is characterized by the group working to find strength from within its own group. Usually, two members pair and become involved in discussion. Bion asserts that whenever two people have this relationship, regardless of their sex, the basic assumption held by the group, as well as the pair, is that the relationship is a sexual one.

Fight—flight is characterized by the group operating as if its purpose is to avoid something by fighting or running away from it. It is a technique used by the group to preserve itself by avoiding or assaulting anything which threatens its continuation. The emphasis is on group, not individual, survival. Given the high incidence of violence associated with organizations such as the Black Panthers, it may be that they are operating in a fight—flight emotional stage.

Dorothy Stock and Herbert Thelen, in *Emotional Dynamics and Group Culture,* have expanded Bion's formulations. Relationships among individuals in the group provide us with another perspective for analyzing group behavior. Each individual has a set of characteristic behavioral tendencies in group situations, a preference for acting in a dependency, pairing, or fight—flight situation. Stock and Thelen, in line with the other theories discussed, conclude that group members will choose other members who satisfy their needs. This may well include choosing members who facilitate operation in the given member's preferred modality (e.g., flight or fight).

Change in member preference is accompanied by shifts in the relationship between the individual and the group culture. A change in the relationship occurs with a reinterpretation of the relationships among culture preference, the member's area of concern, and self-percept (the way in which a member thinks of his own operation in the group situation). Whereas the group culture is the context for individual change, this does not mean that the group itself is static. A group has its own development, characterized by four phases. The first phase, which operates during the first few meetings, is concerned with attempting to define direction and a method of organizing so that work may be accomplished. During this phase, individuals are concerned with expressing *personal* needs and exploring the kinds of gratifications that they may expect in their group.

The second phase, operating during the next few meetings, is concerned with specific *task* problems. There is less intense emotion during this phase, as the group concentrates more on specific task problems than on personal needs.

The third phase, usually of long duration, centers on the expression of *feelings*. Emotion-laden statements are dealt with constructively, or destructively. Constructive use entails using the emotion expressed to increase task effectiveness. Destructive use entails using the emotion expressed to decrease task effectiveness.

The fourth and last phase centers on *high-level work*. There is little affect during this phase; the interpersonal problems have been dealt with effectively, and with the approach of the task resolution, the necessity for group continuation decreases.

The main group problem during these four phases is for the group to channel its available emotional energies into the common task. The main individual problem is to learn how to express personal needs in a way that can be constructively utilized by the group as a whole.

Bion's perspective of group behavior includes each member's behavioral tendencies, preferred culture, basic concern, and self-percept. (A direct assessment of a member's affective approach, that is, his predisposition to express certain kinds of affect, is facilitated by an instrument developed by Stock and Thelen called the Reactions to Group Situations Test [RGST].) These four pieces of information allow for predictions of group performance, how individuals will respond to each other and to the group as a whole. Bion, then, views group development as the reconciliation of opposing forces: personal need satisfaction and effective group performance. Group development also includes a struggle within the group to change from a basic assumption group (dependency, fight—flight, and pairing), to a work group. The group must pass from a dependency group to a flight—fight group to a pairing group before it can effectively achieve the status of a work group. An equilibrium must be established between the emotional and work modes.

Robert F. Bales

Whereas Bion focuses specifically on the dynamic relationship between individuals and the group, and how this relationship gives rise to a group culture, Bales focuses on the group level, on the relationships which exist *because* the group exists. The object of interaction, as with Bion's conceptualization, is to establish an equilibrium between social-emotional considerations and task considerations.

According to Bales, each group goes through three phases of development, and each phase is characterized as a problem demanding solution before the group can progress to a subsequent stage. The first stage is labeled *orientation.* During this phase, members must arrive at a common definition of the situation or problem that must be solved through interaction. During the second phase, termed *evaluation,* the group must establish the values that will guide it. Since each member comes to the group with his own set of evaluative standards, and will attempt to judge the situation and proposed solutions according to them, interaction during the evaluation phase must solve the problem of individual differences in this matter; the group must establish a set of group standards to which every member subscribes, at least nominally, for the purposes of productive group interaction. The third phase Bales discusses is the *control* phase. Because each member will attempt to influence other members of the group, a status hierarchy must be established to deal with the problem of who controls whom. Otherwise, conflicts will ensue and interfere with the task.

While working out these three problems, groups establish an equilibrium in the types and distribution of acts performed. There are four major categories of types of acts members will perform; each type has three subcategories.

1. Positive reactions
    1. Shows solidarity
    2. Shows tension release
    3. Shows agreement
2. Answers
    4. Gives suggestions
    5. Gives opinions
    6. Gives information
3. Questions
    7. Asks for information
    8. Asks for opinions
    9. Asks for suggestions
4. Negative Reactions
    10. Shows disagreement
    11. Shows tension
    12. Shows antagonism

Bales groups the first three subcategories under the heading of *Social-Emotional Area: Positive.* The next six subcategories he groups under *Task Area: Neutral.* The last three subcategories are grouped under *Social-Emotional Area: Negative.* The advantage of this broader classification is that it reduces the twelve subcategories to two basic areas, social-emotional and task, which closely parallel what Bales considers to be the two tasks groups must perform.

Each group has two tasks, an *external task* and an *internal task.* The external task involves adapting to outside control and performing those tasks strictly relevant to task solution. The means used to solve the external task are called instrumental-adaptive. The internal task is to maintain group cohesiveness, solidarity, and agreement. The means used to solve the internal task are called expressive-integrative. A state of equilibrium between external and internal tasks can exist only if positive acts predominate over negative ones. Negative acts tend to disturb the balance and reduce the level of satisfaction directly. The degree to which positive acts predominate depends upon a number of factors, including the situational demands and the levels of aspiration of the group members.

The implication of a theory based on dynamic equilibrium is that no part of the system is independent of the others. Changes in one aspect of the group functioning will affect other parts of group functioning. With this in mind, Bales presents twelve hypotheses which seem to apply to most small groups. These hypotheses concern the dynamic relationships among functional problems, strain, role, status, and control; and among solidarity, status, and performance. Summarized, these hypotheses are given below.

1. As functional problems increase, strain towards defining specific social roles increases.
2. As role importance increases, status increases (the converse is also hypothesized).
3. As roles become more specific and differentiated, inequalitarian (unequal) access to resources and rewards increases.
4. As a group member's importance increases, his status increases (the converse is also hypothesized).
5. As roles become more differentiated, more directive control is exercised.
6. As the directive control of a group member increases, his status increases (the converse is also hypothesized).
7. As status differences widen, strain among members increases.
8. Solidarity between group members of unlike status causes a strain to have the statuses merge.
9. Adaptation to an outer situation demands the recognition of status differences.
10. As solidarity increases, task performance decreases.

11. As solidarity between group members of different statuses increases so does equalitarianism, but motivation to adapt to the outer situation in which the group exists decreases.
12. As solidarity increases between those in authority and those not in authority, there is less formal exercise of authority, and the unpleasant and difficult tasks tend not to get done.

From this list two points emerge. First, as groups solve the three problems of orientation, evaluation, and control, members achieve their goals (tasks) and build solidarity. Second, task achievement and group solidarity tend to oppose each other, so the emphasis of the group shifts from task achievement to building solidarity.

In Bales's theory of group interaction, different forces seek not to integrate, as in Bion's scheme, but to co-exist, each force being satisfied at a given moment, but no one force being the object of concern all the time. Thus Bales suggests an equilibrium in which all aspects of group functioning are interrelated and interdependent.

It may be of interest at this point to try to use Bales's categorization system, called the Interaction Process Analysis. It will take some time to train a few members of the group to use the system effectively, to be able to recognize verbal and nonverbal acts which have observable beginnings and ends and which "fit" the twelve types of acts that occur during group interaction. Once the data have been collected, compare your group's performance with norms that Bales has established. For example, the observed group may have 37 percent socioemotional acts, while the norm established by Bales may be 50 percent. What factors within the group might have contributed to this lower percentage observed?

Members' Perceptions: Fritz Heider and R. D. Laing

Schutz's theory offers a rationale for the existence of groups; Thibaut and Kelley, and Homans offer an explanation for why people remain in a group; and Bion and Bales offer a conceptualization of group interaction as the result of two opposing forces trying to become reconciled. Once a group is formed and continues to exist, additional perspectives allow us to focus on other important determinants of small group behavior.

Although most small group theorists deal with the perceptions that group members have of each other, Heider and Laing conceptualize small group interaction as the interaction of perceptions. Heider details the problems encountered in focusing on perceptions; and the effects of a member's perceptions on his behavior. Laing offers a more specific analysis of the various levels on which members' perceptions may be studied; he also outlines a specific technique for measuring perceptions and using them as the basis for an analysis of small group interaction.

Fritz Heider

Our reactions to the things and people around us are based upon how we interpret incoming data, and we interpret data according to pre-conceived ideas. In receiving and interpreting incoming data, one of our major objectives is to perceive the world we live in as *consistent,* for only when we perceive things as being consistent can we ascribe meaning to them.

Our reactions to other people are based on our perceptions of them. The messages we receive about another individual are not the objective facts about him such as his height, weight, or hair color, for these things are mediated by our senses. What we do perceive are impressions or representations of objective facts. In other words, we sense motives, wants, desires, and feelings, but we are not necessarily aware of the specific cues that may tip us off. It is this sensing which determines percept. Even objective cues, that is, those cues which can be easily verified (e.g., Lawrence is 5'11"), are subject to various interpretations. This is because meaning is partially derived from things outside the objective cue. Two common sources that provide cues to help us derive meaning from a particular stimulus are the *surrounding* stimuli and the *order* of the stimuli. For example, picture two men running, one in front of the other. Now, answer the question: "What is happening? Is the person in front being followed or chased?" The objective cues are present, but it is impossible to determine what the behavior means because we lack surrounding stimuli. Are the two people running being chased by a gang of hoodlums? Did the person in front just kick the person in the rear?

It is important to focus attention on perceptions because our perceptions affect our behavior: (1) it makes possible control over the environment; (2) it determines how we evaluate our behavior, other events, and people; (3) it influences motivation; and (4) it facilitates the formation of bonds between people. Concerning control over the environment, an individual's perception of the environment limits his action possibilities. P (perceiver) controls the environment to the extent that he influences O's (other person) perceptions of it. For example, if P influences O to perceive college students as drug-abusing radicals, he influences the way O will behave when confronted by college students.

How we perceive others determines how we will evaluate them. For example, in the small group setting, if P offers O positive evaluations, he influences O's evaluations of himself and of the other group members. Based on his perception of P's evaluation, O will probably evaluate himself, P, and the group highly.

Perception also affects our motivation. If an individual perceives a situation as dangerous, he will be motivated to avoid it. A different case may involve P influencing O to perceive a situation as so dangerous that O is motivated to action. For example, if P influences O, a college president, to believe that students are planning a violent action on campus, and O perceives the situation as an emergency, he may be motivated to call in the police.

Mutual perception serves as the basis for union or communion between people. For example, there is a functional closeness and interaction in a mutual glance. If P engages in an extended glance, he is seeking intimacy. By deflecting his gaze, he is avoiding communion. The glance, allowing for mutual perception, may facilitate the formation of bonds between the two people. (Try the following one afternoon: maintain eye contact with a passing stranger for a period longer than usual, more than ten seconds, and note the reactions. The other person will probably appear embarrassed, and try to break your contact: the experience is too intense. However, the same experiment with a close acquaintance could elicit an entirely different reaction. The same act is perceived differently.)

Heider's theory of interaction focuses on each member's perceptions of the other members, as well as his perceptions of the elements included in the group process. We perceive objects and events according to our own unique backgrounds and biases, and these perceptions form the basis for our reactions; they affect our behavior, as well as our evaluation of our behavior. Consequently, an analysis of the perceptions of each group member provides the key to an analysis of the behavior exhibited in the small group.

R. D. Laing

Like Heider, Laing focuses on interpersonal perceptions as the crux for analyzing interpersonal behavior. In his book, *Interpersonal Perception: A Theory and a Method of Research* (with H. Phillipson and A. R. Lee), Laing expands the notion of perception to include different levels of perceptions. Your field of experience is filled with your direct view of yourself, your indirect view of others, and your perception of how others view you. Your direct view of yourself, how you view yourself, is your *direct perspective.* Your view of another is also your direct perspective. Your perception of another's perspective is your *metaperspective.*

This analysis can extend indefinitely. From direct perspectives (Laing uses "perspective" as Heider uses "perception") such as "A husband's view of himself," and "A husband's view of his wife," we expand to metaperspectives such as "A husband's view of his view of himself," "A husband's view of his wife's view of himself." A third level, the level of *meta-metaperspectives* may be discussed, "A husband's view of the wife's view of the husband's view of himself," as may fourth, fifth, and even sixth levels, though they are certainly more difficult to tap and of little practical value.

According to Laing, our experience and behavior are always in relation to someone or something other than ourselves. This is because each of us perceives and interprets the behavior of others, and these perceptions and interpretations then become part of our experience. In addition, we form metaperspectives of how we think others perceive and interpret our own behavior. One of the consequences of forming metaperspectives is the tendency for us to alter our own behavior in light of how we think others perceive us. The identity we form based on our metaperspectives, or how we perceive others perceive us, is our *meta-identity.*

Perceptions are not necessarily accurate. *Selective perception* is one of the most obvious communication problems. Based upon our past learning and experience, we selectively attend to some stimuli, while disregarding other stimuli. Since no two people have the same experiential background, each of our perceptions is uniquely biased according to our past experiences. Likewise, the interpretations based on direct perspectives, metaperspectives, and meta-metaperspectives are a product of our unique experiential background. Mismatched expectations and conclusions are the stuff of human reality.

By analyzing the relationships among the different levels of perspectives, Laing derived a model called the *spiral of reciprocal perspectives.* Human beings are constantly thinking about others, and about what others are thinking about them, and what others think they are thinking about them, and so on. By analyzing the different perspectives of individuals, the success and failure of interaction can be assessed. Laing assesses interaction in terms of understanding, being understood, and the feeling of being understood. *Understanding* is defined as conjunction (agreement) between the metaperspective of one person and the direct perspective of another. For example, if I see myself as overweight (my direct perspective), and my wife's perception of me is one of a person who sees himself as overweight (her metaperspective), then there is understanding. Misunderstanding is the disjunction between the two levels of perspectives.

Being understood, or *being realized,* is defined as the conjunction between the meta-metaperspective of one person and the metaperspective of another. For example, if I think that my wife thinks that I think that she is overweight (my meta-metaperspective), and she thinks that I think that she is overweight (her metaperspective), then she is being understood. Being misunderstood, or the failure of being realized, is the disjunction between the persepectives.

The *feeling of being understood,* as opposed to *being* understood, is defined as the conjunction of an individual's direct perspective with his own metaperspective. For example, if I see myself as overweight (my direct perspective) and I think she thinks I am overweight (my metaperspective), then I feel that I am being understood. The *feeling of being misunderstood* is the disjunction between an individual's two perspectives.

The fourth piece of information that can be derived from an analysis of the conjunction and disjunction of various levels of perspectives is simple *agreement* or *disagreement* on issues. Agreement is defined as the conjunction of the direct perspective of one person with the direct perspective of another. For example, if I see myself as overweight (my direct perspective), and my wife sees me as overweight (her direct perspective), there is agreement. Disagreement is the disjunction between the perspectives.

Conjunction or disjunction can exist for the perspectives of the group goal, reactions toward certain members of the group, or even a decision to perform tasks in a certain way.

May 28.   Tonight at the group meeting we did something different. We answered the following question for ourselves, and as we thought each of the other members answered it in turn. The question was, "Is this project almost completed?" The responses allowed were "definitely yes," "yes," "I don't know," "no," and "definitely no." We analyzed the levels of understanding and found that there was more misunderstanding than anything else. No wonder the meeting before this one bogged down so easily. We can't even agree on whether the project is almost done or not!

We spent the rest of the meeting working out some

simple problems concerning how we perceived our progress, starting with figuring out how far we had gotten, and how far we had to go.

At this point do an analysis of a group you are in using Laing's approach. Devise a questionnaire which will tap the direct perspectives, metaperspectives, and meta-metaperspectives of each group member. Focus on what appear to be sore spots or what you think are the most relevant aspects of your group's behavior. For example, you can ask each member to respond to the following (adapted from question 4 of the Interpersonal Perception Method [I.P.M.], which contains a total of 720 questions):

How true do you think the following are?
1. The group depends on me.
2. I depend on the group.
3. I depend on myself.

How would _____ (a group member) answer the following?
1. "I depend on the group."
2. "The group depends on me."
3. "I depend on myself."

How would _____ (a group member) think you have answered the following?
1. The group depends on me.
2. I depend on the group.
3. I depend on myself.

These questions can help you make decisions concerning the degree to which members of the group feel "important," and the degree to which other members agree upon this felt importance. An analysis of the conjunctions and disjunctions of the various perspectives can pinpoint trouble spots. Once revealed, effective strategies may be developed for coping with the problem. Possibly, such an analysis can help the group spend its time more effectively by focusing on important aspects of its interaction. Finally, if used on successive occasions, it can serve as the basis for comparing one point in time with another point in time.

Balancing Perceptions

Both Heider and Laing see the end result of our perceptions as the formation of a *balanced state.* For Heider, a balanced state exists when a member's feeling and evaluations are in alignment with his perceptions. For Laing, a balanced state exists when perceptions among different individuals are congruent.

According to Heider, we perceive other people (O) and things (X), and the way we feel about or evaluate them constitutes our sentiment. The relationship between sentiments and things tends toward a balanced state; that is, when one is positive, the other is positive, or when one is negative, the other is negative. For example, if I like both Fellini films and Mary, and Mary also likes Fellini films, the situation is balanced. It can be diagrammed as follows:

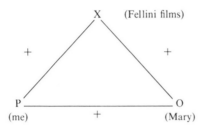

Imbalance would occur when two of the relationships were positive and the other negative, or two negative and the other positive. If Mary did not like Fellini films, the situation could be diagrammed as

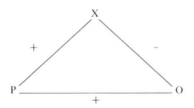

Factors which influence the balance of a situation are similarity, proximity, common fate, good continuation, and past experiences. Individuals who share similar attitudes and beliefs are usually close together, are interdependent so that they affect a joint fate, are sharing a good relationship, and have shared past experiences which are similar, are more likely to be in a balanced state than individuals without these characteristics. For Heider, the group is best conceived as a complex combination of desires, wants, abilities, and perceptions, all of which work to ward off stress by establishing balanced and consistent states.

Group interaction from Laing's vantage point, including an analysis of the various combinations of perspectives, metaperspectives, and meta-metaperspectives, represents group behavior as a complex function of the various combinations of perspectives. Changes in behavior are produced to create balanced states where perspectives are congruent.

Summary

A group may be best conceptualized as existing because it satisfies some need. The need may be an interpersonal one as described by Schutz or, more obviously, the need to accomplish some task for which a group effort is necessary. An individual will remain in a group as long as his need is being satisfied, or as long as the group remains the best potential source for need satisfaction.

In addition to satisfying individual needs, groups have task and social functions which are often in opposition. The main purpose, though, of interaction is to accomplish some goal. This goal may be either task or socially oriented. The extent to which member interaction can solve the problems which arise when individual needs, social-emotional needs, and task demands conflict determines the extent to which the group may be said to be operating effectively.

The most viable approach to analyzing group interaction is on the level of member perceptions. Objective measures of group interaction, such as the number of times a given member speaks to another member, do not provide the most important information: what the members of the group perceive about themselves, their interaction, and their functioning. A member's perceptions direct his behavior in the group; an approach to interaction which does not account for these perceptions can provide only an incomplete picture of small group behavior.

Do you agree with this summary?

Bibliography

Bales, R. F. "A Set of Categories for the Analysis of Small Group Interaction." *American Sociological Review* 15 (1950): 181-87.

―――. *Interaction Process Analysis: A Method for the Study of Small Groups.* Reading, Massachusetts: Addison-Wesley, 1950.

————. "The Equilibrium Problem in Small Groups." In *Small Groups: Studies in Social Interaction,* edited by A. P. Hare, E. E. Borgotta, and R. F. Bales, pp. 424-63. New York: Knopf, 1955.

Bion, W. R. *Experiences in Groups.* New York: Basic Books, 1959.

Heider, F. "Social Perception and Phenomenal Causality." *Psychological Review* 51 (1944): 358-74.

————. *The Psychology of Interpersonal Relations.* New York: Wiley, 1958.

Homans, G. C. *The Human Group.* New York: Harcourt, Brace, 1950.

————. "Social Behavior as Exchange." *American Journal of Sociology* 63 (1958): 597-606.

————. *Social Behavior: Its Elementary Forms.* New York: Harcourt, Brace, 1961.

Kerlinger, F. N. *Foundations of Behavioral Research.* New York: Holt, Rinehart and Winston, 1964.

Laing, R. D. *Knots.* New York: Pantheon, 1970.

Laing, R. D., Phillipson, H., and Lee, A. R. *Interpersonal Perception: A Theory and a Method of Research.* New York: Springer, 1966.

Rosenfeld, L. B. "A Critique of William Schutz's Three-Dimension Theory of Interpersonal Behavior Using His Measuring Instrument FIRO-B." Dissertation, The Pennsylvania State University, 1971.

Rosenfeld, L. B., and Jessen, P. A. "Compatibility and Interaction in the Small Group: Validation of Schutz's FIRO-B Using a Modified Version of Lashbrook's PROANA 5." *Western Speech* 36 (1972): 31-40.

Rosenfeld, L. B., and Frandsen, K. D. "Fundamental Interpersonal Relations Orientations in Dyads: An Empirical Analysis of Schutz's FIRO-B as an Index of Compatibility." Paper presented at the Speech Communication Association annual convention, December 1970.

————. "The Other Speech Student: An Empirical Analysis of Some Interpersonal Relations Orientations of the Reticent Student." *Speech Teacher,* in press.

Schutz, W. *FIRO: A Three Dimensional Theory of Interpersonal Behavior.* New York: Holt, Rinehart and Winston, 1958.

————. "The Interpersonal Underworld." *Harvard Business Review* 36 (1958): 123-35.

Stock, D., and Thelen, H. *Emotional Dynamics and Group Culture.* New York: New York University Press, 1958.

Thibaut, J. W., and Kelley, H. H. *The Social Psychology of Groups.* New York: Wiley, 1959.

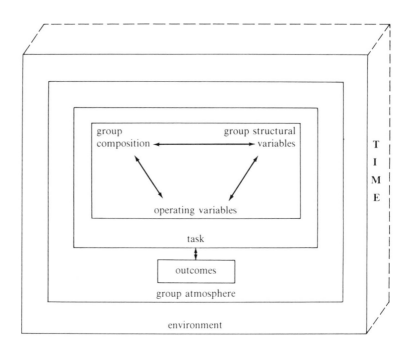

CHAPTER 3

PHASES IN GROUP DEVELOPMENT

The theories presented in chapter 2 dealt with broad questions of group functioning. Although several theories were concerned with the developmental sequence for task performance, the overall concern was for broader interpretation of the group process. In this chapter we will consider theories specifically concerned with the phases of group process. These may be considered subsystem theories, theories concerned with one aspect of the entire system. These subsystem theories provide models for observing group interaction.

Eight different schemas are presented here in chronological order. Each was derived from observation, usually of one type of group —problem-solving, social, or therapeutic. Because each theory reflects the interests and concerns of its author, each may not be applicable to many kinds of groups. But, taken together, these theories do provide some valuable insights into group processes, such as those used for task solution or reaching consensus.

Bales and Strodtbeck   (1951)

The point of departure for Bales and Strodtbeck is Bales's own theory. The phase hypothesis taken from Bales's theory states that groups go through three phases. Interaction moves from problems of orientation to problems of evaluation, and finally to problems of control. As these transitions occur, the number of negative and positive reactions (*disagrees, shows tension, shows antagonism, shows tension release, shows solidarity,* and *agrees*) increases.

Bales and Strodtbeck tested their hypotheses by observing groups consisting of persons assumed to be "normal" and adult or near adult. Each group was under some pressure to maintain group solidarity (e.g., a course grade was at stake) so that disagreements and other negative reactions were thought disruptive. A substantial number of groups operate under similar restrictions.

For a group to go through any of the three phases Bales and Strodtbeck describe, it is necessary that the problems associated with a given phase be unresolved at the beginning of interaction. Hence, concerning *orientation,* group members may individually understand aspects of the group's orientation, but the task of this phase is to reach *group* consensus regarding its orientation. During the *evaluation* phase, group members must reach agreement about the value judgments the group will use to solve its problem. In the *control* phase, the group feels pressured to find a solution. It also expects that future decisions concerning solutions may be necessary.

The shift from one phase of group process to another is mainly one of emphasis. All three phases are in operation at any given time. It is how the group spends its energies, however, which determines which phase of development the group is in. For example, one group, during its seventh meeting, had to deal with a member who had been absent.

March 14.   This is our seventh meeting. Tom showed up after miss-
ing the last three meetings. This became a review meeting.
I was angry with Tom for not having called when he knew
he couldn't make the last meeting, but he was vindicated
when I saw him—his face was still green, even with his tan!
*   At any rate, we spent this meeting helping Tom catch*
up. We told him about the ideas we had for presenting a tape
to the class, and about the put-on role playing we planned.
Our aim was to be exciting, as well as informative.
*   Tom asked questions and, once he felt he had a handle*
on what we had done, started offering ideas. By the next
meeting we should all be on the same wave-length again.

Looking at the interaction in terms of Bales's categories of acts, there was an immediate increase in acts in categories 6 (gives information), 7 (asks for information), and 4 (gives suggestion). These three categories are most closely associated with *orientation,* a phase which was more or less complete by the end of the second meeting. The effect was quite clear: the group regressed to an emphasis on an earlier phase.

The phase movement suggested by Bales and Strodtbeck may serve a number of purposes, the first of which is experimentation. What effects are observed when deliberate manipulation of group processes are introduced into a working group? A second use to which phase movement may be put concerns group analysis. An unsuccessful group product may be the result of inadequate phase movement. For example, does the group have a clear notion of the problem, and their resources, before setting up criteria for evaluation of solutions? If not, then the group should return to the first phase and resolve that phase before proceeding with their work.

It might be interesting at this point to use your knowledge of phase movement during a problem-solving discussion. Organize groups with at least four members. List, in proper order, the problems the group must solve. Now, choose one of the two following topics for discussion (or, better, generate your own problem).

Experience 3-1. Moon Landing Agreement Exercise. Directions: You are a space crew originally scheduled to make rendezvous with your mother ship on the moon's lighted surface. Mechanical problems arise and you have been forced to land 200 miles from the rendezvous. Much of your equipment has been damaged. Your survival hinges upon your reaching the mother ship. The most critical items available must be chosen for the 200-mile trip. Below are the fifteen items left intact after landing. Your task is to rank order them in terms of importance in allowing the crew to reach the rendezvous point. Place the number 1 near the most important item, the number 2 by the second most important item, and so on, through the number 15, the least important.

> **box of matches**
> **food concentrate**
> **50 feet of nylon rope**
> **parachute silk**
> **portable heating unit**
> **two .45 caliber pistols**
> **one case dehydrated Pet milk**
> **two 100-lb. tanks of oxygen**
> **map of the moon's constellation**
> **life raft**
> **magnetic compass**
> **five gallons of water**
> **signal flares**

first-aid kit with injection needles
solar-powered FM receiver-transmitter

There *are* agreed upon answers for this exercise, as well as a method for scoring (see the pages immediately preceding the bibliography of this chapter).

Experience 3-2. Scholarship Agreement Exercise. PROBLEM: To choose *one* of the following to receive a scholarship of $2,000 per year to your school, renewable for four years as long as academic progress is satisfactory to the University.

DUANE, 17, finished high school in three years be-cause, he says, he "couldn't have stood another year of the b.s." His mother, a registered nurse, is a widow with two younger children. In spite of finishing a year early, Duane made a 3.0 in high school. University tests predict he is likely to earn a 2.6 in a science curriculum, 3.1 in non-science. His mother is determined that he become a physi-cian; Duane says his mind isn't made up. Because of the cost of babysitting her youngest child, his mother can provide almost nothing for his college education. Duane has had some emotional troubles; a psychiatrist recommends college because he feels Duane "needs an intellectual challenge."

CARLA, 18, has very high recommendations from a small-town high school where she earned a 3.8 average. In her senior year she accepted an engagement ring from a local truck driver who wants her to get married at once and forget college. She is known to have spent the night in a motel with him a few times. Your school predicts she is likely to earn a 2.6 in science and a 3.3 in nonscience. She wants to become a social worker "to help the poor in the big cities." Her pastor says she has a fine mind, but he predicts she will marry and drop out even if she starts college. Her parents are uneducated, industrious, very poor.

ROY, 21, earned the Silver Star and lost his right hand in Vietnam. He earned a high school diploma in the Army. The university predicts a 2.0 in science and a 2.3 in non-science for him. He is eligible for veterans' assistance but his family needs his help to support a large brood of younger children. Roy wants to major in business, "to make enough money in my life not to have to live like an animal as my parents do."

MELISSA, 26, is a divorcee with a seven-year-old son. She made a 2.8 in high school, "because I goofed around," but tests predict a 2.9 in science at your school and a 3.6 in nonscience. She wants to become an English teacher, "probably in high school but in college if I'm lucky." She was a beauty queen at 18 and is still regarded as beautiful, but says she is bitter toward men and will never.remarry. She receives no child support or family help toward caring for her son. Her present employer, a dress shop owner, gives her a good character reference but predicts she will marry again rather than finish college.

SAM, 19, was offered several football scholarships to Southern colleges, but they were withdrawn in the spring when, after he finished high school, he had his legs injured in an automobile accident. He can get around well but cannot compete in athletics. He made low high school grades but entrance test scores for your school are good; he is predicted to average 2.5 in science or 3.0 in a nonscience curriculum. His father, a laborer, refuses to contribute to college for him. Now that he can no longer play, Sam is determined to become a football coach, though he has been advised it may be difficult without a college playing record.

Follow carefully your list of problems the group must solve. Do not proceed to the next problem until the current one has been solved satisfactorily. Does adhering to the list help or hinder the group? Do you seem to work faster or slower than usual? If some groups did the first exercise, and some the second, were there differences? If so, why? How does Bales and Strodtbeck's phase movement hypothesis explain or fail to explain the interaction in your group? Would you modify their theory? If so, how?

Braden and Brandenburg (1955)

The major portion of Braden and Brandenburg's *Oral Decision Making* is concerned with debate and debate situations. The sections devoted to discussion and group function in general are useful as introductory material for understanding discussion behavior. Braden and Brandenburg's three phases closely relate to each group member's personal-social needs. These needs include the need for conformity, security, preeminence, self-esteem, and affection.

Phase 1: When the group first forms, group members are extremely self-centered, concerned with their own personal-social needs. This egocentricity is dysfunctional to group functioning: decision making is difficult, and the atmosphere is tense. Frustration and conflict are characteristic of this phase.

Phase 2: Members react to their own behavior; they notice that self-centered behavior is detrimental to efficient group functioning. Occasionally members will overcorrect for egocentricity, with a resulting and equally harmful mode of behavior based on "group-centeredness." During this phase, members begin to balance their own self-centeredness with the amount of group-centeredness necessary to produce efficient operation.

Phase 3: Members work out a system for satisfying the personal-social needs of each member in a manner that is not detrimental to group functioning. A balance between individual needs and group needs firmly is established. In addition, group members internalize the group goal during this phase.

Looking at group development in self-centered versus group-centered terms adds a new dimension to our understanding of group dynamics. How important this is depends upon the type of group under observation. It is likely that group members will deliberately avoid self versus group conflicts when a decision is pressing.

Bennis and Shepard   (1956)

Whereas the focus of the two preceding phase theories was on problem-solving groups coping with external problems, the theory of group development proposed by Bennis and Shepard focused on "self-study" groups. The authors observed groups of graduate students enrolled in a course on group dynamics. The task given the groups was to improve their internal communications system. The group goal was "valid communications," a method whereby the group could achieve and test consensus. Such a group is commonly termed the "human relations" group.

According to Bennis and Shepard there are two major phases in group development, each with at least three subphases. The first phase, *dependence,* deals mainly with power relations and the resolution of dependence needs. Dependent members are those who find rules and regulations not only necessary, but comforting. Authority is seen as necessary for the successful resolution of any problem. Counterdependent members, on the other hand, find rules discomforting and view authority as unnecessary in many instances. The dependence phase has three subparts: *dependence–flight, counterdependence–fight,* and *resolution–catharsis.* (The language Bennis and Shepard use closely parallels the language, if not the meanings, employed by Bion). Although Bion was one major influence on this theory, Schutz and Thelen also contributed toward its development.

Dependence–flight is behavior directed at warding off anxiety. Group members seek security by searching for a common goal, by providing each other with personal anecdotes, or by seeking approval from their leader. Problems which may be discussed during this subpart are external to the group, that is, they are not directly related to the group's task. The group is engaged in flight behavior, as well as dependence behavior.

Counterdependence–fight is behavior directly associated with a new view of the trainer or leader. During this subpart, the leader is seen as less than all-powerful, and as incapable of satisfying the needs of group members. Consequently, the group switches from dependency to counterdependency behavior. Expressions of hostility toward the leader are frequent and are likely to be supported by group members.

Two subgroups emerge during counterdependence–fight. The first consists of group members who attempt to establish some kind of authority structure to replace that left by the deposed leader. This is usually accomplished by creating an agenda or electing a new chairman who will take command of the disintegrating group and restore order. The second subgroup is composed of group members who oppose such attempts.

During resolution–catharsis, the third subpart, group members who have not been involved in either of the two conflicting subgroups above, provide leadership which leads to a new orientation toward the group. The power vacuum is filled, member responsibilities are defined. The whole basis for group action shifts. Bonds between group members develop and the group is no longer perceived as helpless and ineffectual.

The second phase of group interaction, *interdependence,* deals mainly with personal relations. In Phase II, the concern switches from dependency (Phase I) to interdependency. Intimacy, friendship, and identification are now group concerns. "While the distribution of power was the cardinal issue during Phase I, the distribution of affection occupies the group during Phase II" (1956, p. 429).

The three subphases of Phase II are *enchantment–flight, disenchantment–fight,* and *consensual validation.* Enchantment–flight is behavior directed at keeping harmony in the group. The group emerges from the resolution-catharsis phase happy and harmonious. But underlying hostilities cause members to resist the harmony. Subgroups begin to appear and enchantment is shifted from the group as a whole to the subgroups. This new organizational pattern is the manifestation of flight behavior—flight from the reality of group conflict.

The second subphase, disenchantment–fight, parallels the second subphase of Phase I. Again, there is a division of the group into two major subgroups. The counterpersonal group resists further intimate contact; the overpersonal groups demands unconditional love. The anxiety created by these subgroups appears openly, such as in the making of disparaging remarks about the group.

Consensual validation, the third subpart, occurs as a result of external pressure on the group. In the groups that Bennis and Shepard observed, there was a time limit to interaction (the length of the course), and a required group evaluation. The counterpersonals resisted evaluation as an invasion of their privacy; the overpersonals resisted it because it appeared to be discriminatory (the group had to rank members according to their value to the group). The independents, those who did not see evaluation and intimacy as threatening, restored confidence in the group by submitting to the evaluation process or by expressing confidence in the group's ability to evaluate its members.

Although the developmental process has been broken into six pieces for purposes of analysis, it is meaningful only if seen as a dynamic process. The phases blend into each other; bits and pieces from each subphase occur during other subphases. The flow is primarily forward through the phases, but regressions and advances are the rule, not the exception.

All groups are, to some extent, "human relations" groups. All groups must deal with members who are defensive and unproductive. Likewise, the members of a given group must attempt to establish productive interpersonal relations. Bennis and Shepard, in attempting to describe the phases of "human relations" groups, have provided observers with a schema for analysis applicable to almost all groups.

Schutz   (1958)

The three perspectives discussed so far view group development as being primarily linear, that is, it begins at a given point in time and, although there may be some slight variation, continues along a straight path to its completion. Deviations from this straight path are seen as logical, but are nevertheless described as aberrations. The developmental sequence outlined by Schutz departs from this notion of linearity. Rather, he views group development as cyclical. The cycle of group development is repeated indefinitely.

Schutz hypothesizes that from their very inception all groups of two or more individuals go through the following developmental sequence: inclusion behavior, control behavior, and, finally, affection behavior. This cycle, inclusion/control/affection, reoccurs until the group disintegrates. During disintegration, the pattern reverses: affection behavior is followed by control behavior, which is finally followed by inclusion behavior. (See Chapter 2, pp. 16-18, for a description of the behaviors which characterize inclusion, control and affection.)

Combining Schutz's notion of development with his notion of interpersonal compatibility allows us to make predictions about the level of group productivity during any particular phase of the cycle. For example, if a given group has high inclusion compatibility and low control and affection compatibility, then the initial stage of each developmental cycle will be characterized as the most compatible.

Parallel situations occur for each of the three interpersonal need areas. It is important to realize, however, that it takes many meetings before a group reaches the affection interval of the cycle. Groups which are of short duration usually exhibit only inclusion and control intervals. Short-lived groups aside, once the first cycle of inclusion, control, and affection appears, it will repeat again and again until it reverses in anticipation of the group's demise.

Analyzing the movement of a group from one interval to the other may result in some valuable insights. If, for example, the inclusion/control/affection cycle does not appear regularly, it may be that the group is experiencing difficulty in one phase. It may be that the group is not, according to Schutz, functioning *as a group.* Observing a reversal in the cycle may predict impending dispersal. Finally, by measuring each individual member's interpersonal needs (using

Schutz's FIRO-B instrument) and determining the inclusion, control, and affection compatibility of the group, predictions may be made concerning group and individual productivity.

Observe and analyze a group and determine which phase (inclusion, control, or affection) the group is in by developing a questionnaire for each member to complete after a meeting, asking them to describe the most important accomplishments and the topics of greatest interest for that meeting. Another method is to analyze tape recordings of the meeting and make your own judgments. Of course, both methods used together will provide the most useful data.

Scheidel and Crowell   (1961)

The different subtheories discussed to this point have attempted to create systems for the analysis of group development, without regard to specific aspects of that development, such as leadership. Bales and Strodtbeck were concerned with general *problems* which directed group development. Braden and Brandenburg focused on *personal-social needs,* and how these needs directed group development. Bennis and Shepard described the *emotional life* of the group and its members. Finally, Schutz was concerned with the satisfaction of *interpersonal needs* in a group.

Scheidel and Crowell, however, conclude that these subsystem theories are inadequate for analyzing *idea development.* Idea development, or the "process of cooperative work in the building of a group judgment which represents the information, values, and thinking of all the members is the crux of the discussion method" (1961, p. 155). The focus of Scheidel and Crowell's work is on what they consider to be the smallest ideational contribution, more simply, a "thought-unit." Each unit is described along the five dimensions listed below:

     I. A   Assertion
       Q   Question
       AQ Assertion-Question (combined in single thought-units)

    II. O   Information
       E   Inference

   III. S   Substantive
       P   Procedural

IV. V   Volunteered
    R   Requested

V.   1   Initiation
    2   Restatement
    3   Clarification
    4   Substantiation
    5   Extension
    6   Simple Response to request
    7p   Positive Modification
    7c   Negative Modification
    8a   Stated Acceptance-approval
    8r   Stated Rejection-disapproval
    9   Synthesis
    10   Summary (1964, pp. 141-42)

The letter(s) or number(s) preceding a given description is used to categorize the thought-unit. "Thus, a unit designated AESV7p would be an assertion of an inference regarding the substance of the discussion. It would be volunteered by the participant and would suggest some modification of the prior idea, although involving affirmation or agreement with the essentials of that prior idea" (1964, p. 142).

An analysis of 811 thought units lead to the formulation of a *spiral* model of ideational development. Whenever an idea was initiated, it was followed by units which built on the idea, such as clarification or restatement. Inferences were also followed by building. Ideational development then involves a back-and-forth movement. An idea is introduced and then is used as the foundation for group development. The fact that a group spends about half its time on clarification, substantiation, or other acts which serve to elaborate an expressed idea, helps insure loyalty to the group's solution.

The groups observed by Scheidel and Crowell consisted of trained discussants. Although this may limit the generalizability of their findings, it does not necessarily detract from their categorization system. The idea that group problem solving is best represented by a spiraling model of individual thought-units provides a new perspective for observing the developmental process.

Before the Scheidel and Crowell system can be used in the analysis of other types of groups, normative data must be generated for them. Otherwise, the results of their study may apply only to the specific groups observed. If this is so, then the notion that the thought units they describe are reciprocally related is a fruitless notion to investigate with other types of groups. The spiral model may not hold for groups composed of naive participants, or groups less task than socially oriented. Modifications may be necessary in the general schema to make it applicable to a wider variety of groups.

Other concerns include the assumption that focusing on idea development is crucial to understanding group development. It may be possible, for example, to include Scheidel and Crowell's system in the broader one provided by Schutz. For instance, it may be that thought-units which help anchor the idea presented also serve to satisfy *inclusion* needs. Do thought units help members affiliate more closely by concentrating them on one idea, and, finally, do such units help the group feel more like a "whole," as opposed to a collection of individuals?

By focusing on the amount of elaboration that takes place, group members may conclude that they spent too little time on clarification, synthesis, or summary, which prevented them from making a firm commitment to the group solution. On the other hand, too many ideas may have been presented with the result that none of them were ever adequately discussed. Scheidel and Crowell's categorization system may help provide the framework to conduct these analyses.

Experience 3-3. Form groups with at least four members each. Decide what developmental sequence you will try to follow in solving a problem. Now, pick a problem and solve it according to the sequence you agreed upon. For example, you may have decided that you will only positively reinforce ideas presented. This might take the form of positive modification, requested clarification, or thought extensions. After the positive acts, you may insist on examining the liabilities of the ideas presented. Or, you may have decided to avoid all forms of reinforcement until the group has exhausted itself of ideas. If time permits, try several different sequences of idea development. Which sequence gives the best results? Why?

Tuckman   (1965)

Tuckman's model, also a linear one, is derived from a review of fifty articles dealing with stages of group development. He presents two developmental sequences: one for the social realm of group activity, and one for the task realm. With slight shifts in emphasis, social and task developmental sequences apply to all groups.

The social development phase is divided into four stages: *testing-dependence, conflict, cohesion,* and *functional roles.* Task development is also divided into four stages: *orientation, emotionality, relevant opinion exchange,* and the *emergence of solutions.*

The first stage in social development, *testing-dependence,* is similar to the dependence–flight stage described by Bennis and Shepard. During this stage, group members appear to be dependent on the leader or trainer for guidance in what is, at first, a new situation. They also engage in testing each other to discover what is and is not allowed in the group. The familiar "cut-up," who insists on seeing how far he can push other members of the group, serves an important function during this stage. Other group members learn about the group from the sanctions placed on the cut-up; the sanctions apply equally to each group member.

The second stage in social development, *intragroup conflict,* is similar to the counterdependence–fight stage described by Bennis and Shepard. Group members, in an attempt to express their individuality and resist group structure, display acts of hostility both toward each other and toward the leader or trainer. The conflicts during this stage usually center around one key issue, that is, to what degree will members become interpersonally involved in the group?

September 16. I felt like a wreck this morning. Just totally turned off about going to class or anything else. I even thought of excuses for missing the group meeting. At first I couldn't figure out why I was so intent on copping out. While approaching the classroom, I realized that I just didn't want to see any of the other group members. Since last Tuesday I had let my imagination distort my involvement with the group. Somewhere in me a phobia of participation was growing. Hell! This is doing nothing but making me miserable and I refuse to let anyone or anything control my life that way. The other group members are probably totally unaware of the whole situation. It's my problem, not theirs. If I feel they are suppressing me and my ideas, I'll let them know about it. At least I might feel better. I will not be swallowed by the group!

Funny, I felt strong enough to attack Tony and his attitude toward my ideas. And yet, I spoke loudly enough to insure that Louise and Ellen heard me. Ellen just chuck-

*led, which I resented, but Tony was extremely apologetic.
These reactions didn't mean as much to me concerning my
relations with the other members of the group as they did
to me and my relations with myself. I had to reconcile the
feeling of having nothing intellectual to offer, the feeling of
dissatisfaction, before I could continue to participate.*

*After class I ran into Judy. She commented on her
feelings. She and I have common feelings of alienation! I
thought I had been feeling sorry for myself because I didn't
seem to have as much credibility as the other members.*

*After this experience I realized that the project was an
assignment, and not solely an opportunity for social engage-
ments. Today and from now on I'll perform as a part of the
group, working with the others to achieve our goal. I don't
have to extend my contacts with these persons any more
than to finish the project.*

My enthusiasm has all but vanished.

The third stage of social development, *development of group
cohesion,* is similar to the resolution–catharsis and enchantment–
flight stages described by Bennis and Shepard. Because of the conflict
in stage two and the emerging desire to work as a cohesive group, the
group overreacts and demands harmonious relations from members.
Members subsequently accept the group and norms are established to
insure its perpetuation. Task conflicts, at this point, are avoided to
insure harmony.

The last stage of social development, *functional role-relatedness,*
builds on the third stage, development of group cohesion. In this
stage, group members establish interpersonal relationships and adopt
different task roles. Both of these behaviors eventually facilitate the
group's problem-solving function.

The following is a summary of the social aspect of group development based on Tuckman's theory: When the group first meets, the
situation is new; members are anxious and uncertain about what to
expect. A good deal of time is spent "feeling each other out." When
the newness of the situation begins to wear off, group members start
to assert their individuality. Once this has been accomplished, the
group re-forms in order to pursue task functions. Each member now
adopts a certain role in the group, these roles being designed to
facilitate task solution.

The first stage in task development, *orientation to the task,* is
similar to Bales and Strodtbeck's orientation phase. During this stage

group members orient themselves to the task by considering the following questions: What are the parameters of the task? What is expected of them in order to solve the task? How will they accomplish the task? What information is necessary in order to accomplish the task?

The second stage in task development is termed *emotional response to task demands,* and is similar to the first phase of group development described by Braden and Brandenburg. During this stage, group members react emotionally to the demands placed on them by the task; each member must reconcile his personal orientation with his group orientation. The more impersonal the task, the less relevant this stage of development. Indeed, it may be reasonable to use the degree of conflict witnessed during this stage of development as an indication of the way in which the task is perceived—as personal or impersonal.

The third stage in task development, *open exchange of relevant interpretations,* takes two forms, depending on whether the task is personal, as in therapeutic groups, or impersonal, as in most laboratory exercises. When tasks are personal, members characteristically discuss themselves and each other. When tasks are impersonal, an exchange of opinions occurs regarding the task. For "self-study" groups, this third stage is similar in part to the consensual validation stage described by Bennis and Shepard. For task groups, this third stage is similar in part to the evaluation stage of Bales and Strodtbeck.

The last stage of task development, *emergence of solutions,* is characterized by task completion. The sequence the group has followed appears to be a logical one: orientation to the problem, emotional reaction to the problem, exchange of opinions and interpretations, and, finally, the suggestion and selection of a solution.

Although task and social development of the group have been separated for closer inspection, it is obvious that they work together. Separating them may help analysis, but only their synthesis provides a true picture of reality. As with the other models of group development, the best way to understand Tuckman's proposed model is to use it. Given the large amount of subjective interpretation necessary to determine what stage a group is in at any given moment (when it may be in a state of change), the best way to use Tuckman's model may be as follows: keep a diary, noting what conflicts arise during meetings, as well as what the major concerns were. Reviewing the diary may reveal your group's stages of social and task development. A simple comparison with Tuckman's model should provide meaningful insights into both the model and *your* group's method of developing as a problem-solving unit.

Fisher (1970)

Another model concerned with one specific aspect of group development is Fisher's model for decision emergence. Fisher is concerned with decision making, typically involving problem solving. He reviews prior attempts to design models of group development and concludes that a model which deals with the nature of group interaction *across time* is needed. His review of the weaknesses in prior models, all of which have been discussed in this chapter, may serve as a springboard for interrelating the subsystem theories from which they grew.

> There have been few attempts to test theoretical conceptions of group task behaviors systematically. Among the most notable of such conceptions are Bales and Strodtbeck's three-phase progression of group development, Bennis and Shepard's four levels of work, and Scheidel and Crowell's spiral process of idea development. Each of these studies, however, possesses serious limitations. Bales and Strodtbeck, for example, reported that groups concentrated on different kinds of problems across time but they did not discuss the interaction process which the groups used to solve those problems. Bennis and Shepard's study was concerned primarily with delineating those socio-emotional variables which obstruct efficient task completion. Only Scheidel and Crowell observed the verbal behavior related specifically to task accomplishment —notably decision-making. Unfortunately, these authors did not report observing aspects of the time dimension which McGrath and Altman consider "absolutely crucial for understanding small group phenomena." (1970, pp. 53-54)

Fisher divided interaction into two categories: task and nontask. Any verbal interaction considered nontask was coded "et cetera" and was eliminated from analysis. Thus, the focus for analysis was on *verbal* interaction, more specifically, only that verbal interaction considered pertinent to a specific decision proposal.

A category system was developed to describe phases in the group's development. Unlike the Scheidel and Crowell system, this one has three major categories.

Dimension One:
A—Asserted
S—Seeking

Dimension Two:
1—Interpretation
2—Substantiation
3—Clarification
4—Modification
5—Summary
6—Agreement

Dimension Three:
(applicable to "1" and "2" categories only)
f—Favorable toward the proposal
u—Unfavorable toward the proposal
a—Ambiguous toward the proposal

Additional Symbols:
O_n—Origin of a decision proposal
(D_n)—Reintroduction of a proposal (1970, p. 55)

Letters and numbers are used to code a given unit of interaction. A unit coded $A2fO_3$ would indicate the following: A = it is an assertion; 2 = the assertion is substantiating something; f = the assertion is a favorable substantiation; and O_3 = the assertion is a favorable substantiation of the third decision proposal which has been introduced for the first time.

From an analysis of ten diverse groups, four phases of group development emerged. Each phase had a characteristic interaction pattern which allowed it to be distinguished from other phases.

Phase one, *orientation,* had significantly more clarification and agreement than other phases, as might be expected, because group members were unsure of themselves and the situation; there were few assertions made during this period. The order in which units followed each other indicates that agreement was used to facilitate social interaction, more than to reinforce ideas. Furthermore, attitudes toward decision proposals were not singled out for reinforcement, and significantly more ambiguous statements were reinforced than unambiguous ones. The first phase was characterized by acts indicative of "getting acquainted, clarifying, and tentatively expressing attitudes" (1970, p. 61). Fisher compares his findings with others and notes the similarity between his first phase and the first phases of Bales and Strodtbeck, Schutz, and Tuckman.

The second phase, *conflict,* had significantly more unfavorable substantiation units and unfavorable interpretation units. The preponderance of unfavorable acts marked this phase as one filled with dispute. Comments were less ambiguous and expressed more tenaciously. Attitudes polarized as the group became more aware of where it was heading and of the consequences of specific proposals being made. The second phase is characterized by acts indicative of dissent, polarization of attitudes, and controversy. As with phase one, the similarity to other models was striking.

The third phase, *emergence,* had significantly fewer unfavorable acts. Characteristic of phase three were interpretation acts followed by interpretation acts, and favorable comments followed by favorable comments. Ambiguous statements reappeared and were once again reinforced. However, in this phase, such acts served to express modified dissent and mediate changes in attitudes. Unfavorable comments changed to ambiguous ones, marking an increase in favorable attitudes toward the group's decisions. Again, Fisher's third phase is similar to phases in other models.

The fourth and last phase, *reinforcement,* had significantly more acts of favorable interpretation and favorable substantiation. Dissent had almost vanished. There were few ambiguous and unfavorable comments. This last phase was devoted to affirming unity.

Fisher's main contribution seems to be confirmation of other theoretical approaches. If similar results can be obtained under diverse circumstances, then the claim for a four-phase developmental sequence certainly will seem justified.

Whether the theorist cuts up the pie of group development into three, four, or more pieces, a pattern seems to have emerged. This pattern is composed of the following elements: *orientation, conflict,* the *emergence* of a group, and the *reinforcement* of accomplishments. According to Fisher, phases can be identified not because the behavior exhibited during any one stage is unique to that stage, but because a preponderance of a particular type of behavior occurs for a given phase.

Lashbrook and Bodaken   (1967, 1971)

Based on Bales's definition of what constitutes a small group, and the principles of sociometrics (see chapter 8), Lashbrook and Bodaken developed a computerized system for analyzing small group interaction. Although no specific theory of group development has been generated on which the analysis is based, it is presented here as another way to view interaction as patterned and meaningful.

The most interesting feature of this approach, called PROANA5 (*pro*cess *ana*lysis for *five*-person groups) is that, unlike other systems of analysis which focus on the verbal or nonverbal content of interaction, this form of analysis is based on patterned or nonpatterned interaction. Patterned interaction is defined as a message, lasting less than 45 seconds, which is relevant to the previous message. Nonpatterned interaction is a message lasting longer than 45 seconds and/or one with low relevance to the previous message. The specific verbal content is not considered in the analysis; its only role is in the determination of whether a message is patterned or nonpatterned. The input data consists of frequency counts for patterned and nonpatterned messages and message direction (e.g., person A speaking to person B).

The analysis performed by the PROANA5 computer program considers the following variables:

1. *Balance of participation:* an effectively interacting group increases the amount of interaction from the first third to the second third of meeting time; interaction then tapers off in the final third.

2. *Communication line usage:* interaction is most effective when all ten possible lines of communication are used.

3. *Clique group formation:* interaction between two members which exceeds the total amount of interaction among other group members during any one period of discussion.

4. *Detrimental clique group formation:* a clique group which lasts for more than one period of interaction will probably have a detrimental effect on the group.

5. *Communication propensity:* one member of the group is selected to receive the majority of communication. This may indicate leadership or deviance from group expectations.

6. *Leadership* (together with the greatest communication propensity): when a member of the group has a large number of nonpatterned interactions, he is designated the procedural leader; if, instead, he has a large number of patterned interactions, he is designated the emergent leader.

7. *Member isolation:* an increase in nonpatterned interaction, together with a decrease in patterned interaction, indicates member isolation.

8. *Member dominance:* when a member's total amount of communication is greater than the total of any two other members' communications, he is said to be a dominant group member.

The analysis provided by PROANA5 is more complex, and certainly richer, than the short summary given here indicates, but these are the basic areas of interaction analyzed.

An example of how PROANA5 can be used may help clarify its value as a tool for investigating group interaction. Schutz's theory of compatibility leads to several hypotheses which may be tested using the PROANA5 form of analysis. For instance, Schutz has hypothesized that compatible groups differ from incompatible groups in their total number of patterned interactions, in clique group formation and in the number of unused lines of communication. A PROANA5 analysis revealed that, although not all hypotheses were confirmed, all differences were in the predicted directions. Compatible groups used statistically significantly more lines of communication and had non-significantly fewer clique groups and patterned interactions. Combining both Schutz's theory and Lashbrook's method of analyzing interaction, meaningful questions could be posed and answered concerning group behavior (Rosenfeld and Jessen 1972).

The developmental sequence a group employs varies according to the nature of the task (personal or impersonal), the nature of the group (therapeutic, social, or professional), the composition of group members ("normal" or not, young or old), and a number of other factors. The value of understanding a group's developmental sequence is obvious: group performance may be facilitated with such information. Many problems of group interaction may be attributed to faulty sequencing. An understanding of typical interaction patterns, such as conflicts which are likely to follow orientation periods, can help the group deal with their own patterns constructively. Each perspective outlined in this chapter may serve as a basis for observation. Together, they offer a variety of approaches to observation, and, combined, they offer a number of insights into the dynamics of small group interaction.

Experience 3-4.   **After each group in the class has met several times, each group should prepare one of its diaries to present to another group as a "scrambled diary." To scramble the diary, place a description of each meeting on a separate sheet of paper, remove all references to dates, then shuffle the papers. The object is to place the meetings in proper order. After this is completed, each group should explain how they accomplished the task.**

ANSWERS AND SCORING DIRECTIONS FOR
THE MOON LANDING AGREEMENT EXERCISE

	Rank
Box of matches	15
Food concentrate	4

50 ft. of nylon rope	6
Parachute silk	8
Portable heating unit	13
Two .45 caliber pistols	11
One case dehydrated Pet milk	12
Two 100-lb. tanks of oxygen	1
Stellar map	3
Life raft	9
Magnetic compasses	14
Five gallons of water	2
Signal flares	10
First-aid kit with injection needles	7
Solar-powered FM receiver-transmitter	5

Answers in order:

1 Two 100-lb. tanks of oxygen
2 Five gallons of water
3 Stellar map
4 Food concentrate
5 Solar-powered FM receiver-transmitter
6 50 feet of nylon rope
7 First-aid kit with injection needles
8 Parachute silk
9 Life raft
10 Signal flares
11 Two .45 caliber pistols
12 One case dehydrated Pet milk
13 Portable heating unit
14 Magnetic compass
15 Box of matches

Scoring. Subtract your ranking number for each item from NASA's ranking number. Add these differences. The lower the sum of the difference scores, the more favorably your rankings compare with NASA's.

Example:

	Your Ranking	NASA's	Difference
Box of matches	8	15	7
Signal Flares	14	10	4

Explanation. These are the answers supplied by the NASA scientists. The answers are split into two groups: physical survival and traveling to the rendezvous.

1. and 2. Without air and water it would be impossible to survive for even the shortest amount of time.
3. The map is necessary for locating your own position, as well as determining the proper direction to the mother ship.
4. Food concentrate supplies the daily food required for what might be several days of traveling.
5. The FM receiver-transmitter may allow for contact with the mother ship, and may serve as a distress signal transmitter.
6. Nylon rope helps in mountain climbing and tying injured together.
7. The first-aid kit contains valuable oral pills or injection medicines.
8. Parachute silk offers protection against the sun's rays.
9. The life raft serves to carry supplies or injured and provides shelter. The CO_2 bottles may serve as self-propulsion devices.
10. Flares may also serve as propulsion devices, and, when in the line of sight of the mother ship, may serve as distress calls.
11. The guns may also serve as the basis for making self-propulsion devices.
12. The dehydrated milk is heavy and useful only when mixed with water.
13. The heating unit is useful only if you landed on the dark side of the moon. The usual problem is overheating, and not cold.
14. The compass is useless since the moon probably has no magnetic poles.
15. The matches are useless because there is no oxygen on the moon.

Bibliography

Bales, R. F. *Interaction Process Analysis: A Method for the Study of Small Groups.* Reading, Massachusetts: Addison-Wesley, 1950.

Bales, R. F., and Strodtbeck, F. L. "Phases in Group Problem Solving." *Journal of Abnormal and Social Psychology* 46 (1951):485-95.

Bennis, W. G., and Shepard, H. A. "A Theory of Group Development." *Human Relations* 9 (1956):415-37.

Bion, W. R. "Experiences in Groups: I." *Human Relations* 1 (1948):314-20.

_____. "Experiences in Groups: II." *Human Relations* 1 (1948):487-96.

_____. *Experiences in Groups.* New York: Basic Books, 1961.

Bodaken, E. M., Lashbrook, W. B., and Champagne, M. "PROANA5: A Computerized Technique for the Analysis of Small Group Interaction." *Western Speech* 35 (1971):112-15.

Braden, W. W., and Brandenburg, E. *Oral Decision-Making.* New York: Harper and Brothers, 1955.

Crowell, L., and Scheidel, T. M. "Categories for Analysis of Idea Development in Discussion Groups." *The Journal of Social Psychology* 54 (1961):155-68.

Fisher, B. A. "Decision Emergence: Phases in Group Decision-Making." *Speech Monographs* 37 (1970):53-66.

Golembiewski, R. T. *The Small Group.* Chicago: University of Chicago Press, 1962. See pp. 193-200.

Hearn, G. "The Process of Group Development." *Autonomous Groups Bulletin* 13 (1957):1-7.

Lashbrook, W. B. "PROANA5: A Computerized Technique for the Analysis of Small Group Interaction." Report 3-67, Speech Communication Research Laboratory, Michigan State University, 1967.

Lashbrook, W. B., and Bodaken, E. M. "PROANA5: A Venture in Computer Assisted Instruction in Small Group Communication." *Computer Studies in the Humanities and Verbal Behavior* 2 (1969):98-101.

Martin, E. A., and Hill, W. F. "Toward a Theory of Group Development: Six Phases of Therapy Group Development." *International Journal of Group Psychotherapy* 7 (1957):20-30.

McCroskey, J. C., and Wright, D. W. "The Development of an Instrument for Measuring Interaction Behavior in Small Groups." *Speech Monographs* 38 (1971):335-40.

McGrath, J. E., and Altman, I. *Small Group Research: A Synthesis and Critique of the Field.* New York: Holt, Rinehart, 1966.

Miles, M. B. "Human Relations Training: How a Group Grows." *Teachers College Record* 55 (1953):90-96.

Philp, H., and Dunphy, D. "Developmental Trends in Small Groups." *Sociometry* 22 (1969):162-74.

Rosenfeld, L. B., and Jessen, P. A. "Compatibility and Interaction in the Small Group: Validation of Schutz's FIRO-B Using a Modified Version of Lashbrook's PROANA5." *Western Speech* 35 (1972):31-40.

Scheidel, T. M., and Crowell, L. "Idea Development in Small Groups." *Quarterly Journal of Speech* 50 (1964):140-45.

Schutz, W. C. "What Makes Groups Productive?" *Human Relations* 8 (1955):429.

———. *FIRO: A Three Dimensional Theory of Interpersonal Behavior.* New York: Holt, Rinehart, 1958.

Smith, A. J. "A Developmental Study of Group Processes." *Journal of Genetic Psychology* 97 (1960):29-39.

Thelen, H., and Dickerman, W. "Stereotypes and the Growth of Groups." *Educational Leadership* 6 (1949):309-16.

Theodorson, G. A. "Elements in the Progressive Development of Small Groups." *Social Forces* 31 (1953):311-20.

Tuckman, B. W. "Developmental Sequence in Small Groups." *Psychological Bulletin* 63 (1965):384-99.

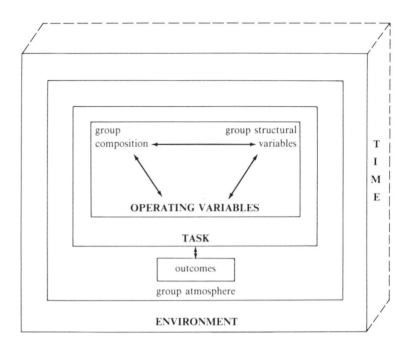

CHAPTER 4

GROUP INFLUENCE

Conformity Behavior

Before discussing conformity behavior in groups, it is necessary to collect some data. You should have enough data from other experiences but it may be too diffuse. The following experience should provide more usable data.

Experience 4-1. Form six groups: group 1 contains *three members*, no more; group 2 contains *seven members*, no less; group 3 contains *four* to *six members*; groups 4 and 5 contain *five members*, no more or less; group 6 contains any number of members. The instructions for each group for this experiment are different, so be sure to read only the instructions for your group.

Group 1: This group contains no more than three members. Your task is to reach consensus in rank ordering the ten experiences, with the most annoying ranked first, or number 1. Complete the task during the class period, or within 50 minutes.

Group 2: This group contains no less than seven members. Your task is to reach consensus rank ordering the ten experiences, with the most annoying ranked first, or number 1. Complete the task within the class period, or within 50 minutes.

Group 3: This group contains between four and six members. Your task is to reach consensus rank ordering the ten experiences, with the most annoying ranked first, or number 1. Complete the task within 15 minutes.

Group 4: This group contains five members, seated as follows:

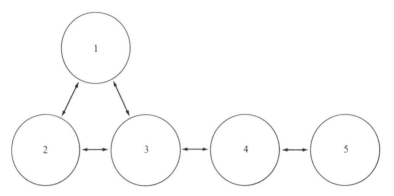

Member 1 may speak to members 2 and 3;
Member 2 may speak to members 1 and 3;
Member 3 may speak to members 1, 2, and 4;
Member 4 may *speak* to member 3 and only nod yes
    or no to member 5;
Member 5 may speak to member 4.

Your group task is to reach consensus in rank ordering the ten experiences with the most annoying first, or number 1. Complete the task within one class period, or 50 minutes.

Group 5: This group contains five members seated as follows:

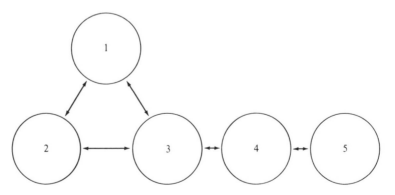

Member 1 may speak to members 2 and 3;
Member 2 may speak to members 1 and 3;
Member 3 may speak to members 1, 2, and 4;
Member 4 may *speak* to member 3 and only nod yes
  or no to member 5;
Member 5 may speak to member 4.

Your group task is to reach consensus in rank ordering the ten experiences, with the most annoying first, or number 1. Complete the task within 15 minutes.

Group 6: The task for this group is to tell the other groups how the ten experiences relate to each other. The report must be short and clear.

Below are ten common situations.
1. Your date is late.
2. Your date gets obnoxiously drunk.
3. A third person is flirting with your boyfriend (girlfriend).
4. Your date talks too much.
5. You're on a bad blind date.
6. You've been stood up.
7. The best way to characterize your date is "extremely unaffectionate."
8. Your date is a poor conversationalist.
9. Your date is inappropriately dressed for the occasion.
10. Your date won't take "no" for an answer.

Conformity is not a dirty word. It is simply behavior reflecting the successful influence of others or the degree to which an individual's behavior corresponds to the group norms, which are implicitly stated rules for behavior in the group. Consider what working in groups would be like if there were no conformity. First, working with others would be extremely frustrating if it were not possible to make certain basic assumptions about their behavior. Second, there would be little chance for consensus or group agreement. For example, we assume that when time is up, and a decision is called for, agreement will be forthcoming: each member will conform to group pressure. Without being able to make this assumption, interaction would be almost impossible. Conformity is essential to group functioning because it introduces order into the group process.

Conformity is influenced by the personality characteristics of the individuals, intragroup relationships, and external pressures. These variables interact in such a way that at a particular time any one may assume greater importance than the others.

The amount of research in conformity and deviation (aberrant behavior) is staggering. Some of the conclusions that have been reached are as follows:

1. Personality characteristics investigated, which may predispose a group member to conform, are:
   a. degree of submissiveness
   b. level of self-confidence
   c. authoritarianism
   d. intelligence
   e. originality
   f. need achievement
   g. need for social approval

2. Intragroup variables which seem to affect conformity are:
   a. cohesion
   b. attractiveness of the group
   c. importance of the group
   d. amount of interaction

3. External pressures which seem to affect conformity are:
   a. group size
   b. group structure
   c. difficulty of the problem or task confronting the group
   d. newness of the situation
   e. pressure for consensus
   f. the degree of crisis or emergency
   g. the degree of situational ambiguity

Fortunately, some propositions are available which relate and organize some of the variables affecting conformity. Before examining these propositions, let us look at a few examples of the kinds of studies done by researchers to help clarify conformity behavior.

Personality Variables

Faust (1959) investigated the relationships among need for affiliation, predisposition to conform, and the amount of group support available for a particular point of view. Individuals were classified according to low, medium, or high need for affiliation and then were asked to discuss the topic of divorce. Faust found that members with a medium need for affiliation conformed to the group decision whether or not their personal decisions were supported by other group members. This action seemed to be motivated by their desire for social acceptance. Members with high need for affiliation conformed more to a particular view even when there was no support for that particular view. Members with a low need for affiliation, usually group leaders of their respective groups, were least affected and influenced by other group members. Faust concluded that "when the individual is unanimously opposed in attitude, he changes his attitude to join his potential friends" (p. 293).

Another personality variable related to conformity is authoritarianism (Rokeach 1961). Any source to which we look for information, or to which we turn to verify information, constitutes an authority. Individuals may display two orientations toward authority, open or closed. An open orientation is based upon the authority's perceived cognitive correctness or accuracy. A closed orientation is based upon the authority's perceived power to mete out rewards and punishments.

Rokeach offers a definition of conformity unlike the one above. According to him, conformity is "a state of mind wherein the person is necessarily unaware that he cannot distinguish, assess, and act independently from an authority" (Rokeach 1961). A person who is unaware why he is conforming, but recognizes that he is, will rationalize his behavior, since conforming behavior is threatening to the self-concept. From this perspective, conformity is not merely a result of social influence or socialization, nor compliance brought about by coercion. It is a state of mind.

The more closed the orientation an individual has toward authority, the more he is predisposed toward conforming behavior. Closed-minded individuals conform more than open-minded individuals, since they do not analyze messages sent to them, but rely instead on the authority's potential punishment or reward. If a group is considering a particular course of action and offers rewards and punishments, a closed-minded individual will conform to the course of action agreed upon. To the open-minded individual, a particular course of action is viewed in terms of the possible alternatives and which of those are most feasible. This individual may behave exactly the same way as the closed-minded person, but the underlying cause of that behavior is different. Thus, the conforming behavior of the open-minded individual does not necessarily indicate that he is a conformist.

Some of the other personality characteristics that have been investigated seem to warrant the following conclusions:

1. The greater the submissive tendencies of a group member, the higher the probability he will conform to the group.
2. The better an individual's self-concept, the lower the probability he will be a conformist.
3. The greater an individual's intelligence, the lower the probability he will be a conformist.
4. The lower an individual's need achievement, the greater the probability he will conform to group norms.

Intragroup Variables

One of the most important intragroup determinants of individual conformity is group attractiveness. The more attractive a group is for an individual member, the greater will be the tendency for that member to conform. If a member of a group is uncertain about his own opinion and he considers the group to be attractive, he is likely to perceive the opinions of other group members as better than his own and, therefore, will conform to the other opinion (Hardy 1957).

The attractiveness of a group depends upon (1) the group's source of attraction and (2) the individual's own orientation in the group. There are at least two possible sources of attraction: control over what the member desires, and the ability to solve a problem of importance to the member. The greater the control a group has over what the member desires, the greater the member's attraction to the group and the greater his conformity to group behavior and norms. When someone joins a fraternity because he wants to meet girls, the fraternity is attractive to that individual because it controls the opportunity for meeting them. Similarly, to the extent that a group is better able to solve or cope with a problem which is important to the individual, the greater will be his conformity to the group. When a problem is so complex or complicated that an individual working alone is unable to solve it, the more likely it is that he will find attractive a group that is able to solve it.

The second consideration when analyzing group attractiveness is an individual member's orientation in the group, that is, whether he is task, socio-emotional (maintenance) or self-oriented. Task-oriented members will find the group attractive to the extent that it is an effective problem-solving machine, and rewards task effectiveness. These members will conform most when they see conformity as a means of achieving the task. Maintenance-oriented members are attracted to a group when it is cohesive and there is a high amount of interaction relating to the feelings and attitudes of group members. These members will conform most when they perceive that their conformity is necessary to avoid mistakes when interacting. Self-oriented members are attracted to a group when they see it as a means for solving their own problems. If the problems of this individual happen to be the same as the group's problems, it may be difficult to assess the source of attraction.

Although success may be defined differently for each type of member, research has focused primarily on task success. Kidd and Campbell (1955) confirmed the hypothesis that success on previous tasks and subsequent conformity are positively related.

A third intragroup variable relating to conformity is status. Generally, individuals with lower status tend to conform to those with higher status. Status definitions vary from group to group. In some groups, status is based upon ritual; violation of rules will bring disapproval. In other groups, status is based on formal power; in others, on intellectual prowess. How the group defines status will determine, to some extent, how much an individual will conform to that group.

Regarding conformity then, the following general conclusions seem warranted. (1) The more important the group is to the individual, the greater the probability of his conforming to the group. (2) The greater the amount of interaction, the higher the probability of conformity. Generally, the more group members are aware of each other's opinions, the greater the probability of attitude convergence. Increased interaction can insure this increase in awareness.

Situational Variables

What would happen if a teacher suddenly informed you that your performance on the next exercise will determine your class grade? For example, he might say, "Experience 4 is worth 100 points to the winning team. Team members may divide the points among themselves and these points may be used to justify an *A* in the course. The team that finishes first gets 100 points. The team that finishes last loses 100 points, and must present evidence why their grade should not be lowered." The pressure is on! The groups are in competition. The situation is one of crisis (especially for those students doing poorly in the course).

Crisis situations usually increase conformity. An examination of behavior during time of *declared* war (as during World War II) indicated that there was a decrease in deviant behavior. In situations considered borderline crises, individuals will rely on the group to determine whether or not a crisis exists. Orson Welles's 1938 broadcast of *The War of the Worlds* caused widespread panic. Cantril (1958) discovered that whether or not the situation was defined as one of crisis depended on observation of the behavior of others. If someone who listened to the broadcast believed that a crisis was at hand, that Martians really were invading, but then noticed other people behaving in a normal, everyday fashion, he re-evaluated the situation. On the other hand, if this person noticed people running through the streets screaming, "The Martians are coming, the Martians are coming," his original fear was confirmed. The basis for deciding if the situation was a crisis came from what appeared to be group consensus (a calm street versus a panic-stricken one).

In a competitive situation, Blake and Mouton (1961b) found evidence of a competition-conformity relationship. Individuals will conform to protect or enhance their own group. The greater the competition between groups, the greater the conformity. Blake and Mouton's findings indicate that individuals in a group, without communicating a course of action to each other, will challenge adversaries and disregard neutrals. Paralleling this, they rate their own group's solution to a problem as higher or superior to other groups' solutions.

To increase the homogeneity of agreement within a group, members will distort information about other groups. Under competitive conditions, members of one group *say* they understand the other group's proposal, but they probably do not. During competition, areas of agreement between competing groups go unnoticed. This helps explain situations in which bargaining or arbitration may fail to bring about agreement. Neither group understands the other's position, although both make loud claims that that is not the case—only the other guy does not understand. Both groups are likely to miss areas of agreement which could provide a basis from which to work. Redefining the situation may help this predicament. For instance, rather than focusing upon the union's obligation to its membership or the organization's profit-loss schedule, the situation may be redefined in terms of how other people are being affected by the strike. The Transit Workers' Union and the City of New York have to see a strike in terms of how it affects *other* New Yorkers.

Other situational factors that affect conformity are group size, group structure, task difficulty, the newness of the situation, and the ambiguity of the situation. Generally, conformity increases as the size of the group increases, but only up until the group contains about four members (Asch 1951). Beyond this, support for a variety of solutions and decisions increases, and the pressure to conform to any particular one decreases.

Group structure which determines the amount of group interaction is indirectly related to conformity. Structures in which positions do not differ according to the number of possible lines of communication and which allow a lot of intermember interaction produce more conformity than structures where only part of the group is responsible for communication. Of course, this variable must be considered simultaneously with the others discussed. For example, crisis seems more important than group structure. If a teacher were to set up several structures which contained isolates, as in Figure 4-1, and specify that group consensus for a correct solution be generated quickly, what do you think would happen? Will member 6 avoid communicating because it takes too long for messages to get from him to the others? Will group members adapt to the structure by effectively ignoring members 5 and 6 in order to solve the problem quickly? If so, will members 5 and 6 conform to the group's decision? If the situation is well defined as one in which speed and then accuracy are of crucial importance, the answer to both questions is yes. Yes, members 1–4 will attempt to ignore 5 and 6, and yes, 5 and 6 probably will accept the decision made by members 1, 2, 3, and 4.

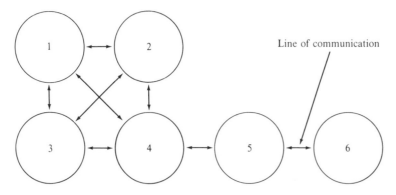

Figure 4–1.   *Group members 1, 2, 3, and 4 can all speak to each other. Member 5 can speak to only members 4 and 6, whereas member 6 can speak only to member 5. This effectively isolates member 6 to a large degree, and member 5 to a lesser degree*

Another situational variable influencing conformity is task difficulty. As the problems a group encounters become more difficult, conformity is likely to increase. This is because members become more dependent on each other for a solution; this increases the importance of the group for the members, which, in turn, leads to greater conformity. If the problem becomes too difficult and it is clear that the group will be unable to provide a solution, the group loses its importance and attractiveness for its members and conformity decreases.

The relationship between task difficulty and individual ability is also important. If the task is extremely difficult and an individual perceives himself as totally inadequate to help the group, conformity decreases for him. Newness of the situation is another variable that affects conformity. Generally, conformity is greatest in a situation which is new but resembles another situation the group encountered and in which conformity occurred. The closer the situation is to a prior one successfully handled, the greater the probability of conformity.

The last variable under this heading considers how much ambiguity is encountered. How clear are expectations for group members? Research findings indicate that the more ambiguous the situation, the greater is the probability of conformity in the group. The autokinetic situation, in which an individual traces the movement of a stationary light in a dark room (the light *appears* to move), is highly ambiguous. Group pressure in this situation was effective—80 percent of the subjects conformed to group pressure (Sherif and Sherif 1956). In a less ambiguous situation, such as when individuals must judge which of three lines is the same length as a standard line, less than 33 percent of the subjects conformed to group pressure (Asch 1951).

Other Considerations

An important question concerning conformity is, "What kind of conformity are you talking about, verbal or behavioral conformity?" We see and hear much about those who are willing to give lip service to some particular cause, but are not willing to devote their own time and efforts for it. Eliciting behavioral conformity may be different from eliciting verbal conformity. The most desirable type of conformity, of course, is a combination of the two.

The last consideration concerns propensities of individuals to conform. Studies indicate that conformers are likely to be first offspring in their families, and appear to come from unfriendly, intolerant family environments with inconsistent and rejecting parents. Being "well born," that is, being born into wealth and power, is presumed to be another determinant of conformity, since individuals from such a background may fear that not conforming may result in a loss of power and wealth. Finally, conformity thrives best in situations which reward it. It should be clear that the personality characteristics of the individuals involved, the intragroup relationships that exist, and the situational variables all interact to produce conformity.

The importance of any one consideration is relative to how it interacts with the others. Thus, predicting or trying to manipulate factors to obtain group conformity is a complex and difficult task. Nevertheless, an understanding of the factors which relate to conformity behavior should increase your effectiveness as a group member.

Compliance, Identification, and Internalization

Up to this point, no distinctions have been made concerning the various types or levels of conformity. Conformity was broadly defined as behavior reflecting the successful influence of other people on individuals, and fine distinctions have not been made. Even though several individuals may display overt behavior which we label as "conformity," the underlying processes that lead to the behaviors may differ. These underlying differences must be considered in any discussion of conformity behavior.

Kelman (1958) distinguishes three processes of influence. Although each process leads to conformity behavior, each allows us to predict the specific form of behavior which will occur under various conditions. "*Compliance* can be said to occur when an individual accepts influence because he hopes to achieve a favorable reaction from another person or group. He adopts the induced behavior not because he believes in its content but because he expects to gain specific rewards or approval and avoid specific punishments or disapproval by conforming. Thus the satisfaction derived from compliance is due to the *social effect* of accepting influence" (1958, p. 53). *Identification* exists when an individual conforms to maintain or establish what he considers a satisfying self-defining relationship to the group. He literally "takes on the role," creating a situation in which he believes in his responses, but not necessarily the specific content of those responses. Satisfaction comes from the *act* of conforming. When an individual who does not care to wear a suit to work does so because he wants to be regarded favorably by his work group, the suit itself is irrelevant; what is relevant is the *act* of wearing the suit. This is identification conformity. *Internalization* demands the most commitment. In this extreme case, the individual conforms because both the act *and* content of the act are rewarding. The conforming behavior is congruent with his value system and is likely to be integrated with his existing values. Satisfaction is due mainly to the *content* of the new conformity behavior.

Accepting the influence of others is a function of many variables. One important factor is the relative power of the influencing agent. Generally, if the agent's power is high, conformity is likely to be high.

Kelman found that, if the source of power is based on means-control, the ability of the source to control the means for action, conformity will tend toward *compliance*. If the source of power is based on attractiveness, conformity will tend toward *identification*. Lastly, if the form of power is based on credibility, the degree to which the source is perceived as trustworthy, competent, and dynamic, conformity will tend toward *internalization*.

The form that conformity takes is important only insofar as it allows us to predict what circumstances will insure conformity behavior. It should be clear from the discussion so far that it does not take stringently controlled circumstances to insure compliance conformity from an individual. The circumstances that insure internalization, however, must be more rigorous.

Kelman hypothesizes the following in regard to the conditions necessary for the three forms of conformity. If the form of conformity is compliance, then conformity behavior will be observed only if the influencing agent offers constant surveillance of the individual. If the form of conformity is identification, then conformity behavior will be observed only when the individual perceives his relationship to the influencing agent as salient. Finally, if the form of conformity is internalization, then conformity behavior will be observed when the *issue* is perceived as relevant, regardless of the salience of the relationship to the agent, or the agent's surveillance.

Kelman's three-pronged approach to the study of conformity behavior provides us with understanding which cannot be attained by focusing on the individual variables discussed earlier and their interrelationships. Viewing *each* variable in terms of its consequent form of conformity, as well as combinations of variables and their consequences, leads us to better predictions of behavior.

Public Versus Private Conformity
The focus so far has been on public performance, although Kelman has implied the public versus private distinction. In a crisis situation, conformity is likely to increase, but when the individuals involved in the decision are personally removed from the crisis, they are likely to support the group decision in *public* but deny support in *private*. The same thing occurs under more common circumstances. Classroom groups display *public* conformity in the classroom to create an image of harmony and cohesiveness but, in *private*, each member may bewail his group and cry that he has been forced to behave unnaturally.

Which forms of conformity behavior are likely to be public and private, and which merely public? Compliance is *exclusively* public conformity. Identification is *primarily* public conformity. Internalization is *both* public and private conformity.

> *Thursday, November 11   Dave seemed to be the center of attention this morning. I went with him to the Audio-Visual Department to get the equipment for our presentation. He complained all the way. He was angry with several members of the group. I cannot figure out why he wasn't angry with me, too.*
>
> *Throughout the presentation he planned and executed his revenge. At the beginning he stepped out to get some hot chocolate, leaving the group and class waiting. Then, casually, during the project, he corrected and supplemented the various introductions each of us gave. Each of us can recall what he did, although the interruptions were not noticeable to the class. We were pretty angry at the time. Whether he did this for class attention or recognition doesn't matter. If he did it to annoy the other members of the group, he succeeded.*
>
> *Then Tony remarked to the class that the members of our group liked each other so much that we wanted to remain together as a group! This was ridiculous! I may have enjoyed working on the project, but now that it's over, I'm glad. We may have looked cohesive during our presentation, but that was only to insure that we worked smoothly.*

Now try to analyze the results of experience 4-1. Each group performed essentially the same task, but with different instructions. These instructions should have led to differences in the conformity behavior. Group 1 had a small number of members and no time limit; Group 2 had a large number of members and no time limit; Group 3 had an average number of members and a very short time limit; Group 4 had an average number of members placed in a specific structure which created one (possibly two) isolated positions and there was no time limit; Group 5 was similar to 4, but had a definite time limit; and Group 6 was given a highly ambiguous situation, since the number of members, time limit, and specific task were not precisely specified.

What differences would you have predicted? Were these differences observed? Why, or why not? What must we specify in order to predict conformity behavior? What things are almost impossible to control?

Effects of Group Influence on Problem Solving

If members are aware of each other's judgments, judgments tend to converge. This finding has been confirmed by a number of studies investigating a variety of situations. Simpson (1939), in an early study, found that divergency of opinion on a re-ranking of artistic pictures *after* discussion decreased approximately 27 percent. In a later study (1960), he found that, after discussion, group members felt more confident in their responses to the Minnesota Teacher Attitude Inventory. Utterback (1950, 1956) found that, on issues discussed at inter-collegiate conferences, individuals tended to shift their opinions toward prediscussion majority viewpoints about half the time. New positions were also accepted. This second finding points to the fact that individuals affect and are affected by the group.

What happens when a vocal minority exists in a group? Does the minority conform to the majority, does the majority yield to the vocal minority, or do both subgroups shift to accommodate each other? To answer these and other questions, Grove (1965) manipulated group composition with respect to attitudes toward the topics discussed, public or private expression of attitude, and presence or absence of discussion. He found that discussion produced more attitude convergence than either public or private expression. Interestingly, the single deviate in each group altered his own attitude, as well as the attitudes of the other members. Grove's results seem to indicate that the final group attitude, as well as final individual attitude, differs from both the initial majority and minority positions.

The influence of majority and minority positions on each other suggests that the group process is a self-correcting one: incorrect majority and minority ideas will be filtered out during group discussion. The group, as a whole, is more likely to accept suggestions that ultimately prove viable and reject suggestions which are not tenable (Utterback 1962). As more suggestions and sides are aired, the probability of the best solutions being accepted increases.

Although group discussion generates pressure toward uniformity, the influence members have on each other constitutes only one of the many influences that exist. Other influences derive from sex differences, situational differences, and individual differences, such as intelligence.

Groups Versus Individuals

Although it may sound like heresy in this age of "group think," it should be quite obvious that under many conditions groups are *not* useful. Before considering the conditions which affect the decision of whether to employ a group or an individual to solve the particular problem at hand, take time to do the following.

Experience 4-2. Divide your class into small groups with four to six members each. Select several individuals to work alone. Ask each group and each individual to generate test items for an examination on small group dynamics. Groups should follow a brain-storming procedure, that is, each idea generated should not be subject to discussion until all ideas have been exhausted. The object, for both the groups and individuals, is to generate as many items for the examination as possible.

Experience 4-3. Divide the class as in experience 4-2. Ask each group member, as well as each individual, to estimate the temperature of the room. Group members should add their estimates together, then divide by the total number of members to obtain a group average. Now obtain a class average for all the groups.

Experience 4-4. Divide the class as in experience 4-2, and solve the following problem: A farmer must cross a river but he has a problem. He has a bale of grass, a wolf, and a lamb with him, and the boat can hold only the farmer and *one of the three at a time.* If he leaves the lamb alone with the grass, the grass will be eaten. If he leaves the wolf with the lamb, the lamb will be eaten. How can he transport the wolf, the lamb, and the grass safely to the other side?

Experience 4-5. Divide the class once again as for the other experiences. This time develop a short crossword puzzle on any topic. Each puzzle must have at least ten words.

Experience 4-6. The last experience is similar to the fifth one. This time, the groups and individuals must *complete* a crossword puzzle. Do not use any of the puzzles generated during the fourth problem; use one from your daily newspaper or a magazine.

By now you are exhausted. Good. You should be able to generate a list of guidelines for using either a *group* or an *individual* for problem solving. Generate such a list and compare it with the one at the end of this chapter. What modifications are necessary (for both lists)?

As mentioned earlier, we live in an age when groups are employed for virtually all types of problem solving, in spite of the fact that they may not be the most efficient way to find a solution. As our society becomes more complex, and problems become more involved, the trend toward relying on groups probably will increase. The complexities of modern life, the innumerable facts which can affect significant decisions, force leaders of industry and government to seek counsel and help when making decisions.

Early research in group discussion attempted to compare the relative advantages and disadvantages of individuals and groups. This research focused on the outcomes or products of the two methods, not the processes each used. According to Dickens and Heffernan (1949), the following conclusions were supported by the research.

1. Discussion tends to draw extreme judgments toward a middle ground; extreme judgments become less extreme.
2. After discussion, judgments tend to improve in accuracy or correctness.
3. The majority opinion in a group exerts a great deal of influence upon individual member's decisions.
4. Correct answers are supported more tenaciously by the group than incorrect ones.
5. The greater the range of responses permitted by a given problem, the greater the superiority of the group method over the individual method for finding solutions.

Much of this research, though, offers little support for the claim that two heads are better than one. Results are ambiguous; in many cases it has been shown that average individual judgments were probably as good as, and perhaps superior to, the judgments made after group discussion (Harnack 1964, pp. 21–22).

Marjorie E. Shaw (1932), however, has provided some clear evidence in favor of group superiority. Giving groups and individuals complex problems that called for rational solutions (such as experience 4-4), she found that groups produce more correct solutions than individuals, but at the expense of greater time. Groups tend to check errors and reject incorrect suggestions; individuals rarely are able to accomplish this.

Shaw's work was confirmed by Barnlund (1959). Barnlund had his groups solve reasoning problems that involved arguments in which personal feelings were likely to be strong. In order to control for the effects of differing abilities, Barnlund matched group members for ability. His results were clear: groups rather than individuals were superior in solving the assigned tasks. He also found that combined critical thinking was more likely to catch and correct deficiencies in evidence and reasoning than an individual effort. In addition, he hypothesized that group interaction seemed to have a stimulating effect upon the performance of individuals.

This last hypothesis has been tested under a variety of conditions (Triplett 1897; Travis 1925; Begum and Lehr 1963). Whether bicycle racers worked alone, were paced, or were in competition (Triplett), and whether an audience was present (Travis; Begum and Lehr), the effect was consistent: the presence of other people has either *no* effect or a *facilitating* effect on performance. If the task is a motor one, as in the Travis study, the effect is likely to be facilitative. If the task is more cognitive in nature, the effect of an audience is likely to be trivial.

Ewbank and Auer (1954, p. 115) concluded that group thinking is superior to individual thinking when there are a variety of points of view on the problem, a large number of suggestions for the solution of the problem, or a large number of effective criticisms for the proposed solutions.

The Task

The type of problem encountered determines group performance. If only a few steps are necessary to solve the problem, and if the solution is easily verifiable by others who possess the relevant facts, the group probably will function at the level of its best member. In other words, in such a case it would be as reasonable to use the "best" person as it would to use a group to solve the problem. Simple problems in math and reasoning, such as the fourth experience above, are examples of this type of problem.

The solution to the fourth problem is easily verified and has few steps. The final group solution is equal to that of the best member. The solution to experience 4-4 follows: the farmer takes the lamb across first, then goes back for the wolf, drops the wolf off and picks up the lamb to be returned to the original side, where he leaves the lamb and carts the grass to the wolf's side, dropping off the grass and returning for the lamb to complete the crossing.

The probability of the group exceeding the level of the best member increases as the problem more nearly approximates the following requirements. The problem has multiple parts; no one group member possesses all of the information necessary to solve it or has access to all the parts. Examples of this situation are common. For instance, presidential committees usually are designed to insure that experts in different areas are brought together to solve a problem that demands the pooling of diverse bits of knowledge. In your own group projects, one of the earliest steps is dividing the task into its presumed component parts so that different members can gain the necessary expertise to finally solve the problem. The problems are too complex for any one member to solve successfully. Pooling the group's resources, however, allows not only for the group to solve its problem, but also to exceed the performance level of its best member.

Another consideration is necessary at this point. If group members have high task compatibility, the probability of the group exceeding the level of the best member increases. This seems a reasonable conclusion, given the hypotheses generated by Bales (see chapter 2). As social solidarity (Bales's terminology) increases, task performance decreases, and motivation to adapt to the external situation also decreases.

The third situation that exists because of the nature of the task is the case where the group's level of performance falls below the level of the best member. This situation most likely occurs when the solution is difficult to verify and when the members engage in nontask-solving behavior, such as interpersonal conflicts. You probably have experienced the following situation. A member of your group offers a solution, but he is unable to explain how or why it will solve the problem. As a consequence, the group ignores him. Later it discovers that his solution was correct. But because the solution could not be verified (in this case explained), the group fell below the level of its most proficient member.

The second condition, that is, when the group engages in nontask behavior, occurs more often than the first one. Interpersonal conflicts are cómmon to all groups. Each of the subsystem theories discussed in chapter 3 includes, in some form, a conflict phase that is part of the developmental process. If a group cannot cope with and finally resolve interpersonal conflicts, its task behavior is severely impaired and its performance level will fall below that of the most proficient member.

There is a clear relationship between task difficulty and the problem-solving abilities of groups and individuals. It may have been implied that problems with few steps and easily verified solutions are easy. This is not necessarily so. For example, problems in mathematics, which require few steps and have highly verifiable solutions, may not be considered easy at all. Ask someone in a calculus class. By the same token, multifaceted problems may be easy once the relevant information is made available. The difficulty in such a case may not be finding an adequate solution; it may simply be finding the time to go to the library and do the research.

The easier a problem, the greater the probability that the most capable members can master it alone. With an easy problem, group members have little to offer each other. Seeking a group solution would be a waste of time and effort. If the problem is more difficult, each member is more likely to contribute in some way to the overall solution. Pooling, therefore, is beneficial, and the group solution may well be worth the extra time and effort involved.

Generally, then, the best kind of problem for group problem solving is one of moderate difficulty for the group members, characterized by multiple parts and a wide variety of solutions, each of which is verifiable.

Groups Versus Individuals: Speed

The relationship between the speed with which individuals and groups work and the type of problem they encounter has already been touched upon. The fewer the steps and the more easily verifiable a problem is, the better it is suited to individual work. Thus, given a concrete problem, the smaller the group, the faster a solution will be generated. Conversely, the more abstract the problem (such as a move in chess), the more time smaller groups will consume.

Groups are time consuming when measured in man-hours. An individual working ten hours uses as many man-hours as ten individuals working one hour. This means that even if a group finishes a task faster than an individual, it may still consume many more man-hours. Both individuals and groups must become oriented toward the problem, but the expression of diverse viewpoints in a group consumes a great deal more time. One explanation for this greater consumption of time is that groups must pass through certain developmental stages before they can function as problem-solving units.

Similarly, groups characteristically pass through a conflict stage unnecessary for individuals. The third stage of group development, the emergence of a group, also is not applicable to individuals. Finally, the emergence and reinforcement of solutions take longer for groups, since more solutions are offered and a greater number of people need reinforcement. In order to derive the benefits offered by group work, it is *necessary* to consume more time than an individual might take for the same problem.

One consolation to the increased time consumption of groups is illustrated by the notion that groups are "slow but sure." Groups usually produce more and better solutions, but at a price. The question, then, becomes, "Which is more important, the time or the solution?" If the solution has few, if any, consequences, or is to serve only a temporary function, then individual problem solving may be the desired course of action. If the solution is more important than problem-solving time, or when it appears that it will be impossible to reverse the effects of the solution, then group problem solving may be in order.

Groups Versus Individuals: Risk

Experience 4-7: Read the first situation. Now decide what probabilities for success you must have in order to switch to the second alternative. Probabilities available are 1, 3, 5, 7, or 9 chances out of ten that the alternative will occur. Selecting 10 (that is, there is no chance involved) is essentially a refusal to accept the alternatives. How much risk are you willing to tolerate in the first situation? The second? The third?

1. What risk are you willing to assume in order to accept the alternative in the following case. John may stay

in the English class with which he preregistered and, given the teacher's past performance, be assured a grade of B, or he may switch to another class with a more exciting teacher whose past grading record indicates no assurance of any particular grade. Given this situation, you might say to yourself, "If the chances are 1 in 10 of receiving at least a B in the more exciting class, I would make the switch." At the other extreme, you might say to yourself, "I would never make the switch unless I am *guaranteed* a grade of at least a B in the more exciting class." Somewhere in the middle of these extremes is the position, "If the chances are 5 in 10 of receiving at least a B in the more exciting class, I would make the change."

2. A man may continue to date the woman he is presently dating. She is nice looking and intelligent but would refuse to see him again if she knew that he asked another woman out. He may continue to date woman #1, or he may ask a prettier, more intelligent woman out with no assurance of success.

3. A teacher with tenure may stay in his present school system with an adequate salary or he may go to another system with a higher salary, but no assurance of being given tenure.

After each individual in the class has responded to the situations above, divide the class into groups with four to six members each. Each group now must reach consensus on the probabilities necessary to accept the alternatives in each situation.

What happened in the groups? Did the probability of success necessarily increase (indicating a more conservative decision) or decrease (indicating a riskier decision)? Discuss the effects you think you observed and their possible causes.

It has already been noted that the presence of other people has an effect on the number and quality of decisions a group generates. Groups tend to stimulate individual productivity. A more subtle effect of the presence of other people is revealed in how much risk a group is willing to assume as opposed to how much *individuals* are willing to assume. Generally, groups are likely to make riskier decisions than individuals.

Comparing group-centered and leader-centered groups, Ziller (1957) found that group-centered decisions were riskier than leader-centered decisions. Since Ziller's study, a great many other researchers have focused on the "risky-shift phenomenon." Stoner (1968) found that prediscussion decisions were less risky than postdiscussion decisions. Wallach, Kogan, and Bem (1962), increasing the diversity of situations under which the risky-shift phenomenon was observed, came to substantially the same conclusion as Stoner. Wallach and Kogan (1965) confirmed the earlier findings and specified that regardless of whether or not the group reached consensus, if discussion took place, the risky-shift phenomenon occurred.

Although the mere occurrence of the risky-shift phenomenon is of interest, without understanding the reasons for its occurrence it becomes a simple curiosity. A number of explanations have been offered. Three of the most reasonable explanations are that (1) a high value is placed on risk in the American society and (2) there is a diffusion of individual responsibility when a group operates by consensus. A third explanation concerns the greater influence of the risky individual on the group.

The first explanation of the risky-shift phenomenon was proposed by Brown (1965). Our society values risk, so it is logical that risk takers have high status. During discussion the average level of risk individuals are willing to take becomes evident. That level becomes the baseline for group "risk." To be considered risky, a member must exceed the group baseline. As individuals try to gain status, the amount of risk they are willing to assume increases. Eventually, the level of risk the group is willing to assume becomes higher than a simple average of the initial individual positions.

Individuals may shift for reasons other than status. Individuals perceive that they are greater risk takers than others (Levinger and Schneider 1969). Asked to respond to twelve choice dilemmas in three ways—own choice, believed choice of other students, and best choice —it was found that students see themselves as greater risk takers than others and that they admire even greater risk takers. This causes shifts toward greater risk.

Another reason individuals may shift and become more risky in groups is that they feel it is expected of them. Consider the time that a group of which you were a member "insisted" on your becoming more risky than you would prefer. For example, in New York it is not uncommon for otherwise respectable groups of young boys to steal hub caps from cars. Although individual members may not want to participate in this activity because of the risk involved, they often go along because other members expect that they will take the risk. The effect is cumulative; the group becomes more risky.

The second explanation of the risky-shift phenomenon concerns diffusion of responsibility. Wallach et al. (1962) favored this hypothesis which considers the individual's responsibility to the particular decision and his responsibility to act as the group's representative. Whereas an individual must assume the responsibility for his own decision, he does not have to assume *as much* responsibility for his group's decision. By the same token, whereas an individual must be the spokesman for his own decision, he does not have to feel as responsible for being the spokesman for his group's decision. As individual responsibility decreases, the amount of risk taking increases.

Group consensus is one of the best methods groups use for diffusing individual responsibility. Consider the hospital panel which must decide which of several patients will be awarded use of a kidney machine and who, because of age or lack of equipment, will die. How does this decision relate to the risky-shift phenomenon? How do the criteria used relate? Are members of the panel willing to take greater risks with certain patients because, if they are proven wrong, the blame, like the decision-making responsibilities, diffuses? Risk, diffusion of responsibility, and group consensus are interrelated. As your knowledge and experience with small groups improves, try to trace the influence each element has within various contexts.

The third explanation of the risky-shift phenomenon deals with the influence risk-taking individuals have on their groups. Since group members value individuals who take greater risks than they themselves take and perceive them to be more forceful in group discussions (Wallach, Kogan, and Burt 1965), Marquis (1962) suggests that higher risk takers will have greater influence on the other members.

It is possible, of course, that the high risk takers have other qualities that contribute to their greater influence. High risk takers are characterized as colorful and dynamic, two highly influential characteristics, while conservative group members (low risk takers) are usually characterized as dull and drab. Therefore, the influence these members have may logically be attributable to characteristics other than risk taking.

Taken together, all three explanations contribute toward a better understanding of the risky-shift phenomenon. Each one directs our attention to some of the crucial variables involved. Whether one explanation is more feasible than another probably depends on the specific circumstances, the nature of the task, the consequences of the decision, and the amount of time available for generating a decision.

Propositions Contrasting Group and Individual Performance

Collins and Guetzkow, in *A Social Psychology of Group Processes for Decision Making* (1964), have developed a list of propositions contrasting group and individual performance (pp. 54-55). These propositions are discussed below.

> PROPOSITION 2.1 When several individuals work collectively on a single task their activities will (a) overlap and/or (b) make a division of labor possible.

This proposition results in two consequences. (1) There will be an informal series of checks where information of tasks overlaps. (2) Because of the division of labor, more information will be at the disposal of the group than at the disposal of any one individual, which will increase the probability of better decisions.

> PROPOSITION 2.1-A. For tasks involving random error, combining several individual estimates or solutions into a single group product will increase accuracy.

In an earlier experience you were asked to estimate the temperature of the room. How accurate was your individual estimate? How accurate was your group estimate? How accurate was the total class estimate? Accuracy should have increased at each step because the difference between the actual temperature and the predicted or guessed temperature is random, that is, it does not vary systematically from individual to individual. For every individual who guessed too high, there was undoubtedly one who guessed too low. By averaging the different estimates, the highs and the lows tend to cancel each other out. Thus, the group estimate should be more accurate. The larger the group, the more accurate should be the final estimate, since the probability of having as many high as low estimates is increased.

> PROPOSITION 2.1-B. For tasks which involve creating ideas or remembering information, there is a greater probability that one of several persons will produce the information than that a single individual will produce it by himself.

The second experience in this chapter concerned generating items for an examination on group dynamics. What was the average number of items produced by the individuals working alone? What was the average for the groups? According to proposition 2.1-B, the group average should be higher, since the group should have more of the information necessary to generate items. The presence of additional people may also stimulate greater activity which results in higher production.

PROPOSITION 2.1-C. Groups will be efficient when the critical demands of the task emphasize the gain (a) from a duplication of effort and/or (b) from the division of labor.

Simple problems in mathematics are best done by individuals. As problems become more complex, and more information and greater checks are necessary to insure accuracy, groups become more efficient than individuals.

PROPOSITION 2.2 When several individuals are limited to a single product, it will be selected from available ideas and information.
PROPOSITION 2.2-A. The final group product will exclude some of the ideas and information potentially available to each member.
PROPOSITION 2.2-B. The accuracy and quality of the final group product will be increased through the elimination of inferior individual contributions.

Groups are superior to individuals in many cases because a greater amount of information is at their disposal. But this does not imply that the accessible information is infinite in quantity. The group may still lack valuable information after all available information is pooled; some critical information may be omitted. In producing a product, the group will pick and choose pieces of available information and sort out what appears reasonable from what appears unreasonable. The more meticulous the group in winnowing their information, the greater will be the probability of a superior product.

PROPOSITION 2.3 A group of individuals working together will usually consume more man-hours when compared to (a) an equal number of individuals working separately and (b) a group with fewer members.

It is this greater amount of interaction that accounts for the greater time consumed by larger groups, Also, developmental processes are similar for both small and large groups. When comparing different size groups attempting to solve the same task, the smaller groups should work faster. Did this happen when you were solving the problems posed in this chapter? Did the groups of four finish before the groups of six? Finally, how do individuals compare with groups? Remember that comparisons are being made in terms of man-hours, not "real" hours. (Calculate man-hours by multiplying the number of members of a group by the number of hours spent working.)

> PROPOSITION 2.4. When an individual works in the presence of other persons, a variety of social motives becomes relevant which are not evoked when an individual works alone.

An example of this concerns the use of foul language. Although a person working alone may not hesitate to cry out with some obscenity when a solution to a problem is not forthcoming, the same person probably would hesitate in a group. Furthermore, a person working alone may not feel that he has to "prove" anything, whereas in a group he may feel that he has to live up to certain minimum standards to keep in good standing. Thus, he may work harder in a group.

> PROPOSITION 2.4-A. The presence of other individuals will frequently increase individual productivity, although the effect may be temporary.
> PROPOSITION 2.4-B. The presence of other individuals may increase the defensiveness of the individual, although the effect may be temporary.
> PROPOSITION 2.4-C. The presence of other individuals can constitute a distraction and lower productivity.

Groups, unlike individuals, must go through developmental stages before becoming effective working units. Until problems associated with the socio-emotional aspects of group development are solved, interpersonal relations may prevent effective task functioning. Usually, social problems are resolved as the group enters the third phase of group development, group emergence.

> PROPOSITION 2.5. The quality of the group product frequently increases when group members utilize social sources of knowledge.
> PROPOSITION 2.5-A. The group is most likely to accept a member's ideas (a) when they are well supported by evidence, (b) when they are logically sound or internally consistent, and (c) when they are consistent with past experience.

PROPOSITION 2.5-B. Social (or personal-centered) influence frequently causes the better alternatives to be chosen.

PROPOSITION 2.5-C. The social weighting given to the majority opinion (i.e., conformity) frequently causes the better alternatives to be chosen.

PROPOSITION 2.6. Group members may collectively achieve more than the most superior members are capable of achieving alone.

Examine your own groups, both the long- and short-lived ones, and see if you can present evidence for these propositions. Under what circumstances does increased interpersonal social activity, which leads to increased social influence, produce a better product? What criteria did your group use for taking a contribution seriously? Did you examine the evidence for the contribution, as well as its internal consistency? Did you evaluate the source and not the contribution, allowing members with high status more leeway in presenting evidence? Did the majority members have more influence? Were their solutions better than the others offered? Finally, under what circumstances did your various groups achieve more than the most proficient or superior members? What kinds of problems were you working on? What were the group members like?

Criteria for Choosing a Group or Individual Problem-Solving Procedure

The following are important aspects to consider in deciding whether to use an individual or a group to solve a particular problem. Depending upon the particular circumstances, some will be more important than others. Which are most important can only be determined by the task and socio-emotional functions your group must perform. A yes response indicates that a group should be used to solve a problem; a no response indicates that an individual should be used.

1. Are many steps required to solve the problem?
2. Are there many parts to the problem?
3. Will the solution be difficult to verify?
4. Are the individuals involved likely to perceive the problem as an impersonal one?
5. Will the problem be of moderate difficulty for the individuals who constitute the group?

Human Interaction in the Small Group Setting

6. Is a great deal of information required to solve the problem? Would a single individual be unlikely to possess it?
7. Does the problem demand a division of labor?
8. Are many solutions desired?
9. Are many man-hours required for the problem's solution?
10. Will individuals have to assume a great deal of responsibility for the solution?
11. Are the proposed solutions likely to be diverse?
12. Are the attitudes concerning the problem likely to be diverse?
13. Is it unlikely that group members will engage in nontask-oriented behavior?

Bibliography

Aronson, E., and Mills, J. "The Effect of Severity of Initiation on Liking for a Group." *Journal of Abnormal and Social Psychology* 59 (1959): 177–81.

Asch, S. E. "Effects of Group Pressure upon the Modification and Distortion of Judgments." In *Groups, Leadership and Men,* edited by H. Guetzkow, p. 177–90. Pittsburgh: Carnegie Press, 1951.

Back, K. W. "Influence through Social Communication." *Journal of Abnormal and Social Psychology* 46 (1951): 9–23.

Barnlund, D. C. "A Comparative Study of Individual, Majority, and Group Judgment." *Journal of Abnormal and Social Psychology* 58 (1959): 55–60.

Bass, B. M. "Conformity, Deviation, and a General Theory of Interpersonal Behavior." In *Conformity and Deviation,* edited by I. Berg and B. M. Bass, pp. 38–100. New York: Harper, 1961.

Begum, B. O., and Lehr, D. J. "Effects of Authoritarianism on Vigilance Performance." *Journal of Applied Psychology* 47 (1963): 75–77.

Berenda, R. W. *The Influence of the Group on Judgments of Children.* New York: King's Crown Press, 1950.

Blake, R. R., and Mouton, J. S. "Conformity, Resistance and Conversion." In *Conformity and Deviation,* edited by I. Berg and B. M. Bass, pp. 1–37. New York: Harper, 1961a.

———. "Competition, Communication, and Conformity." In *Conformity and Deviation,* edited by I. Berg and B. M. Bass, pp. 199–229. New York: Harper, 1961b.

Bochner, A. P., and Tucker, R. K. "A Multivariate Investigation of Machiavellianism and Task Structure in Four-man Groups." Paper presented at the Speech Communication Association annual convention, December 1971.

Brown, R. *Social Psychology.* New York: Free Press, 1965.

Cantril, H. "The Invasion from Mars." In *Readings in Social Psychology,* edited by E. E. Maccoby and T. M. Newcomb, pp. 291–99. New York: Holt, Rinehart and Winston, 1958.

Collins, B. E., and Guetzkow, H. *A Social Psychology of Group Processes for Decision Making.* New York: John Wiley and Sons, 1964.

Crutchfield, R. S. "Conformity and Character." *American Psychologist* 10 (1955): 191–98.

Deutsch, M. "An Experimental Study of the Effects of Cooperation and Competition upon Group Process."*Human Relations* 2 (1949): 199–232.

————. "Some Factors Affecting Membership Motivation and Achievement Motivation." *Human Relations* 12 (1959): 81–95.

Deutsch, M., and Gerard, H. "A Study of Normative and Informational Social Influences on Individual Judgment." *Journal of Abnormal and Social Psychology* 51 (1955): 629–36.

Dickens, M., and Heffernan, M. "Experimental Research in Group Discussion." *Quarterly Journal of Speech* 35 (1949): 23–29.

Ewbank, E., and Auer, J. J. *Handbook for Discussion Leaders.* New York: Appleton-Century-Crofts, 1954.

Faust, W. "Group Versus Individual Problem Solving." *Journal of Abnormal and Social Psychology* 59 (1959): 68–72.

Festinger, L., Schachter, S., and Back, K. *Social Pressures in Informal Groups: A Study of Human Factors in Housing.* New York: Harper, 1950.

Freedman, J. L., Wallington, S. A., and Bless, E. "Compliance without Pressure: The Effect of Guilt." *Journal of Personality and Social Psychology* 7 (1967): 117–24.

Gerard, H. B. "Deviation, Conformity, and Commitment." In *Current Studies in Social Psychology,* edited by I. D. Steiner and M. Fishbein, pp. 263–76. New York: Holt, Rinehart and Winston, 1965.

Goldberg, S. C. "Influence and Leadership as a Function of Group Structure." *Journal of Abnormal and Social Psychology* 51 (1955): 119–22.

Grove, T.G. "Attitude Convergence in Small Groups." *Journal of Communication* 15 (1965): 226–38.

Hamblin, R. L. "Leadership and Crisis." *Sociometry* 21 (1958): 322–35.

Hardy, K. "Determinants of Conformity and Attitude Change." *Journal of Abnormal and Social Psychology* 54 (1957): 289–94.

Harnack, R. V. "A Study of the Effect of an Organized Minority upon a Discussion Group." *Journal of Communication* 13 (1963): 12–24.

Harnack, R. V., and Fest, T. B. *Group Discussion Theory and Technique.* New York: Appleton-Century-Crofts, 1964.

Harvey, O. J., and Consalvi, C. "Status and Conformity to Pressure in Informal Groups." *Journal of Abnormal and Social Psychology* 60 (1960): 182–87.

Hollander, E. P., and Willis, R. H. "Some Current Issues in the Psychology of Conformity and Nonconformity." *Psychological Bulletin* 68 (1967): 62–76.

Homans, G. C. *The Human Group.* New York: Harcourt, Brace and World, 1950.

Jackson, J., and Saltzstein, H. D. "The Effect of Person-Group Relations on Conformity Processes." *Journal of Abnormal and Social Psychology* 57 (1958): 17–24.

Kelley, H. H. "Two Functions of Reference Groups." In *Readings in Social Psychology,* edited by G. E. Swanson, T. M. Newcomb, and E. L. Hartley, pp. 410–14. 2d ed. New York: Holt, Rinehart and Winston, 1952.

Kelman, H. C. "Compliance, Identification, and Internalization." *Journal of Conflict Resolution* 2 (1958): 51–60.

Kidd, J. S., and Campbell, D. T. "Conformity to Groups as a Function of Group Success." *Journal of Abnormal and Social Psychology* 51 (1955): 390–93.

Kiesler, C. A., and Kiesler, S. B. *Conformity.* Reading, Massachusetts: Addison-Wesley, 1969.

League, B. J., and Jackson, D. N. "Conformity, Veridicality, and Self-esteem." *Journal of Personality and Social Psychology* 68 (1964): 113–15.

Levinger, G., and Schneider, D. J. "Test of the 'Risk Is a Value' Hypothesis." *Journal of Personality and Social Psychology* 11 (1969): 165–69.

Marquis, D. G. "Individual Responsibility and Group Decision Involving Risk." *Industrial Management Review* 3 (1962): 8–23.

Milgram, S. "Liberating Effects of Group Pressure." *Journal of Personality and Social Psychology* 1 (1965): 127–34.

———. "Some Conditions of Obedience and Disobedience to Authority." In *Current Studies in Social Psychology,* edited by I. D. Steiner and M. Fishbein, pp. 243–62. New York: Holt, Rinehart and Winston, 1965.

Rokeach, M. "Authority, Authoritarianism, and Conformity." In *Conformity and Deviation,* edited by I. Berg and B. M. Bass, pp. 230–57. New York: Harper, 1961.

Schachter, S. "Deviation, Rejection, and Communication." *Journal of Abnormal and Social Psychology* 46 (1951): 190–207.

Shaw, M. E. "A Comparison of Individuals and Small Groups in the Rational Solution of Complex Problems." *American Journal of Psychology* 44 (1932): 491–504.

Shaw, M. E., and Reitan, H. T. "Attribution of Responsibility as a Basis for Sanctioning Behavior." *British Journal of Social and Clinical Psychology* 8 (1969): 217–26.

Sherif, M., and Sherif, C. W. *An Outline of Social Psychology* Rev. ed. New York: Harper and Row, 1956.

Simpson, R. H. "The Effect of Discussion on Intra-Group Divergencies of Judgment." *Quarterly Journal of Speech* 25 (1939): 546–52.

———. "Attitudinal Effects of Small Group Discussions: Shifts on Certainty-Uncertainty and Agreement-Disagreement Continua." *Quarterly Journal of Speech* 46 (1960): 415–18.

Stoner, J. A. F. "Risky and Cautious Shifts in Group Decisions: The Influence of Widely Held Values." *Journal of Experimental Social Psychology* 4 (1968): 442–59.

Travis, L. E. "The Effect of a Small Audience upon Eye-Hand Coordination." *Journal of Abnormal and Social Psychology* 20 (1925): 142–46.

Triplett, N. "The Dynamogenic Factors in Pacemaking and Competition." *American Journal of Psychology* 9 (1897): 507–33.

Utterback, W. E. "The Influence of Conference on Opinion." *Quarterly Journal of Speech* 36 (1950): 365–70.

———. "Measuring the Outcome of an Intercollegiate Discussion Conference." *Journal of Communication* 6 (1956): 33–37.

———. "Majority Influence and Cogency of Argument in Discussion." *Quarterly Journal of Speech* 48 (1962): 412–14.

Wallach, M. A., and Kogan, N. "The Roles of Information, Discussion, and Consensus in Group Risk Taking." *Journal of Experimental Social Psychology* 1 (1965): 1–19.

Wallach, M. A., Kogan, N., and Bem, D. J. "Group Influence on Individual Risk Taking." *Journal of Abnormal and Social Psychology* 65 (1962): 75–86.

———. "Diffusion of Responsibility and Level of Risk Taking in Groups." *Journal of Abnormal and Social Psychology* 68 (1964): 263–74.

Wallach, M. A., Kogan, N., and Burt, R. B. "Can Group Members Recognize the Effect of Group Discussion upon Risk Taking?" *Journal of Experimental Social Psychology* 1 (1965): 379–95.

Wechsler, D. "Conformity and the idea of Being Well Born." In *Conformity and Deviation,* edited by I. Berg and B. M. Bass, pp. 412–23. New York: Harper, 1961.

Whyte, W. F. *Street Corner Society: The Social Structure of an Italian Slum.* Chicago: University of Chicago Press, 1943.

Whyte, W. H., Jr. *The Organization Man.* Garden City, New York: Doubleday, 1957.

Ziller, R. C. "Four Techniques of Group Decision Making under Uncertainty." *Journal of Applied Psychology* 41 (1957): 384–88.

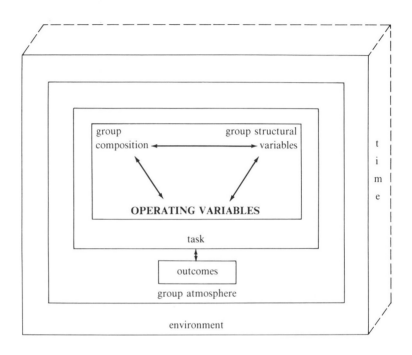

group
composition ←——————→ group structural
variables

t
i
m
e

OPERATING VARIABLES

task

outcomes

group atmosphere

environment

CHAPTER 5

ROLE BEHAVIOR

Clear your heads. Forget about the title of this chapter. Lean back and take a deep breath. Get ready to respond honestly and openly in the following experiences. A note is necessary at the outset: some instructions are for subgroups of the groups you form, and those subgroups *only.* Do not cheat.

Experience 5-1. Below are eleven statements to which you are going to respond individually. The letters before the statements are as follows: TA, which represents Total Agreement; A, which represents Agreement; U, which represents Undecided; D, which represents Disagreement; and TD, which represents Total Disagreement. After each person in the class completes the eleven statements, form small groups with four to six members. The group task is to arrive at a unanimous decision for each response. Do not use conflict-reducing techniques, such as averaging or vote by majority decision. The group may reword the statements to facilitate agreement.

TA A U D TD   1. Each member of this larger group should be required to give some form of graded oral report.

TA A U D TD   2. I could take any of my friends home to meet my parents.

TA A U D TD   3. A person should always stand for what he feels is right, even if losing friends is at stake.

TA A U D TD   4. I wouldn't be afraid to experiment with some of the drugs found in this area (the campus).

TA A U D TD   5. If I caught a friend cheating, I would report him to the teacher.

TA A U D TD   6. It is necessary to have an examination for me to demonstrate that I have done all the work.

TA A U D TD   7. Better discipline is needed in our schools.

TA A U D TD   8. I am not afraid of being "shot down" when asking for a date.

TA A U D TD   9. We have little control over what we communicate to others about ourselves.

TA A U D TD   10. Congruence between feelings and verbal and non-verbal behavior is desirable.

TA A U D TD   11. Examinations are necessary to insure that assigned work has been completed.

Experience 5-2. Divide the class into halves, "teachers" and "students." Have the "students" leave while the "teachers" are given instructions. The "students" *may not* read the instructions for the "teachers"; "teachers" *may not* read "students' " instructions. "Students' " instructions will be read first; therefore, all "teachers" are to leave the room. Then "teachers' " instructions are to be read, with the "students" out of the room.

After the instructions are given, randomly pair a "student" with a "teacher." Observe what happens.

Instructions for Students: You have failed the first two examinations for the course and the teacher has called you into his office. Select one of the following roles to play. Be sure not to appear inconsistent.

1. *Hostile.* You are sure that the teacher is against you. Other people did well, but you are sure it is because the teacher likes them.

2. *Understanding.* You sympathize with the teacher. You see the problem you are creating and feel bad for taking up the teacher's valuable time.

3. *Disturbed.* You feel that you are emotionally ill. You saw the school psychologist once about a year ago and have been using that meeting to its best advantage with every teacher who will listen. The problem is not the work,

the teacher, or the school, it is your inability to *deal* with the work, the teacher, and the school.

4. *Masochist.* You enjoy being beaten with words by your teachers. Every time the teacher says something negative about your work, you top it with something more negative.

5. Portray any other style with which you have come into contact (or used).

Be sure you are familiar with what you are supposed to do before leaving the room and allowing the "teachers" to come in.

Instructions for teachers: You requested the student who just knocked on your door to come to see you. He has failed two tests so far. Select one of the five roles below to play. Be careful not to be inconsistent while you attempt to accomplish two purposes: (1) discuss the examinations with an emphasis on the student's poor work and (2) without appearing obvious, motivate the student to do his best on future examinations.

1. *Hostile.* You are forced to teach when you would prefer to do research. The student is failing and you are *obliged* to help him.

2. *Moralizer.* You prefer to discuss the moral problems involved, e.g., the value of hard work and really trying. You will, of course, lapse into stories of your background, giving examples of your own diligence.

3. *Clinical.* You get right down to work analyzing the problem objectively and coldly. The student is to listen to *you* work out the problem.

4. *Therapist.* You are sure the student's problem is an emotional one. Therefore, you encourage him to tell you his life story. You listen thoughtfully. You offer no help for his poor work and, instead, have the student make suggestions. You nod your head a good deal of the time.

5. Portray any other style with which you have come into contact.

Experience 5-3. Have volunteers act out the following situations in front of the class.

    1. Three people—mother, father, daughter (about ten

years old). The daughter asks her parents where babies come from. She and a friend just argued about *how* mothers become pregnant.

2. Three people—two workers and a personnel director. The two workers, both from minority groups, have been summoned to the personnel office because of complaints from the foreman that they have been late every day for a week.

3. Three people—brother, sister, and sister's boyfriend. The brother has just come home from a date. He finds the sister and her boyfriend on the couch, undressed. The brother cannot avoid the situation, since he turned the light on as he walked in.

Now that some data have been collected, a discussion of roles and role behavior becomes meaningful. What is a role? How do we know it when we see it? Is it helpful or harmful to group functioning? What are some of the problems associated with roles? And finally, how can we use our knowledge of roles to create more effective groups?

Roles are sets of behaviors. We identify different roles by the various behaviors they require. Each role has its own set of behaviors. For example, if we were to observe someone warming bottles of formula, holding an infant and cooing at it, changing its diapers, and exclaiming over the infant's antics, we would possibly identify the role as that of "parent." More specifically, the role may be called "mother" or "father."

We engage in a number of different roles any given day. We may play the role of son or daughter when getting up in the morning, the role of student in school, of store clerk after school, and so on. At any time, we may play multiple roles. A student who constantly supports the teacher is effectively engaging in two roles: student and reinforcer.

The role we engage in at a given moment depends on a number of factors, including where we are, whom we are with, the mood we are in, the time of day, what we desire, what we think is desired of us, and so on. For example, inviting a customer to your house in the evening calls for certain types of role behavior. You are a salesman, a gracious host, and a "nice" guy. The same meeting for lunch would call for different behaviors. You are no longer a host because you are in a restaurant; you are still a "nice" guy, but in a different way, and, since both you and the customer have to get back to your jobs, you are a little less relaxed and a little more aggressive. The customer, depending on the situation, will expect different role behaviors of you.

Role playing is not "bad," it is not something only actors engage in to deceive audiences. Roles are related to the self in a very meaningful way. The self directs each role, that is, it selects each specific role, how it will be "played," and the degree of commitment to playing it. The roles are intimately connected with self. When this connection is tenuous or nonexistent, we label the situation in terms of "role conflict" or, in less extreme cases, in terms of "role distance."

At least four important perspectives are available for looking at role behavior. The broadest perspective is provided by Sarbin and Allen (1968). Goffman (1959, 1961a,b) offers two more specific ones. Within these perspectives others may be worked out for particular situations, such as task-oriented small groups or socio-emotional oriented small groups. But these narrower, more specific perspectives are meaningful only if taken in the larger context. Consequently, before looking at the specific roles that are manifest in small group behavior, the fourth perspective, we will look at the broader perspectives.

Sarbin and Allen

Three questions can be asked of role behavior. Taken together, these questions provide background for an analysis of role behavior. (1) Is the behavior *appropriate,* that is, does it satisfy the requirements for the particular situation or context in which the individuals find themselves? (2) Is the behavior *proper,* that is, does it meet the standards for that role? For example, if a woman beats her infant often and in a cruel fashion, we conclude that she is *not* enacting the role of mother properly. (3) Is the behavior *convincing,* that is, do we conclude that the person is indeed occupying the role legitimately?

Sarbin and Allen suggest that the more roles an individual can effectively assume, the better off he is to meet the demands of social life. The individual who can assume few roles can function in only a few situations. Consider the individual in your own group who enacts only one role—"playboy." This may be functional when the group is engaged in a social activity, but when the task becomes of prime importance, the same individual now is looked upon with scorn.

Sarbin and Allen find it meaningful to look at several dimensions of role behavior: expectations, location, demands, skills, self-role congruence, the audience, and what they call the broad consideration of complex role phenomena. The dimensions of enactment that are of practical consideration are the number of roles, the commitment to them, and the time spent on a given role. The level of role involvement varies on a continuum from noninvolvement to what Sarbin and Allen call sorcery and witchcraft. They define eight distinct steps (Sarbin and Allen 1968, p. 492 ff.)

1. *Noninvolvement:* there are no expectations for action, as characterized by lapsed membership in a club.
2. *Casual role enactment:* there is little effort and, consequently, little effect, as characterized by the customer in a supermarket.
3. *Ritual acting:* slightly more involvement which requires necessary performances, as characterized by the stage actor.
4. *Engrossed acting:* little separation between self and role, as characterized by the stage actor who "becomes" the character.
5. *Classical hypnotic role taking:* the self is engaged to a high degree, as characterized by the hypnotic who can convincingly behave as if he is blind.

The other levels of involvement are, in order, (6) *histrionic neurosis,* (7) *ecstasy,* and (8) *bewitchment.* These involve progressively more involvement up to the last level which concerns those individuals who believe they are the objects of sorcery and witchcraft; they are completely "taken over."

The last consideration in the enactment dimension is *time.* How much time does an individual spend in a given role? Why do some roles demand more time than others? Why does a given individual spend more time in some roles than others do?

Roles are enacted in social situations, and these situations influence the roles. A given role may be viewed in terms of its expectations: the expectations of the role player, such as the rights and privileges he assumes, and the expectations of others, such as the obligations and duties they assume the role player will take on. The different perspectives from which roles may be viewed occasionally result in some conflict. What the role player assumes his duties to be may or may not agree with what others assume them to be. What the role player assumes are his privileges (such as owning a key to the men's locker room), others may not assume. The less defined the role, the higher the probability of conflict.

The degree to which performers conform to role expectations determines in part whether their role behavior, or enactment, is seen as convincing, proper, and appropriate. A common situation may help clarify the relationship of role expectations to these three considerations. A student comes into class, sits down quietly, and directs his attention to the front of the room where the teacher is lecturing. The student nods agreement at the appropriate places and smiles indulgently at the bad puns. When called upon to answer a simple question, the student stammers and sputters his way to a red face. The teacher calls on someone else. Until the time the teacher called on the student, the student enacted all the behaviors expected of his role as student. He was alert and responsive. His behavior fit the context, and so was appropriate; it met the standards for the role, and so was proper. Once the teacher called on him, the situation changed. It became clear that he was not really "up" on the material and that he really was not engaged in the role of student. His involvement was minimal. He failed to meet the demands of the situation and the role.

This example shows how context affects expectations. The location in which actors find themselves helps determine the roles they play. A role is appropriate to a given *situation,* which includes not only the surrounding physical environment but also the behavior of other people, the cues they give concerning their expectations for different roles, and the cues they give about their own roles.

The physical environment affects the roles selected. Talking serious business when occupying adjoining stalls in a bathroom is difficult at best. Likewise, cheerful patter and lighthearted joking is out of place at a funeral. Place is one of the cues which helps us select the proper role. The cues others give of their expectations also affect the roles selected. Nonverbal cues often let us know what is expected of us. In the small group situation you may have noticed that, when an idea is needed, one person may be singled out for increased eye contact. The others in the group are looking to that member for the idea and, by so doing, are asking that he assume a particular role. The last category of cues are those others give about their own roles. Badges, signals, uniforms, even age convey information about the roles others enact. You will probably assume the role of "good driver" when a policeman is nearby.

The number of roles an individual may select is limited by the expectations of others, the roles others are playing, and the situation. *Role demands* help assure that an individual assumes a *particular* role. Role demands are implicit expectations for certain behaviors; they may be considered norms or folkways. For example, when a man and woman are driving together and have a flat tire, the role demands make it clear that the man will change the tire.

Implicit in everything mentioned about roles so far is the notion that a given individual will be *able* to assume an appropriate, proper, and convincing role. However, individuals differ in abilities and skills, and these differences affect the readiness to perform some role. Effective role enactment is related to two skills: cognitive and motor. Cognitive skill is the ability to read cues from others correctly, to understand the context, and to infer proper role expectations for the position. Motor skills include control of the voice and body to insure proper performance. For example, an actor who has not mastered vocal variety is not likely to be convincing.

Role and self may be parallel or equated. As already mentioned, roles are directed by self, self being the references the individual makes about himself. The greater the congruence between self and role, the higher the probability that role enactment will be appropriate, proper, and effective. The greater the incongruity between self and role, the higher the probability of self–role conflict. For example, a humane judge may be required, because of his role as judge, to sentence a criminal to death. Often, what is assumed to be self–role conflict is really role–role conflict. If a medical doctor must treat his own wife, this may cause a conflict between his role as doctor and his role as husband.

Socialization is often directed at differentiating which behaviors are appropriate for males and females. This differentiation produces what we call sex roles. For instance, we assume that women should be more proficient in domestic activities, such as cooking and housekeeping, while men should be more facile with auto maintenance. These stereotyped behaviors are the results of socialized sex roles. The more related a task is to the accepted sex role for an individual, the greater the likelihood that he will perform it effectively.

Let us consider now the possible effects of an audience on role performance. Audiences which are real and present are easy to visualize; absent and imaginary ones are difficult to visualize. An example of an absent but nevertheless real audience are members of a reference group. How many times have you modified your behavior because your peers would approve? Your peers may have been absent, but they still constitute a real audience. An absent audience may be partly imaginary. A politician assumes a certain role because he wants to appeal to the new voters between eighteen and twenty-one years of age. The audience is absent, and its qualities may be largely derived from myth.

Finally, Sarbin and Allen conclude that an audience has at least four effects on role enactment. First, if the audience accepts the role as appropriate, they are, in essence, validating its enactment and providing public confirmation of its reality. When radical college students taunt policemen with shouts of "pig," they are denying the policemen's role enactment and publically disconfirming the reality of the role. How are the policemen to respond? What alternatives are open to them? Is their role still viable? What role should they assume?

Second, the audience guides the performance of the performer. When students ask a teacher questions concerning the material presented, they may be indicating that something is wrong with his role enactment: he may be ambiguous. When questions expand the scope of the material and provide new insights, they can indicate that the teacher's role enactment has been particularly engaging and stimulating.

Third, the audience reinforces the performer. Expressions of approval and disapproval help the performer enact his role, encouraging the appropriate behaviors and discouraging those which are inappropriate.

Fourth, by constant observation, the audience helps the performer maintain a consistent enactment over time and place. As a role is repeated over time, it becomes more stable, the probability of successful role enactment increases, and the probability of conflict decreases.

The complexity of role playing (audiences, other interacting individuals, a complex environment, and a host of expectations and demands) virtually insures that trouble is part of the performer's reality. One difficulty performers encounter is role conflict. Role conflict occurs when a performer is called upon to enact two or more contradictory roles. There are two basic forms of role conflict: *interrole* conflict and *intrarole* conflict. Interrole conflict occurs when two or more roles have incompatible role expectations. For example, middle-class black Americans may experience interrole conflict when they earn enough money to leave the ghetto but realize that in leaving, they will be leaving their black brothers and sisters. In this case there is conflict between the expectations of different (multiple) roles.

Intrarole conflict, on the other hand, exists when there are two or more incompatible role expectations for a single role. For example, the role of foreman in a large industry is defined differently by the workers and the management. The workers expect the foreman to represent them, to understand and support their contentions with higher level management. On the other hand, management sees the foreman as *their* representative. Whose expectations shall the foreman meet?

Role behavior is complex and dynamic. It involves many interdependent factors. No simple classification scheme of role behaviors enacted in small group settings can do justice to the rich and complex relationships which function in small groups.

Goffman (1959)

Goffman's major theme, expressed in *The Presentation of Self in Everyday Life,* is similar to Sarbin and Allen's perspective on role behavior. Goffman's perspective is that of the theatrical performance: all the world is a stage, and the roles an individual assumes are selected and played much as an actor selects and plays a given role for an audience.

The part of an individual's performance which regularly functions in a general and fixed fashion is called the performer's *front.* Front helps others define the situation. Performers must act consistently to insure that their projected definition of the situation, their personal fronts, are consistent. This is important because the performer will conceal activities, facts, and motives which are inappropriate for the particular situation in which he finds himself.

Imagine the role of teacher. It appears to be fixed, that is, there is little variation among different performers. This is because the teachers' consistent, fixed behavior helps students define the situation as a learning environment. What would happen if the teacher interacted with his students as if they were potential research helpers? Would these actions be consistent with his role as a teacher?

If we view the world as a stage, we can divide it into two distinct areas: *front* and *back.* The front region is occupied only by the actors. Any particular performance actors give is done in the front region. They treat the audience politely and behave in an appropriate manner. The behavior exhibited in the back is less regulated than in the front. Here, off the stage, however, the actors' behavior may intentionally contradict what goes on in front of the audience. Of course, no member of the audience is allowed access to the back stage—it would spell disaster for the performers trying to maintain a consistent front.

Many groups formed to do class projects confirm Goffman's insights concerning front and back stages. Group process papers usually consider two aspects of performance: performance in class and performance during meetings outside of class. In class there appears to be no intragroup conflict; the groups seem to work like well-oiled machines. Out of class, however, conflicts abound. Some are so shattering that certain members may be asked (impolitely) to find another group. When asked why they appear to be so much in control of their interpersonal transactions *in class,* the usual response is, "If it is obvious that there *is no real consistency,* how can we hope to make the desired impression?" Consistency in performance and consistency in the perceived effects are very much related to each other.

A group must devise strategies to keep back region secrets from the audience, since revealing a secret may effectively destroy the performance. There are three different kinds of secrets, each concerned with a different aspect of role enactment in the back region.

Dark secrets are facts which the team conceals because they are incompatible with its projected image. For example, if a group of individuals collecting money for a charity secretly knows that it will keep the money for itself, it will keep that secret from its audience. To reveal the secret would destroy its image and insure that it would receive no money.

Strategic secrets are intentions and capabilities of the team which are concealed from the audience. For example, if a team wants sympathy it may appear weak and in trouble when, in reality, no such trouble or weakness exists.

Inside secrets are those which mark an individual as a member of the group and, consequently, help the group gain identity. The group which performed in class as if there were no intragroup conflicts was using the knowledge of intragroup conflicts as an inside secret. Only the members of the group knew the secret, and this secret helped them define themselves as a group.

Because groups have secrets, a member may take on one of two discrepant roles. The first type of discrepant role is informer, someone who pretends to be a member of the team, is allowed into the back region, gains information, and then sells out the team to the audience. The second type of discrepant role is that of the shill, someone who acts as though he were a member of the audience but is, in reality, in league with the performers.

Maintaining a consistent front is difficult. It involves trying to conceal activities and motives that are inconsistent with the front, trying to insure that secrets are kept, and deferring access to audience members to the back stage area. But performers, audiences, and outsiders all observe techniques designed to save the show, to insure proper role enactment.

Occasionally, incidents occur which threaten the validity of the performance. Audience members may inadvertently enter the back region or performance area. For example, walking through a hospital, you may have wandered into the room where doctors and nurses drink coffee and try to ease the tensions inherent in their profession. How do they react? What do you do? Usually, they act surprised, and you perform a hasty retreat. Another type of incident may be the result of poor team coordination or one team member's mistake. For example, a juggler may miss a ball tossed him by his partner. The third type of incident is more intentional than the first two types. An individual member may act in a way to purposely destroy the polite appearance of consensus among the team members. An example of this type of incident occurred during a group presentation when one group member corrected another group member on a small point of information. Later, he corrected another member. The group tried to cover up the incident by joking about the corrections, but the effect on the group was obvious—hostility, because he was not keeping the group's secret.

Joking is only one defense against incidents, and it is necessarily employed after the fact. The best defense is to prevent incidents from occurring. The effect of *dramaturgical loyalty* is to prevent incidents by invoking loyalty among the group members to keep the secrets. The group in which one member corrected two others during a performance lacked dramaturgical loyalty.

Dramaturgical discipline is exhibited by each group member who is not carried away by his own performance. The role enactments of each member must appear complementary. If one member gets carried away with his own performance, role enactments are no longer complementary and the front appears inconsistent. A third defense a group might employ to guard against incidents is called *dramaturgical circumspection.* In dramaturgical circumspection, a group must decide how tight or loose their performance can be in order to maintain a consistent front. The more the audience knows about the group, the looser it can be in its performance.

Whereas a group responds to incidents with defenses, the audience and outsiders employ protective defenses to help the performers maintain a consistent front. Audiences and outsiders help by granting the performers civil inattention after they have made an embarrassing mistake, or by voluntarily staying away from back regions unless invited. With audience and performers working together, the probability of maintaining a consistent front, and thus completing a successful performance, is increased.

Goffman's dramaturgical metaphor adds dimension to the Sarbin and Allen perspective, thereby broadening our own perspective of roles and role enactment. Whereas Sarbin and Allen concentrate on individuals, Goffman concentrates on groups. Given that small group behavior is a function of both individual role enactments and team "role enactments," both perspectives seem applicable.

Before analyzing your role enactment during the three experiments completed at the beginning of this chapter, let us review one more perspective presented by Goffman in a more recent work.

Goffman (1961b)

In Part II of *Encounters: Two Studies in the Sociology of Interaction,* Goffman discusses the notion of *role distance.* Although Sarbin and Allen discuss role enactment and what might be classified as role distance, the specific focus offered by Goffman allows us a better understanding of this important phenomenon.

Goffman defines "role" in a narrower sense than it has been used so far in this chapter. He suggests that a role consists of the acts an individual would engage in were he to act solely in terms of the normative demands (the expectations) made upon someone in his position. Note the distinction between this and other definitions. Whereas other definitions define a role in terms of the behaviors performed, Goffman's definition focuses on the expected behaviors which *may* be performed. The concept of role performance is akin to what we have so far been calling role enactment; it is the actual behavior of the performer. Because there are variations in the ways individuals will enact the same role, it is necessary to consider a role as the *typical* response of individuals in a particular situation. Thus we have the concepts of *typical* role behavior and *actual* role behavior.

Goffman indicates that roles may be *played,* and *played at.* This distinction is similar to the one Sarbin and Allen make concerning the levels of involvement a performer may have for his role. Ritual acting, which exists when the performer is involved with his role only to the extent that he can be sure of giving an adequate performance, may constitute "playing at" a role. The stage actor who gives an excellent performance without ever really "becoming" the character also may simply be "playing at" being the character. If, on the other hand, he "becomes" the character, then he is said to be "playing" rather than playing at his role.

Role enactment is based on two assumptions, both of which operate when roles are being played *at*, as opposed to being played. The first assumption is that an individual enacting a particular role is identifying with what he is doing at that particular time. The second assumption is that informational cues provided by the total environment confirm the first assumption. When an individual plays *at* a role, it may or may not be obvious that the first assumption is not being maintained. The individual may not be accepting the role as part of his identification and the audience may or may not know it. However, the situational cues may make it clear to both the performer and audience that the performer is playing at the role.

Role distance exists when there is an effectively expressed separateness between the individual and his role. This situation occurs when the performer is playing *at* his role, and both he *and* the audience know it. In some cases, performers will go out of their way to separate themselves from their roles. For instance, a judge bound by law to execute a prisoner may revert to role distancing behavior, that is, he may say that the responsibility for the action reverts back to his role, and he, as an individual, would not sentence a man to death.

What are the advantages to be gained from role distancing? Remember that any individual plays a great many roles, yet is highly involved with only a few. There may be roles that he is forced to engage in, via role expectations, that he simply would perfer to avoid. Role distancing then alerts the audience not to take his enactment as part of his identity.

Role distancing also becomes important when the performer enacts a role to indicate what he chooses *not* to claim. This occurs when a performer's *actual* behavior is intended to distort the *typical* behavior required for a particular role. For instance, when a group member is called upon too often to be secretary, he may use role distancing to disassociate himself from the role by taking inadequate notes.

Third, role distancing may be employed when the performer wants to stress that a particular role is only *part* of his identity. Remember, during the conflict stage of group development, each member tries to establish his own identity within the group (to counter feelings of being swallowed by "group identity"). As members establish their own identities, roles become easier to adopt. A member can enact a given role because he knows that other members regard him as *more* than the role: he has already established himself as a complex individual. The transition from the conflict stage to the task stage may well be marked with role distancing designed to insure that the other members know the enactment of a particular role is not to be taken as the performer's *total* identity.

Unless a performer clearly states *why* he is using role distancing, the audience may not understand his motives. First, they may think the performer is alienated from his role, i.e., they may not see the role as reflecting his actual self. A second explanation the audience may provide for role distancing is opposite from the one just discussed. Whereas the first explanation dealt with the performer's possible alienation, this one suggests that he may feel secure enough in his role to engage in role distancing without affecting his performance. If this reason is ascribed to the role distancing behavior, the performer is perceived as extremely secure, and as a consequence his status may rise. Similarly, a performer may feel that he is so firmly "validated" in a given role that role distancing could have no harmful effects on how his performance is perceived.

Before going further, pick one of the three experiences at the beginning of this chapter and analyze behaviors you observed. Make a list of all the typical roles played, or played at, in the small group setting. An analysis of the first experience should indicate consistencies in behavior patterns. These consistencies should help identify the roles that were enacted. Next, how did the task affect the roles? Did some of the statements strike you as more personal than others? If so, what do you think is the effect of a personal task on the roles enacted in a group? What expectations did the members have for each role? How were these expectations revealed? For example, did some group members simply state what they felt an individual should do in a given role? Were any roles enacted because of role demands? Did someone finally emerge as leader because no one else did and he felt someone *had* to? What kinds of skills were necessary to perform the roles you observed? Were the number of individuals who could fill the demands of a particular role limited because of the skills necessary? Did you observe any self–role conflict, or any role–role conflict? How was this conflict manifested? Did anyone engage in role distancing behavior? If so, why? Finally, how did the roles enacted fit the larger patterns of group development and interaction?

Benne and Sheats

One of the oldest and most useful guides for observing role enactment in small group discussions is provided by Benne and Sheats (1948). They divide roles into three broad categories: group task roles, group building and maintenance roles, and self-centered roles. The three categories are considered separately below, but it should be clear that any given role may serve a number of group functions. Some additions to their schema have been made.

Group Task Roles

1. *Initiator–Contributor:* contributes ideas and suggestions; proposes solutions and decisions; proposes new ideas or states old ones in a novel fashion.

2. *Information Seeker:* asks for clarification of comments in terms of their factual adequacy; asks for information, or facts relevant to the problem; suggests information is needed before making decisions.

3. *Information Giver:* offers facts or generalizations which may relate to personal experiences and are pertinent to the group task.

4. *Opinion Seeker:* asks for clarification of opinions made by other members of the group and asks how people in the group feel.

5. *Opinion Giver:* states his beliefs or opinions having to do with suggestions made; indicates what the group's attitude should be.

6. *Elaborator–Clarifier:* elaborates ideas and other contributions; offers rationales for suggestions; tries to deduce how an idea or suggestion would work if adopted by the group.

7. *Coordinator:* clarifies the relationships among information, opinions, and ideas, or suggests an integration of the information, opinions, and ideas of subgroups.

8. *Diagnostician:* indicates what the problems are.

9. *Orienter–Summarizer:* summarizes what has taken place; points out departures from agreed upon goals; tries to bring the group back to the central issues; raises questions about the direction the group is heading.

10. *Energizer:* prods the group to action.

11. *Procedure Developer:* handles routine tasks such as seating arrangements, obtaining equipment, and handing out pertinent papers.

12. *Secretary:* keeps notes on the group's progress.

13. *Evaluator–Critic:* critically analyzes the group's accomplishments according to some set of standards; checks to see that consensus has been reached.

Group Building and Maintenance Roles

1. *Supporter–Encourager:* praises, agrees with, and accepts the contributions of others; offers warmth, solidarity, and recognition.

2. *Harmonizer:* reconciles disagreements; mediates differences; reduces tensions by giving group members a chance to explore their differences.

3. *Tension Reliever:* jokes or, in some other way, reduces the formality of the situation; relaxes the group members.

4. *Compromiser:* offers to compromise when his own ideas are involved in a conflict; disciplines himself to admit his errors so as to maintain group cohesion.

5. *Gate-Keeper:* keeps communication channels open; encourages and facilitates interaction from those members who usually are silent.

6. *Feeling Expresser:* makes explicit the feelings, moods, and relationships in the group; shares his own feelings with others.

7. *Standard Setter:* expresses standards for the group to achieve; may apply standards in evaluating the group process.

8. *Follower:* goes along with the movement of the group passively, accepting the ideas of others, sometimes serving as an audience.

Self-Centered Roles

1. *Blocker:* interferes with progress by rejecting ideas or taking the negative stand on any and all issues; refuses to cooperate.

2. *Aggressor:* struggles for status by deflating the status of others; boasts; criticizes.

3. *Deserter:* withdraws in some way; remains indifferent, aloof, sometimes formal; daydreams; wanders from the subject; engages in irrelevant side conversations.

4. *Dominator:* interrupts and embarks on long monologues; authoritative; tries to monopolize the group's time.

5. *Recognition Seeker:* attempts to gain attention in an exaggerated manner; usually boasts about past accomplishments; relates irrelevant personal experiences, usually in an attempt to gain sympathy.

6. *Confessor:* engages in irrelevant personal catharsis; uses the group to work out own mistakes and feelings.

7. *Playboy:* displays a lack of involvement in the group through inappropriate humor, horseplay, or cynicism.

8. *Special-Interest Pleader:* acts as the representative for another group; engages in irrelevant behavior.

Group task roles help the group solve its task problem. Group building and maintenance roles help the group solve its socio-emotional problems. Self-centered roles solve individual problems.

Very often a simple analysis of the roles being enacted in a given group provides an explanation for the group's success or failure. The following diary entry, written after the third group meeting, reveals the firm foundation the group built, a foundation based on diverse and complementary role enactment.

> *November 19.   This group is fantastic! Here it is only the third meeting and already we're flying! I think our success is tied to the roles which are starting to become solidified. Each time we meet we fall into a pattern. I seem to be the initiator or information provider. I read the material and try to outline ideas to be discussed at each meeting.*
>
> *John, on the other hand, develops the ideas. He takes my suggestions and tries to find a way to use them in our class presentation. He is able to sort those things which will work from those which will not work.*
>
> *Denny volunteers to do most of the leg work which invariably accompanies John's suggestions. He typed our questionnaires and has already started looking for the material we'll need for the presentation.*
>
> *Concerning leadership, it shifts constantly. We've each become the leader in our own area. And each leader has two willing followers in the other members! The work has been divided evenly, and this helps us feel as if we are all important to the group.*
>
> *We all play a variety of roles, although we each concentrate on a few. And all the roles seem to work well together. We can concentrate easily on the task at hand.*

Obviously, not all the roles will be played by all the group members. Some members will feel more comfortable in particular roles (allowing for self–role congruence) and, therefore, will tend to spend more time in those roles. Also, not all the roles are necessary for proper group functioning. Some roles are more important than others under certain conditions. As the task gets more complicated, the role of clarifier becomes more important. Similarly, as problems become more personal, the roles of tension reliever and supporter become more important. You should have noticed an increase in tension relievers during the third role-playing exercise at the beginning of this chapter.

As a final exercise, to help cement the notions discussed in this chapter, do an analysis of the roles played, or played at, during any one of your group's meetings. Are enough roles being enacted to insure proper group functioning? What roles are missing, and what effect does their absence have on your group's development? What were the primary roles enacted at a given meeting? What does this tell you about the meeting? What happens when roles are *not* complementary? In the second experiment, what happened when a hostile teacher and a disturbed student were paired? Does this have any relevance for your own group? Answering these and other questions which pertain to the unique interaction in your own group should provide you with a clearer understanding of the importance of role behavior.

Bibliography

Bales, R. F., and Slater, P. E. "Role Differentiation in Small Decision-Making Groups." *Family, Socialization, and Interaction Processes,* edited by T. Parsons and R. F. Bales, pp. 259-306. New York: Free Press, 1955.

Benne, K. and Sheats, P. "Functional Roles of Group Members." *Journal of Social Issues* 4 (1948):41-49.

Bible, B. L., and McComas, J. D. "Role Consensus and Teacher Effectiveness." *Social Forces* 42 (1963):225-33.

Borgatta, E. F. "Role and Reference Group Theory." In *Social Science Theory and Social Work Research,* edited by L. Logan, pp. 16-25. New York: National Association of Social Workers, 1960.

Brilhart, J. K. *Effective Group Discussion.* Dubuque, Iowa: Wm. C. Brown, 1967.

Cannon, W. B. " 'Voodoo' Death." *American Anthropologist* 44 (1942): 169-81.

Carter, L., Haythorn, W., Shriver, B., and Lanzetta, J. "The Behavior of Leaders and Other Group Members." *Journal of Abnormal and Social Psychology* 46 (1950):589-95.

Coe, W. C., and Sarbin, T. R. "An Experimental Demonstration of Hypnosis as Role Enactment." *Journal of Abnormal Psychology* 71 (1966):400-406.

Coutu, W. "Role-Playing Vs. Role-Taking: An Appeal for Clarification." *American Sociological Review* 16 (1951):180-87.

Ehrlich, H. J., and Rinehart, J. W. "The Study of Role Conflict: Explorations in Methodology." *Sociometry* 25 (1962):85-97.

Gerard, H. B. "Some Effects of Status Role Clarity and Group Goal Clarity upon the Individual's Relations to Group Process." *Journal of Personality* 25 (1957):475-88.

Goffman, E. *The Presentation of Self in Everyday Life.* Garden City, New York: Doubleday, 1959.

———. *Asylums.* Chicago: Aldine, 1961a.

———. *Encounters: Two Studies in the Sociology of Interaction.* Indianapolis: Bobbs-Merrill, 1961b.

Gross, N., Mason, W. L., and McEachern, A. W. *Explorations in Role Analysis.* New York: Wiley, 1958.

Kagan, J. "Acquisition and Significance of Sex Typing and Sex Role Identity." In *Review of Child Development Research,* edited by M. L. Hofman and L. W. Hofman. New York: Russell Sage Foundation, 1964.

Mead, G. H. *Mind, Self, and Society.* Chicago: University of Chicago Press, 1934.

Milton, G. A. "The Effects of Sex-Role Identification upon Problem Solving Skill." *Journal of Abnormal and Social Psychology* 55 (1957):219-44.

———. "Sex Differences in Problem Solving as a Function of Role Appropriateness of the Problem Content." *Psychological Reports* 5 (1959):705-8.

Sarbin, T. R., and Allen, V. L. "Role Theory." In *Handbook of Social Psychology,* edited by G. Lindzey and E. Aronson, 1:488-567. 2d ed. Reading, Massachusetts: Addison-Wesley, 1968.

Stanislavski, C. *An Actor Prepares.* New York: Theatre Arts Books, 1961.

Steiner, I. D., and Field, W. G. "Role Assignment and Interpersonal Influence." *Journal of Abnormal and Social Psychology* 61 (1960):239-45.

Toby, J. "Some Variables in Role Conflict Analysis." *Social Forces* 30 (1952):323-37.

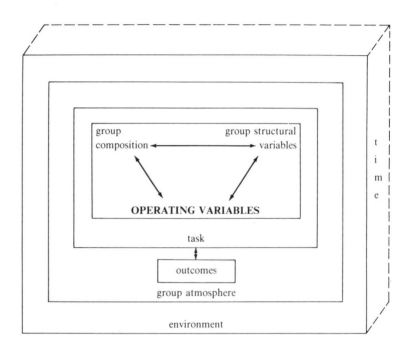

CHAPTER 6

LEADERSHIP

If asked at this point in time who the leader of your group is, you would probably be able to name some particular group member. And, if you compared your answer with the answers of other group members, you probably would find that your answers would agree. If you don't agree, you probably could talk out the reasons for your disagreement. Rarely are people's perceptions of leadership solely a matter of opinion.

Everyone knows something about leadership, but few can articulate that something adequately. What makes a leader a leader? Why did you pick Jane as the leader and not Jim? What are the variables you considered in making your choice? Before beginning data collection, tackle these questions. Re-form groups that you have been in before or get into the groups that exist for your group projects. Now, individually answer the following question: "Who is the leader of your group?" Discuss your answer with the other group members. How much agreement is there? Why are there differences? From your discussion, extract those considerations which appear crucial for determining who the leader is. Create a list of the variables, rank ordering them from most to least crucial.

Once your group has completed this task, discuss your conclusions with the other groups. How much difference is there in your lists? Can you explain the differences? Is it necessary to consider more variables than you originally thought necessary? Why are these other variables important? Is it possible, at this point, for the entire class to generate a list of critical variables that are applicable to all situations?

Now we can collect some data which should prove useful for an analysis of the concept of leadership.

Experience 6-1. Form three groups of equal size. Each group has separate instructions, so please do not read the instructions for any group other than your own.

Instructions

Group 1: Your task is to gather all the objects on the list and be the first group to return to the room. Note that _____ (the name of a group member indicated by the person directing the exercise, most likely the teacher) is to be the leader—*and no one else.*

Group 2: Your task is to gather all the objects on the list and be the first group to return to this room. Before you begin your hunt, *select a leader.*

Group 3: Your task is to gather all the objects on the list and be the first group to return to the room.

The following is the list of objects:
1. One flat stone.
2. One library book with a red cover checked out from the college library on the day this experiment takes place.
3. One small bag of potato chips or pretzels purchased in the student union on the day this experiment takes place.
4. Today's copy of the student newspaper dated the day this experiment takes place.
5. A copy of the student newspaper published during the week prior to the week this experiment takes place.
6. One sheet of computer printout paper (with or without printing) with three signatures on it, no one of which belongs to any member of your group.
7. One yellow-topped computer card.

Experience 6-2. Form five groups. The following general instructions are for all the groups. Following the general instructions, specific instructions are given for each one of the five groups. Do not read instructions that are designated for other groups.

General Instructions: Pretend that a bomb has been dropped and ten people are left in a bomb shelter. There is only enough food and oxygen to accommodate seven people until the fall-out has reached a safe level. These seven will have to create a new society. Your group must reach a unanimous decision on which three people must go.

1. A seventy-year-old minister
2. A pregnant, hysterical woman

3. Her husband
4. A laboratory scientist
5. An electrician
6. A famous writer
7. A female vocalist
8. A professional athlete
9. An armed policeman
10. A high school girl

After fifteen to twenty minutes dissolve the groups and have volunteers role play each one of the bomb shelter inhabitants. Each actor should present the best possible case for why he should be spared. After the role playing, re-form your original groups and rediscuss the problem. Arrive at a final decision.

Specific Instructions:

Group 1: You must finish first.

Group 2: Majority and minority opinions are allowed for your group.

Group 3: The group will be expected to justify its selection to the other groups.

Group 4: According to a group of well-known psychologists, there is a "correct" solution to the problem. Try to come as close to the professional opinion as possible.

Group 5: According to a group of well-known psychologists, there is a "correct" solution to the problem. If the group answer agrees with the psychologists' solution, the group may use this exercise to justify an *A* in this course.

Leadership has been studied most from two different perspectives: (1) the *trait approach* which considers the traits of recognized leaders in relation to those of nonleaders; and (2) the *functional approach* which considers how a group leader actually performs. The trait approach dates back to the 1940s. The functional approach is currently one of the popular ones.

The Trait Approach

In a series of twenty studies, Bird (1940) isolated seventy-nine traits as belonging to the "leadership personality." The number of traits may have been due to the variety of situations he analyzed, however, of the seventy-nine traits, only four were common to four or more investigations. His conclusion was that particular personality traits of a leader may be a function of the situation, e.g., in one type of situation the leader may have to be very intelligent, in another he may have to be very dependable.

Stogdill (1948) grouped Bird's characteristics, asserting that leadership characteristics may be classified according to these five categories: (1) *Capacity,* such as intelligence and judgment; (2) *Achievement,* such as knowledge and scholarship; (3) *Responsibility,* such as dependability and aggressiveness; (4) *Participation,* such as cooperation and humor; and (5) *Status,* such as popularity and position.

If the group's task is to generate new solutions to familiar problems, which category would be most important for predicting who the leader is likely to be? In this case, capacity and achievement are probably more important than responsibility, participation, and status. On the other hand, if the group task is to resolve personal conflicts, the participation and responsibility categories would probably be more important. Stogdill's conclusion that leadership is not situation specific is untenable, at least from a common sense viewpoint.

A different approach to the study of leadership traits proved more productive than the approach taken by Bird. Adopting the same position as R. D. Laing, making *perceptions* the focus of attention, Geier (1967) focused on *perceived* traits rather than *objectively measured* traits. In other words, whether a person is intelligent or not is irrelevant; what matters is if he is perceived as intelligent.

Geier interviewed group members in leaderless groups to determine which factors seem to exclude individuals from the leadership role. His approach was unique in that it made use of unstructured questions yielding introspective data. His major objective was to determine if patterns might be revealed which would help explain emergent leadership. An analysis of the data revealed that the pattern of leadership emergence was essentially the same for each group. First, there was a painless elimination of leader contenders who possessed what group members perceived as negative characteristics. Second, there was an intense struggle for leadership by the remaining contenders.

In the first stage most members exhibited a desire for the leadership position. The characteristic that eliminated the greatest number of contenders during this stage was the perception of being uninformed. Second in importance for leader rejection was nonparticipation; extreme rigidity was third. During the second stage, marked by an intense struggle for leadership, each member was fully aware of the struggle. Remaining contenders were progressively eliminated on the basis of other characteristics such as offensive verbalization. According to Geier, then, there is no single "leadership personality." The leader is best defined as the person perceived to assume most frequently the functions of leadership; he is not simply the individual who initiates, encourages, or facilitates group ideas. One member might achieve leadership through intellect, another through his interest and helpful attitude. Leadership does not reside exclusively in the individual, but in his functional relationship with fellow members and the goal at hand.

The trait approach is a weak one for at least two reasons. First, it is difficult to define operationally a given trait. For example, how would you define the trait labeled "cooperative"? How would you know when you saw it? Second, traits do not fully explain the manifest behaviors in the group. Is a particular trait the best explanation for why the group members behaved toward the leader as they did, or is it best to look for other explanations? Was the group hostile toward the leader because he stifled their freedom, or because task completion time was approaching and an important piece of the course grade was riding on the outcome?

It is a fruitless venture to try to analyze leadership from a trait approach. There appear to be too many variables that interact with "traits" to warrant any general conclusions. Although it may be possible to outline leadership traits for specific situations, the sheer number of specific situations seems to rule out the feasibility of such efforts in order to make useful generalizations. It is, therefore, not surprising that the trait approach has been abandoned.

The Functional Approach

The functional approach defines the leader as the individual who performs actions that assist the group achieve its goal. In this case, leadership is a function that is to be performed, and not a certain kind of individual.

In chapter 3, dealing with phase development in groups, it was suggested that groups have to solve certain problems in order to become functioning units. The problems can be broadly divided into two areas: task and socio-emotional. Concerning the task, the group has specific problems that it must solve, such as gathering information, generating viable solutions, and achieving consensus. Problems in the socio-emotional development of the group often involve the resolution of interpersonal conflicts and personality clashes. R. F. Bales (1950, 1955, 1956, 1958; Bales and Slater 1955; Borgotta and Bales 1956; Slater 1955), noticed the tendency for leadership to be differentiated into two specific functions. As might be expected, these functions focus on task and socio-emotional demands. Generally, the members selected by the group as *most liked* were not perceived by the group as having contributed most to task accomplishment or giving directions for task accomplishment. On the other hand, the individual who was seen as most helpful in solving the external task (by contributing the best ideas for solving the problem) was usually perceived as the person most helpful in solving the internal task, by guiding the discussion and keeping it moving. Supporting evidence for this split in leadership function comes from a variety of other sources (Olmstead 1959; Hollander and Webb 1955; Cattell and Stice 1954; Gibb 1950).

Besides being differentiated on the basis of questionnaires completed by the group members, task and socio-emotional leaders can also be differentiated by their behavior patterns. An analysis of the interaction of the group members chosen as highest on socio-emotional criteria reveals that they initiate and receive more interactions in the socio-emotional categories of interaction; they show solidarity, tension release, and agreement. An analysis of the group members chosen as task specialists reveals that they initiate and receive more interactions in the task area and the negative socio-emotional areas; they give and ask for questions, opinions, and information, as well as show disagreement, tension, and antagonism.

Earlier it was suggested that an important consideration when analyzing group attractiveness is the individual member's orientation in the group. Members may be task oriented, socio-emotional or maintenance oriented, or self-oriented. Task specialists are task oriented. They gain satisfaction from the group because it is an effective task machine which rewards *task effectiveness*. This would indicate that the task specialist is less motivated to receive positive affective responses from other group members. On the other hand, socio-emotional or maintenance-oriented members gain satisfaction from the group because it is cohesive and because there is a great deal of interaction focusing on the feelings and attitudes of the group members. This indicates that the socio-emotional specialist is more motivated to receive positive affective responses from the other members than the task specialist. Under these circumstances, the task specialist discriminates more among the group members and is more likely to criticize members and categorize them according to their task effectiveness. The socio-emotional specialist discriminates less among the group members and is less likely to criticize them. He attempts to maintain peace and cohesiveness in the group.

Both leaders are essential to insure proper group functioning. The socio-emotional specialist helps the group through its social development: testing-dependence, conflict, cohesion, and the building of functional roles. The task specialist helps the group through its task development: orientation, emotionality, relevant opinion exchange, and the emergence of solutions. (See chapter 3 for Tuckman's description of the stages of development.) Though each specialist directs his efforts in a particular area, it is obvious that the two do not operate in isolation. Proper task and social development go hand-in-hand: without progress in one area, progress in the other is retarded, if not impossible.

The task and socio-emotional specialists complement and balance each other. They tend to interact more with each other than any other pair of members and tend to agree more with each other. This cooperation gives the task specialist the support of the socio-emotional specialist, thus the disturbance caused by the task specialist in the affective areas (through his use of directives and negative responses) is countered. In groups where there is no cooperation between the two leaders, consensus is almost impossible to attain. The group is split from within: the task-oriented and maintenance-oriented members do not develop a good working relationship, the group is seen as having contradictory purposes (task versus social), and proper phase development is never realized.

The following diary entry describes the possible effects of a conflict between the task and socio-emotional leaders.

April 18. This meeting was unique. It was the first time I observed any overt hostility. Chuck was discussing his idea for a model of small group communication in a rather vague manner, whereupon Norah started yelling at him, insisting that he stop being so vague, and that he start using some concrete examples. Chuck became defensive. The group atmosphere was tense.

This was the first meeting that focused on the task. Until now we would meet and rap, drink, go to a movie, or watch television. But now we have less than a month to get our project presentable. And we haven't even settled on a topic yet!

Janice, who finally showed up after missing the last few meetings, tried to introduce a new idea. She was ignored by just about every member.

Things were getting worse.

Finally, they came to a head. Norah, who was definitely our socio-emotional leader and, therefore, played an enormous part in our group given our social orientation, withdrew from the discussion. She was in charge of just about every meeting before this one, but now Chuck took over. There was a conflict between the task and socio-emotional leaders because prior to this meeting we had need of only one leader, and Norah filled that role. They never had to work together, and now they couldn't. Given the lateness of the date and the general anxiety from not having a meaningful topic for our project, the task orientation for the meeting won out over the social orientation.

Norah withdrew farther and farther away from the discussion. Nothing very constructive in the way of a project was accomplished.

The Two Approaches Working Together

In a study by Haiman (1955), authoritarianism (trait) was seen as relating to the type of leadership that was deemed most appropriate (function) by group members. According to Adorno et al. (1950), authoritarianism is characterized by a strict adherence to conventional values, including the rejection of those opposed to the conventional values. There is a preoccupation with power and the leader–follower dimension, including the rejection of those members considered subjective or imaginative. Authoritarianism can best be considered as a continuum with authoritarian and nonauthoritarian poles. Where an individual falls on the continuum is determined by the Adorno F-Scale. The most usual type of study relating authoritarianism to leadership is typified by the questions: What predictions of discussion leadership can we make with a knowledge of the authoritarian personality? Are authoritarian group members more likely to see the task or the socio-emotional specialist as more important to the group? Is the authoritarian group member more task or socio-emotionally oriented?

Haiman developed a questionnaire to discriminate viewpoints concerning discussion leadership. He then gave the scale to subjects who had completed the F-Scale. Results show a significant correlation between the two measures indicating that there is a relationship between authoritarianism and leadership attitudes.

The three items (of ten) best discriminating between authoritarians and nonauthoritarians reveal one relationship between a trait and a preferred leadership function. These items are (1) "The best procedure is for the leader to plan the agenda and then keep the members of the group to it"; (2) "When two group members cannot seem to get along, the best thing to do is ignore the problem and carry on"; (3) "The leader should be immediately recognizable to an outside observer" (p. 143). The first two items clearly indicate task preference. Indeed, the second item not only relegates the socio-emotional specialist to a secondary position, but virtually eliminates any necessity for the function!

In a study by Haythorn et al. (1956), groups formed were composed of either four authoritarian or four nonauthoritarian individuals. Again, the F-Scale was used to measure authoritarianism. Both groups were to discuss, compose, and record a script involving a human relations problem for a movie scene. At task completion, each subject was asked to rank order the group members who were most responsible for the solutions to the problems encountered. The group member with the highest average rank was designated the emergent leader. A significant difference was found between the two groups. "The fact that F minus [nonauthoritarian, equalitarian] subjects engaged in more 'positive affect acts,' showed greater concern for the feelings of others by asking for expressions of opinion more frequently, and engaged in fewer directive acts was interpreted as reflecting the essential differences between 'autocratic' and 'democratic' group climates" (p. 71).

As the Haiman study indicates, predictable differences exist in leadership based upon knowledge of the group members' authoritarianism scores. Authoritarian groups are task oriented, as are authoritarian group members; nonauthoritarian groups are more socially oriented, as are nonauthoritarian group members.

Leadership Styles

As with many other concepts, leadership is best represented by a continuum. At one end of the continuum is individual-centered leadership, characterized by the "free-rein," or laissez-faire, leader; at the other end is leader-centered leadership, characterized by the autocratic, or dictatorial, leader. In the center of the continuum is group-centered leadership, characterized by the democratic, or equalitarian, leader. Effective leadership is not simply defined as any one of the three places on the continuum described; it is defined in terms of group variables. The question is not which type of leadership is best, but rather, when is a particular type of leadership best?

A group-centered leader actively encourages group members to direct, coordinate, and evaluate the group's activities. He accepts the group members as individuals, not as objects to be manipulated. He trusts the group to make sound decisions. The goals of the group-centered leader include helping the group to develop and creating an atmosphere that will enable the group to utilize its resources.

A leader-centered leader assumes the major, if not all, responsibility for directing, coordinating, and evaluating the group's activities. Group members are objects to be manipulated, objects whose judgments are doubted. The goals of the leader-centered leader are to create an atmosphere that will enable him to direct the group's activities without interference from group members and to set up his own criteria for judging the group's value.

In a recent study by Sargent and Miller (1971), the communication behaviors of democratic and autocratic leaders were contrasted. It was found that autocratic leaders attempted to answer more questions posed within the group than democratic leaders. This behavior is consistent with the view that the autocratic leader wants to direct group behavior and insure that his views are represented. In general, it demonstrates the autocratic leader's concern with group productivity.

Democratic leaders, on the other hand, posed more questions and encouraged alternative approaches and speculations from the group. The democratic leader was concerned with having the group reach *its* decision, rather than accepting *his.* Alternatives were encouraged, as were their evaluation. Generally, the democratic leader and autocratic leader differed in their orientations to the group, with the democratic leader being more group-centered and the autocratic leader being more leader-centered.

Several studies have focused on the differences between groups with group-centered and leader-centered leaders; Wischmeier (1955) concluded that leader-centered leaders are perceived as more valuable in terms of overall contribution to the group than group-centered leaders. He also observed that group-centered discussions generally were judged to be better than leader-centered discussions: they were perceived as having friendlier atmospheres, more member involvement, and greater cooperation. A later study by Storey (1964) supported these conclusions and added two other dimensions for differentiating the two types of leadership in groups. Group-centered groups seemed to produce greater satisfaction with their decision; they also had a higher rate of interaction. Groups with a nondirective, democratic leader liked their groups more than those with directive, autocratic leaders. Differences in productivity are inconclusive, although it appears that groups with leader-centered leaders are more productive (Shaw 1955; Morse and Reimer 1956).

An individual must consider a number of factors to determine where he falls on the leadership continuum. The first, and most important, concern is the individual's assumptions about people. Douglas McGregor, in *The Human Side of Enterprise* (1960), developed two theories to explain human behavior. The two theories, referred to as Theory X and Theory Y, are two ends of another continuum. McGregor explained the basic differences between these two theories as follows: "The central principle of organization which derives from Theory X is that of direction and control through the exercise of authority . . . the central principle which derives from Theory Y is that of integration: the creation of conditions such that the members of the organization can achieve their own goals best by directing their efforts toward the success of the enterprise" (1960, chapters 3 and 4). It is important for the individual trying to determine his own "centeredness" to examine which of McGregor's two theories most closely approximates his own position.

The assumptions about people included in these theories are useful for checking our own assumptions. Theory X assumptions include the following:

1. People dislike work and try to avoid it.
2. People have to be coerced to get them to work adequately toward the achievement of organizational objectives.
3. People prefer to be directed, avoid responsibility.
4. People have little ambition, all they want is security.

Assumptions of Theory Y include:

1. People expend themselves in work as naturally as in play.
2. People need not be coerced to work, they will exercise self-direction and self-control in meeting objectives.
3. People are committed to their objectives to the extent that their achievement is rewarded.
4. People learn to accept responsibility.

5. People are normally imaginative and creative in their solutions to problems.
6. People are only partially utilized, they have greater resources than are normally tapped.

Although an analysis of the assumptions we make about people is one of the most important steps toward determining our place on the leadership continuum, other important factors to consider are: (1) how secure you are in ambiguous situations; the less secure you are, the greater the tendency is for you to be a leader-centered leader; (2) the extent to which your motives for leading the group are tied up with personal self-satisfaction; and (3) the extent to which your self-satisfaction is derived from the group's goal attainment. In other words, is your leader role differentiated from a self-centered role? These considerations will help determine where you fall on the leadership continuum *independent* of a particular group. But, of course, the circumstances of a particular group will have effects on the resultant leadership behavior. Some of these factors are considered below under the heading of Other Variables.

Two other approaches are available for differentiating leadership styles, although the use of the leadership style continuum is the one most widely used. Levine (1949) emphasizes the interaction between leadership and membership—both have their responsibilities. Leadership is of four basic types or styles, all of which are culturally prescribed. *The charismatic leader* is characterized by one who affects and inspires his membership by the strong expression of emotionality. He perceives and responds to those in a large group and is able to express group goals and solidarity in vivid, dramatic, and emotional terms. While the emphasis for this leader is the expression of feelings and not the solution of problems, he can nevertheless make the problems clearer to the membership. The main problem with the charismatic leader is that he often fails to see his role in relation to the goals of the group. In order to be effective, he must understand what the group goals are, and how other leadership styles might help meet them. *The organizational leader* is concerned with the day-to-day problems of administration and organization. He is pragmatic but relies on superficial signs of group success, such as speed and quantity (as opposed to quality). *The intellectual leader* provides the group with perspective, particularly in the interpretation of less immediate goals. He has the ability to view the group problems objectively and unbiasedly. However, he does not encourage member participation. In order to be effective, he must see himself less as a "consultant" and more as an integral part of the group. *The informal leader* is usually an opinion leader. He is close to the membership in important ways, such as status, and is usually not recognized as leader. His problem occurs when he is recognized as a leader and thereby is forced to adopt one of the other styles, all of which are unsuitable for him. It is necessary to understand that leaders need not be "on top" and decisive at all times in order for the role of informal leader to be an effective one.

The last general schema for differentiating among leadership styles is offered by Barnlund and Haiman (1960). The *leaderless group* is one in which there is no nominal leader; everyone shares in the coordination of group activity. This kind of shared leadership is most common to rap sessions and discussions among office workers not under pressure to generate solutions. Under these circumstances, direction and ideas come spontaneously from all members and the group moves from point to point by achieving consensus. No distinction is possible between leader and participant, since everyone engages in both roles. This type of leadership is not to be confused with the leadershipless group in which no members perform leadership functions. The leaderless group has a number of advantages over other types of groups, including the advantage of drawing on a number of talents to perform leadership functions, of generating greater involvement on the part of the membership, and of developing leadership skills in the greatest number of group members.

The *single leader* style fills the need for a symbol who embodies the group's spirit. Group members can point to a single individual as leader and thus gain the psychological support given by the knowledge that a division of labor has been accomplished. Such a designated leader is seen as impartial during times of crisis. The *leader in reserve* is an appointed leader who serves only when he is needed. If the group assumes the responsibility for its activity, the leader in reserve does not interfere. His two main functions are (1) to clarify abstract points and (2) to help the group members generate their solutions. *Nondirective leadership* is a style characterized by a leader who refrains from controlling, advising, or directing group members in order to avoid detrimental influence stemming from his power position. This leader serves as a therapist or counselor, reflecting back to the group what he believes are their ideas and feelings so as to make them more sensitive to their own behavior. *Experimental leadership* is the last form of leadership to be considered. In experimental leadership, each member consciously tries out different methods of influencing the other members in an attempt to determine what, for him, is the most productive and satisfying role.

The first experience at the beginning of this chapter attempted to create three different styles of leadership in as many groups. The first group, with its appointed leader directed to assume all of the responsibility for the group, should have had a directive or authoritarian leadership style. The second group, with its selected leader, should have had a less directive, democratic leader. The third group, with no appointed leader and no instructions concerning leadership, should have had a leadership style which approximated shared leadership or, in some cases, anarchy. What happened in your groups? Who won? Was one type of leadership more effective in helping the group to reach its goal? What pressures made one type of leadership more viable than the others? Did the three styles conform to styles depicted on the continuum or Levine's definitions? If not, why not? Did the leader appointed in the first group fail as a directive leader? Is it possible to force a leadership style on a group, or are there too many uncontrolled variables?

Leadership Effectiveness: Variables to Consider

A. The Contingency Model (Fiedler 1964, 1967)

Different types of groups require different types of leadership. Three important conditions affecting the exercise of power, and thus influencing the leader's role, are: the leader-member relations, the task structure, and position power, the power inherent in the leadership position irrespective of the person who occupies that position.

The *leader-member relations* exemplify the affective relationship between the leader and membership in a given group. Is the leader well liked? Is he respected? Are the members loyal to and confident in the leader? The greater the degree of certainty in and positive agreement to each of these questions, the more power the leader holds and the less he needs official recognition or rank.

The *task structure* concerns the external demands placed upon the group. External demands usually focus upon the specific task a group has. Regardless of how a task may be classified, it will affect how the leader operates. As the task becomes more ambiguous, the decisions less verifiable, the means to task solution greater, and the number of possible solutions larger, more pressure is placed on the specific abilities of the leader to keep the group operating efficiently;

concomitantly, leader power, the ability of the person to mete out rewards and punishments, and the degree to which rules and by-laws support his actions, is less effective under these circumstances.

Classifying a group on leader-member relations, task structure, and position power, and comparing this classification with the type of leadership in operation, clarifies the circumstances affecting leader effectiveness. Directive leaders function best under very negative or very positive circumstances, such as unfavorable leader-member relations and an unstructured task, or favorable leader-member relations and a highly structured task. On the other hand, nondirective, permissive leaders function best under less extreme circumstances, such as when the leader-member relations are unfavorable and the task is highly structured. Because a number of factors affect leadership, it should be obvious that suggesting that one leadership style is more effective than another is a simplistic view. Whether a particular style of leadership will be effective depends upon other variables.

Analyze the results of the experiences at the beginning of this and other chapters in terms of the relationship between the leadership style exercised, the leader-member relations, task structure, and position power. Did the behavior of the group you were in confirm Fiedler's conclusions concerning leader effectiveness? If not, why not? What other variables are important when considering leader effectiveness? What relationship exists between the three-dimensional classification schema and styles of leadership that fall between directive and nondirective?

B. Other Variables

External conditions of the group, other than the task structure, which may be important include the time limit imposed on the group and the consequences of the group's action. Generally, if a group is operating under an extremely severe time limit, more directive leadership is necessary, since nondirective leadership, aimed at having each member fulfill his own potential, takes more time than directive leadership. As the pressure for completion becomes more apparent, the leadership is likely to become more directive. You may have noticed this in the group you work in. The group may start as "democratic," and may appear "democratic" throughout most of its operation, but once a solution is called for, one or two members emerge to direct the group more forcefully and specifically toward the assigned goal(s). Even consensus is often a function of time—compromises are easier to reach when there are only ten minutes left of the class period!

The relationship between the consequences of action and effective leadership style is an interesting one. When the consequences of action are either very important or very unimportant, shared leadership is likely to be the most effective leadership style. For example, when the decision in industry to produce a new model car has multimillion dollar consequences, the probability of one individual assuming the responsibility for the decision is low. Group members seek comfort in a group decision, and shared leadership is the likely result. Likewise, when the consequences of action are unimportant, as when a group of friends are deciding which movie to watch, the probability of one individual assuming the responsibility for the decision is low because it has little relevance for him. When the consequences fall in between these two extremes, other considerations, such as time and task structure, are probably more important.

Internal conditions which influence leadership style include the characteristics of the group members and their expectations concerning leadership. In groups where there is little motivation, the only effective style of leadership is directive. Without directive leadership, the group will not function properly, if at all. If the problem is such that a good deal of intelligence (imagination? creativity?) is necessary to solve it, and few or no members possess that amount, then leadership will probably fall to the most intelligent member(s). Directive leadership, in this case, may provide the only effective means of involving the less intelligent members in the group process.

Member expectations are variables often neglected. Do the group members expect directive leadership? Do they expect to be manipulated and/or ordered? Or do they expect to be an integral part of the decision-making process? Different organizations have different characteristic styles, and the individuals in these organizations come to expect a particular leadership style in their groups. An attempt to employ a particular style of leadership without regard to member expectations may hinder, more than help, a particular group. Colleges have fairly heterogeneous student populations. A wide variety of ages, backgrounds, abilities, and desires are represented in almost every class. Examples of different leadership style expectations probably abound in your own class.

Common Leadership Functions

The leader role is a complex one, demanding a wide range of skills to meet a variety of necessary functions. Although any number of group members may perform any number of leadership functions, the important point is that they are performed. Leader performance may be measured in terms of the number of functions performed and the degree of effectiveness with which they are performed.

Leader task functions include studying the problem and the group objectively. Understanding the biases, interests, abilities, and expectations of group members is important for determining what leadership style may be most effective. Of course, an objective analysis of the problem is necessary to insure that, if the group needs help in understanding the problem, the leader is able to provide it.

Once the group forms, it is the leader's obligation to "break the ice." The first few minutes of any group's life are uneasy ones; individuals are afraid to speak out, or simply, as yet, uninterested in doing so. Opening remarks, introductions, and general questions are all techniques that may be used to help the group over these first minutes. During discussion, the leader must be sure each member understands what is happening, which may necessitate summarizing, clarifying, or probing. Members have to differentiate between ideas, feelings, the problem, and the solutions. The leader has to watch for problems arising from lack of such differentiation, and be prepared to clarify.

Different groups have their own unique developmental rates and styles. Developmental problems have to be recognized and corrected within the time limits set for interaction. The leader, therefore, must keep one eye on his watch, one eye on the task problem, another eye on the quality of interaction, and still another eye on the problems within the group. These demands make him physiologically unique, if nothing else.

The leader must encourage participation from all the members of the group. When a member does not interact, the leader has to discover why and apply corrective measures. Does the member feel inadequate? Does he feel intimidated? Is he uninterested in the group? Each member of the group may prove useful. Not to encourage and insure member interaction may prove a waste of good resources.

Leaders must also encourage critical and creative thinking. By creating an atmosphere in which members feel secure, the leader can provide an atmosphere in which free exchange of ideas can take place without fear of hostile criticism. A parallel function for the leader may be to clarify the criteria for performance and evaluation.

The socio-emotional functions of the leader can be summarized under the heading of Establishing Healthy Interpersonal Relations. Value conflicts and personality conflicts should be avoided because of their detrimental effects on the group. One technique for resolving interpersonal conflicts is to ask each of the individuals involved in the conflict to state the position held by the other member. After this, the discussion continues providing that each person may not begin his own talk without first summarizing the other person's position, to the other's satisfaction. Differences in this area are usually the result of a lack of understanding of the other person's value system. This exercise should resolve the conflict by providing the necessary information.

A group's socio-emotional development makes many demands on a leader, forcing him to develop a variety of strategies to keep the group from dissolving. During the early stages, group members will be feeling each other out to discover boundaries. The leader must guide the group through this stage to keep hostilities from developing. During the stage when group members are asserting their individuality, the leader must devise a means for the group to remain, in fact, a group. This is a crucial stage; often groups never develop beyond it. The leader must point out differences, explain them, and help the group resolve them quickly. Groups that go beyond the conflict stages and develop cohesion usually have resolved interpersonal problems. Problems arising after the development of cohesion are usually easy to handle. The basic hostilities are gone, so open discussion of interpersonal conflicts is a viable approach to these problems.

The purpose of effective leadership is to help the group grow and realize its potential to solve its task efficiently and pleasantly. While doing all this, the leader probably should remain a transparent figure: the person not really there. He should be seen as another member of the group, and little else. He is a guide, a helper, and an active member —not a dominator.

Go back now to the second experience at the beginning of this chapter. Analyze the leadership behavior exhibited in each of the groups in order to clarify some of the points made.

Bibliography

Adorno, T. W., Frenkel-Brunswik, E., Levinson, D., and Sandford, R. *The Authoritarian Personality.* New York: Harper, 1950.

Bales, R. F. *Interaction Process Analysis: A Method for the Study of Small Groups.* Cambridge, Massachusetts: Addison-Wesley, 1950.

———. "The Equilibrium Problem in Small Groups." In *Working Papers in the Theory of Action,* edited by T. Parsons, R. F. Bales, and E. A. Shils, pp. 111-61. Glencoe, Illinois: Free Press, 1953.

————. "Adaptive and Integrative Changes as Sources of Strain in Social Systems." In *Small Groups: Studies in Social Interaction,* edited by A. P. Hare, E. F. Borgotta, and R. F. Bales, pp. 127-31. New York: Knopf, 1955.

————. "Task Status and Likeability as a Function of Talking and Listening in Decision-Making Groups." In *The State of the Social Sciences,* edited by L. D. White, pp. 148-61. Chicago: University of Chicago Press, 1956.

————. "Task Roles and Social Roles in Problem Solving Groups." In *Readings in Social Psychology,* edited by E. E. Maccoby, T. M. Newcomb, and F. L. Hartley, pp. 196-413. 3rd ed. New York: Holt, Rinehart and Winston, 1958.

Bales, R. F., and Slater, P. E. "Role Differentiation in Small Decision-Making Groups." In *The Family, Socialization, and Interaction Process,* edited by T. Parson, R. F. Bales et al., pp. 259-306. Glencoe, Illinois: Free Press, 1955.

Barnlund, D. C. "Experiments in Leadership Training for Decision-Making Groups." *Speech Monographs* 22 (1955): 1-14.

————. "Consistency of Emergent Leadership in Groups with Changing Tasks and Members." *Speech Monographs* 29 (1962): 45-52.

Barnlund, D. C., and Haiman, F. S. *The Dynamics of Discussion.* Boston: Houghton Mifflin, 1960.

Bass, B. M. *Leadership, Psychology, and Organizational Behavior.* New York: Harper, 1960.

Bird, C. *Social Psychology.* New York: Appleton-Century, 1940.

Borg, W. R., et al. "Relationship between Physical Proficiency and Measures of Leadership and Personality." *Personnel Psychology* 12 (1959): 113-26.

Borgotta, E. F., and Bales, R. F. "Sociometric Status Patterns and Characteristics of Interaction." *Journal of Social Psychology* 43 (1956): 289-97.

Bowers, D. G., and Seashore, S. E. "Peer Leadership within Work Groups." *Personnel Administration* 30 (1967): 45-50.

Carter, L. F. "On Defining Leadership." In *Group Relations at the Crossroads,* edited by M. Sherif and M. O. Wilson, pp. 262-65. New York: Harper and Row, 1953.

Cartwright, D., and Zander, A., eds. *Group Dynamics: Research and Theory.* Evanston, Illinois: Row, Peterson, 1960.

Cattell, R. B. "New Concepts for Measuring Leadership, in Terms of Group Syntality." *Human Relations* 4 (1951): 161-84.

Cattell, R. B., and Stice, G. F. "Four Formulae for Selecting Leaders on the Basis of Personality." *Human Relations* 7 (1954): 493-507.

Emery, D. A. "Leadership through Motivation by Objectives." *Personnel Psychology* 12 (1959): 65-79.

Fiedler, F. E. "A Contingency Model of Leadership Effectiveness." In *Advances in Experimental Social Psychology,* edited by L. Berkowitz, 1:-146-90. New York: Academic, 1964.

———. *A Theory of Leadership Effectiveness.* New York: McGraw-Hill, 1967.

Filley, A. C., and Jesse, F. C. "Training Leadership Styles: A Survey of Research." *Personnel Administration* 28 (1965): 14-21.

Fleishman, E. A., and Peters, D. R. "Interpersonal Values, Leadership Attitudes, and Managerial Success." *Personnel Psychology* 15 (1962): 127-43.

Geier, J. "A Trait Approach to the Study of Leadership." *Journal of Communication* 17 (1967): 316-23.

Gibb, C. A. "The Sociometry of Leadership in Temporary Groups." *Sociometry* 13 (1950): 226-43.

Golembiewski, R. T. "Three Styles of Leadership and Their Uses." *Personnel* 38 (1961): 34-45.

Haiman, F. S. "A Measurement of Authoritarian Attitudes Toward Discussion Leadership." *Quarterly Journal of Speech* 41 (1955): 140-44.

Haythorn, W. W., Couch, A., Haefner, D., Langham, P., and Carter, L. F. "The Behavior of Authoritarian and Equalitarian Personalities in Groups." *Human Relations* 9 (1956): 57-74.

Hollander, E. P., and Webb, W. B. "Leadership, Followership, and Friendship: Analysis of Peer Nominations." *Journal of Abnormal and Social Psychology* 50 (1955): 163-67.

House, R. J. "Leadership Training: Some Dysfunctional Consequences." *Administrative Science Quarterly* 12 (1968): 556-71.

Laird, D., and Laird, E. *The New Psychology for Leadership.* New York: McGraw-Hill, 1956.

Levine, S. "An Approach to Constructive Leadership." *Journal of Social Issues* 5 (1949): 46-53.

Lewin, K., Lippit, R., and White, R. K. "Patterns of Aggressive Behavior in Experimentally Created 'Social Climates'." *Journal of Social Psychology* 10 (1939): 271-99.

Lippitt, R., and White, R. K. "The 'Social Climate' of Children's Groups." In *Child Behavior and Development,* edited by R. G. Barker, J. Kounin, and H. Wright, pp. 485-508. New York: McGraw-Hill, 1943.

McGregor, D. *The Human Side of Enterprise.* New York: McGraw-Hill, 1960.

Morse, N. C., and Reimer, E. "The Experimental Change of a Major Organizational Variable." *Journal of Abnormal and Social Psychology* 52 (1956): 120-29.

Newport, G. "Study of Attitudes and Leadership Behavior." *Personnel Administration* 25 (1962): 42-46.

Olmstead, M. S. "Orientation and Role in the Small Group." *American Sociological Review* 19 (1959): 741-51.

Preston, M. G., and Heintz, R. K. "Effects of Participatory Vs. Supervisory Leadership on Group Judgment." *Journal of Abnormal and Social Psychology* 44 (1949): 345-55.

Randall, E. V. "Motivation through Leadership Action." *Personnel Journal* 40 (1968): 104-8.

Sargent, J. F., and Miller, G. R. "Some Differences in Certain Communication Behaviors of Autocratic and Democratic Leaders." *Journal of Communication* 21 (1971): 233-52.

Shaw, M. E. "A Comparison of Two Types of Leadership in Various Communication Nets." *Journal of Abnormal and Social Psychology* 50 (1955): 127-34.

Slater, P. E. "Role Differentiation in Small Groups." *American Sociological Review* 20 (1955): 300-310.

Stogdill, R. M. "Personal Factors Associated with Leadership: A Survey of the Literature." *Journal of Psychology* 25 (1948): 35-71.

Storey, A. W. "Responsibility Sharing Vs. Strong Procedural Leadership." *Central States Speech Journal* 15 (1964): 285-89.

Verba, S. "Leadership: Affective and Instrumental." In *Small Groups and Political Behavior: A Study of Leadership,* pp. 161-84. Princeton, New Jersey: Princeton University Press, 1961.

Vroom, V. H., and Mann, F. C. "Leader Authoritarianism and Employee Attitudes." *Personnel Psychology* 13 (1960): 125-40.

Wischmeier, R. R. "Group-Centered and Leader-Centered Leadership: An Experimental Study." *Speech Monographs* 22 (1955): 43-48.

Zdep, S. M., and Oakes, W. I. "Reinforcement of Leadership Behavior in Group Discussion." *Journal of Experimental Social Psychology* 3 (1967): 310-20.

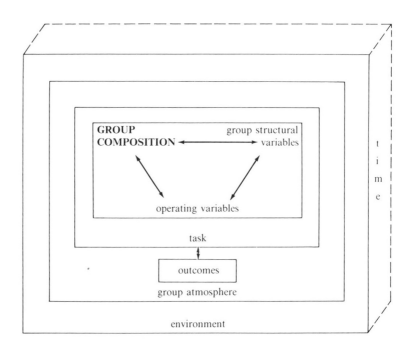

CHAPTER 7

SELF-CONCEPT AND SMALL GROUP BEHAVIOR

Who are you? Are you who you say you are? Fill in the following blank: I am ———. How many different things can you write down? Now, think about each answer you wrote. How do you know you are correct?

Time to collect some data.

Experience 7-1. Each person needs a 3 by 5 index card and a crayon. If I did not know you and I wanted to know you, you would probably tell me your name. But, unless I could associate you with an object or symbol which is relevant, I probably wouldn't remember you. Therefore, on the 3 by 5 card, do not write your name. Instead, draw the object, thing, or symbol which best represents you. Why did you choose that one?

Experience 7-2. Divide the class into pairs. The pairs should spread out as much as possible. Each member of your pair must complete the following:
1. Draw three circles on a piece of paper.
2. Divide each circle into six parts.
3. Label the fist "wheel" *what,* the second *why,* and the third *how.* Now, look at the person opposite you for a few minutes. Do not talk! In the first wheel, write six adjectives which describe your first impressions of your partner. Avoid writing obvious and trivial things, such as the color of your partner's hair (unless it is particularly important to

143

you). Now, exchange papers with your partner. Look over what was written about you and circle one of the six words that you want your partner to expand upon. The reason you circle a particular word may be curiosity, anger, or simply because you cannot believe that such a word was applied to you. The reason may be personal or not. Exchange papers again. You now have the paper on which you wrote your impressions of your partner. One of your impressions should be circled. In the second wheel, labeled "why," write down six words which expand and explain the circled word.

Exchange papers again. Discuss with your partner any aspect of this exercise that interests you. For example, you might wish to discuss the value of first impressions or the reason for circling a particular word in the "what" wheel. Include value judgments in your discussion of the circled word. For example, is "intelligent" good or bad? If the judgment is good, fill in the "how" wheel with six ways to increase the strength of the impression. If the impression is judged bad, generate six ways to decrease it.

Experience 7-3. Form pairs again. Try to avoid someone with whom you are already familiar. Isolate yourselves from other pairs as much as possible.

Take between three and five minutes each and talk about how you see yourself. While your partner is talking, you should remain silent, providing no feedback of any nature. When he is through talking, you are to mimic him, showing him a mirror image of his thoughts, his voice, and his mannerisms. You are not to evaluate anything he said.

Experience 7-4. This is similar to experience 7-3. First, form pairs. Again, try to find an unfamiliar person to work with and isolate yourself as much as possible.

First, one person is to talk about himself for three to five minutes. He may talk about anything—school work, his relationships with family and friends, even personal hang-ups. Do not provide the first person with any feedback. It

> might be worthwhile for the second person to sit with his back toward the first.
>
> When the first person is through talking, the second person picks up the conversation *as if he were the first person,* only this time he makes judgments. For example, suppose the first person finishes with the phrase, "and that's how I came to switch from the medical school to the school of engineering." The second person might begin by saying, "I'm confused. I can't make up my mind whether I want to be a doctor or not."
>
> When the second person has finished, switch roles and start over.

People react to us. They tell us things about ourselves and we listen. Often we react to what they say. We circle adjectives and ask for explanations. We ask for confirmation of our self-concept, which we may or may not receive; then we adjust accordingly. How we see ourselves, and how we think others see us, direct our behavior. In the small group setting we learn about ourselves because others are learning about and reacting to us. The relationship between self-perception and the perception of others is one of interdependence.

George Herbert Mead

This brings us back to the first question: Who are you? How do you know? According to George Herbert Mead (1934), the "self" is a social emergent: we are the impact of others upon us. Our experience of ourselves is indirect; we experience our "selves" by coming into contact with others who act as a mirror. "Selves must be accounted for in terms of the social process and in terms of communication" (Mead 1934, p. 29).

Four basic concepts make up Mead's emergent self. Self is dependent upon (1) a social situation, (2) the capacity for the use of significant symbols, (3) some mechanism for self stimulation, and (4) the ability to "get into" the experience of the other. An examination of each of these four requisites provides a meaningful framework for understanding the relationship between self and other in the small group.

Starting with the fourth concept, communication is essential to the social process; it is the key to society. Language is the means that enables an individual to take on the attitudes of the others in a common activity. Getting into the other's experience is essential to the emergent self.

Language allows us to take on another's attitudes and is a means for self stimulation. If our words stimulate us similar to the way they stimulate others, then we are using symbols properly. The proper use of symbols allows us to conceive of ourselves as objects. This is necessary if we are to determine the effect of our language on others. If we cannot determine this, we cannot use the language, and thus we eliminate the possibility of developing a self. "When the conversation of gestures can be taken over into the individual's conduct so that the attitude of the other forms can affect the organism, and the organism can reply with its corresponding gesture and thus arouse the attitude of the other in its own process, then a self arises" (Mead 1934, p. 167). Mead maintains that the distinguishing trait of selfhood resides in the organism's ability to be an object to itself by taking on the role of the other and through the proper use of symbols.

The relationship between language and meaning hinges on the concept of "significant symbol." Mead defines a significant symbol by writing, "When gesture means the idea behind it and arouses that idea in the mind of the other individual, then we have a significant symbol" (1934, p. 45). He concludes that, "when we have a symbol which answers to a meaning in the experience of the first individual and which also calls out that meaning in the second individual . . . it becomes language" (1934, p. 46). Meaning is, therefore, social in nature; it is the calling out of the same response in ourselves and others.

More important than the formation of a community of meaning is a consideration of how meaning evolves. Meaning evolves through social interaction and in the threefold relationships among gesture, adjustive response, and the resultant of the given social act. "Response on the part of the second organism to the gesture of the first is the interpretation . . . of that gesture [and indicates] the resultant of the social act which it initiates and in which both organisms are involved" (Mead 1934, p. 80). There would be no necessity for gestures if it were not for interaction because, as interaction makes meaning possible, so does language "make adjustment possible among the individuals implicated in any given social act" (Mead 1934, p. 46). All of this implies cooperative interaction and the belief that it is possible to come to social agreements.

Finally, self can only emerge in a society. The only way to "be" is to be interpersonal. "Selves can only exist in definite relationships to other selves" (Mead 1934, p. 164). The relationship between selves and society is not one-way, with society simply allowing for the development of selves. The relationship is interdependent: "As a man adjusts himself to a certain environment, he becomes a different individual; but in becoming a different individual, he has affected the community in which he lives. It may be a slight effect, but insofar as he has adjusted himself, the adjustments have changed the type of environment to which he can respond and the world is accordingly a different world" (Mead 1934, p. 215).

The concepts of self, society, communication, meaning, and significant symbol are central to Mead's perspective. Two other concepts, also important to Mead's conception of the relation between man and man, and man and society, are: (1) the significance of the act and (2) the broader concept of the generalized other. These two concepts are extremely useful for explaining the relationships among group members, the existence of role behavior, and the development of norms.

According to Mead, the ultimate unit of existence is the act, conceived as the self-caused ongoing behavior of the individual which is initiated by some desire and directed to its goal by the elements available in the environment. The act, therefore, determines the individual's relationship to the environment. Elements in the environment are utilized or not, considered important or irrelevant. The environment, on the other hand, changes because of the act. Because of this dynamic relationship between an individual, his act, and the environment, the outcome of behavior is, to a large extent, unpredictable. The environment is in flux, new elements are added, and old elements are subtracted, with the passage of time. *To perform an act takes courage.*

The "generalized other" is society's representative in the individual; it is through the generalized other that society exercises control over the individual. The reason that society exercises control over the individual is that the individual contains, as part of his self, an "I." The "I" is associated with creativity, freedom, subjectivity; it is the always unpredictable, surprising part of ourselves. The generalized other is constituted in the "me." The "me" is the combination of attitudes, roles, meanings, pressures, values; it is the predictable, conforming, social part of ourselves. The "I" and "me" together form a self, the "I" asserting and the "me" limiting the assertion.

At this point, it will be useful to engage in two exercises, both of which are presented to emphasize points made by Mead which seem particularly relevant to small group behavior.

Experience 7-5. Divide the class into small groups of four to six members. Each group completes the same task:

> Spell out your first name in reverse. Look at your reversed name. It spells some strange new word. Pretend that this is a word that comes from a language of an alien species on the planet Mars. Roll this alien word over your tongue, and decide how it is pronounced on Mars. Now write out a definition of the word as it would appear in a Martian dictionary. (Malamud and Machover 1969, p. 252)

When each individual in the group has finished this, choose one of the words, with its definition, to relate to other groups. Be sure that the other groups cannot hear your decision.

When all the groups are finished, have one group simply call out the word, without its definition. How many people from other groups know what it means? How many people can guess what it means? Now, tell the other groups the definition of the word. Why is it that everyone now knows what the word means?

In the first situation there was no social interaction, in the second there was. *Meaning comes from social interaction.* Generally, each group will develop unique meanings for a set of words. In other words, the group becomes its own society in that it may ascribe particular meanings to symbols which are significant only to the members of the group.

Also, consider how you are able to define your own name when it is spelled in reverse. Your name, which is *you* can be looked at as an object. Your ability to conceive of yourself as an object enables you to ascribe meaning to the letters, even in reverse.

Experience 7-6. "Every family has its own favorite expressions, proverbs, slogans, advices, admonitions, or warnings. ... List all the repetitive sayings [you] can recall from [your] own families and then read them aloud in a go-around" (Malamud and Machover 1969, p. 247). Some examples which may be useful to stimulate things are: "Date whom

> you will, but marry someone of your own kind," and, "Shut
> out the lights; do you own shares in the light company?"
> Each of your family sayings have implicit value judg-
> ments. The two given here, for example, imply different
> things. The first statement implies that it is bad to marry
> someone not like yourself; the second implies that it is good
> to be thrifty. What were the value judgments implicit in
> your own family sayings? How do you think these sayings
> affected you? What do you do today that may be a result of
> the family sayings you grew up with?

Family pressures are an integral part of the socialization process.
The sayings you grew up with, and the value judgments they imply,
form part of the generalized other, the "me" part of your self. What
happens when your "me" is confronted with other "me's" in a group?
Can a clash of values be traced back to each individual's socialization
process? Are norms carried over into the groups from the general
society (e.g., "men do not curse in front of women") as easily as they
are because they form part of almost everyone's "me"?

Mead's analysis of the self's developmental process provides
many insights into group behavior. Analyze your own group in terms
of the self-society-communication-meaning-act-generalized other
framework. Your own group's interaction, *socially reflexive* behavior,
and maintenance of order in a continuously changing social organization may become more meaningful and richer.

Self-Concept: Affects and Effects

An esoteric definition of self-concept is provided by Mabel and Rosenfeld (1966): self-concept is "a phenomenological unitary configuration
of symbolic constructs with the self as a reference which the individual
derives from experience and utilizes as a frame of reference for self-
evaluation and understanding, and in the perception of behavior related to the self" (p. 381, n. 2). What this boils down to is that the
self-concept is derived from experience and projected into future behavior. How an individual evaluates himself today reflects how others
evaluated him in the past and affects how he will evaluate others in
the future.

A number of hypotheses have been generated from Mead's "self-
identity" theory. Two that have been tested are: (1) A person's self-
identity is largely determined by others, i.e., it is a function of how

one thinks the public perceives him, and how the public, in actuality, does perceive him. (2) People use the same or similar categories in perceiving themselves and others.

Galloway (1967) conducted an experiment to test the relationship between self and other evaluation. Individuals were placed in groups in which three members evaluated the other two members either positively or negatively. As predicted, group members who received positive evaluations judged themselves and the other members of the group higher than those members who received only negative evaluations.

Several studies have explored the relationship between past experience and self-concept. Does past success foster a good self-concept, and past failure a bad one? Krieger (1966) studied the relative influence of individual and group success on self-evaluation. Subjects were assigned to any one of the following possible combinations: individual success or individual failure, and group success or group failure. Success and failure were controlled by the experimenter. After a success or failure experience in either the group or individual setting, subjects were asked to evaluate themselves. The results were consistent: regardless of the setting, success raises self-evaluation and failure lowers it.

The effect of self-evaluation on the evaluation of others was demonstrated in a study by Jones and Ratner (1967). Interpersonal evaluation is a function of at least two factors, self-evaluation and commitment to that self-evaluation. Subjects were induced to adopt low self-appraisals by receiving low test scores. After making this low self-appraisal, subjects were given the opportunity to express either a commitment or a lack of commitment to the appraisal. Next, subjects were placed in three-person groups in which one of the other members offered only positive evaluations of the subject and the other offered only negative evaluations. The subject was then asked to evaluate the other two members of the group. The results showed that a subject highly committed to his low self-appraisal evaluated the group member offering negative evaluations more highly than the member offering positive evaluations. Jones and Ratner concluded that commitment to a low self-appraisal protects the subject from the "behavioral implications of accepting praise" (p. 446). The group member who accepts praise has an image to uphold: he must be a good group member, effective in solving difficult tasks. Thus, the more committed a person is to a low self-appraisal, the less important are the consequences of his acts, in this case the evaluation of others. This implies that "the extent of a person's commitment to a low self-appraisal is inversely related to his tendency to devaluate a peer sending negative evaluations" (Jones and Ratner p. 447).

A great deal of research emphasizes the importance of the acceptance or rejection of membership in reference groups on an individual's self-concept. A membership group is a group that socially influences the individual by providing the standard by which he guides himself. These groups are the mirrors that reflect the perceived public identity conceived by Mead. Also, as the name implies, a membership group is any group to which the individual belongs. Reference groups, on the other hand, are those groups to which the individual does not belong, but which are nevertheless important to him. An individual aspires to acceptance in a reference group.

The Symbolic Interactionist Theory focuses on an individual's social surroundings. This theory states that an individual's social surroundings provide the situation in which three aspects of self-perception form: "(a) the real self-image, as the ego defines himself to himself; (b) the looking glass self, as the ego thinks others think of him; (c) the ideal self, as the ego would like to be" (Manneheim 1966, p. 270). A study by Manneheim (1966) attempted to relate the consequences of the reference group theories and the symbolic interactionist theory. His hypothesis considered the effects of reference group consensus on an individual's self-concept. The reference group's consensus is perceived by the individual as the looking-glass self. The effect of the reference group's consensus is transmitted through the looking-glass self and influences the real and ideal self-conceptions.

Subjects in the Manneheim study completed two questionnaires: a reference group questionnaire designed to determine an individual's important reference groups, and self-description questionnaires designed to determine an individual's self-image, his reference groups' image of him, and his membership groups' image of him, the latter two being transmitted through the looking-glass self. Results showed that individuals tend to change their self-image over time in the direction of the perceived reference group's image. Also, individuals who change their reference groups often have more changes in self-concept. Finally, there are some individuals who, despite frequent changes in reference groups, maintain a consistent, stable self-image.

Self-concept is, to a large extent, determined by others, but only to the extent that it is communicated and perceived. Because of the relationship between self-concept and communication, the small group setting is ideal for examining the effects of self-concept on a member's evaluation of himself and others and on his role behavior.

The experiments of Galloway and Jones and Ratner focused on self- and other evaluation in the small group setting. Galloway's experiment demonstrated that an individual's evaluation of the other group members is dependent on how the others evaluated him. Jones and Ratner's experiment extended this conclusion to include the effects of self-appraisal. Low self-appraisal (poor self-concept) reverses the effects discovered by Galloway: members with low self-appraisals do not devalue group members offering negative evaluations.

If members' evaluations represent the membership group's image of the member, then these evaluations may be considered an important factor in determining the member's looking-glass self. Thus, evaluations from prior groups, how they were communicated, and how they were perceived will determine how an individual will perform in subsequent groups. Jones and Ratner would predict that group members with poor self-concepts will behave in a manner consistent with their poor self-concepts and will generally be unproductive members. Members with good self-concepts also will behave consistently and will generally be productive group members.

The degree to which an individual is able to be influenced and the degree to which he can influence the group is also determined in part by self-concept. Farkash (1967) conducted an experiment to determine the relationships among self-esteem, authoritarianism, and the degree to which an individual was persuasible. Subjects were given a questionnaire designed to elicit their opinions on a given topic. They also completed tests to measure their self-esteem and authoritarianism, as well as their interest in and amount of information on the topic. Groups were formed with low and high self-esteem individuals, low and high authoritarian individuals, and pro and con opinion individuals. Each subject was presented with a communication on the topic that was contrary to his own opinion and told that the communication came from an authoritative or nonauthoritative source. Results indicated that authoritative sources change more opinions than nonauthoritative sources. Interestingly, low self-esteem subjects with a pro opinion were more easily swayed than low self-esteem members with a con opinion. This may indicate that low self-esteem group members may be more easily influenced to adopt a negative opinion than a positive one. Also, there is an inverse relationship between self-esteem and opinion change: the higher one's self-esteem, the more difficult it is to influence an opinion change.

Another study (Macbride and Tuddenham 1965) related self-confidence and resistance to group pressures. Each subject was placed in a group with five members; each group was given a simple perceptual judgment task. The other four members of the group, who were confederates, expressed consensus on the wrong answers. Approximately thirty percent of the subjects conformed to the wrong answers. Conforming subjects were then given the opportunity to modify their judgments through a series of nonpressure trials. But, high and low scores were manipulated by the experimenters. As expected, judgment modification was predicted by the scores received on the nonpressure trials: high scorers modified their judgments, low scorers did not. A change in the degree of confidence in the ability to perform the task determined the judgment modification, and self-confidence was determined by success or failure experiences. Consequently, if a group member perceives himself as effective in past experiences, he will be more resistant to group pressure in current situations, yielding an inverse function of confidence.

Hechbaum (1954) arrived at similar conclusions using two other variables: social reality and the concept of dependence. *Social reality* refers to those situations in which the only source of verification is group agreement. For example, the Freddie Fastbuck problems (see chapter 8) have highly verifiable answers, whereas the only verification available for some exercises (e.g., the first exercise in chapter 5) was group verification, or agreement. *Dependence* refers to the extent to which a given group member relies on the other group members for establishing the social reality of an issue.

Hechbaum's conclusions were as might be expected: the lower the member's self-confidence, the more verification he needs for opinions he holds; competence to judge issues in the past promotes confidence to express opinions on new issues; the more isolated a group member perceives his view, the greater the probability he will lose some confidence in his ability to perform in the new group; and, finally, the more competent a person perceives himself to be, the less his self-confidence will be influenced by disagreement with the other members of the group.

In a more recent study (Hope and Kerly 1971), the relationship between self-concept and academic aptitude was the focus of attention. Although it would seem that the relationship would be a positive one, that is, the better the self-concept, the greater the academic aptitude, such is not the case. Scores on the Scholastic Aptitude Test did not differ significantly for high and low self-concept freshmen. The only relationship between these two variables confirmed in the study concerned students pursuing a B.A. degree for future economic benefits. These students did not seem to fully realize the demands of their curricula. Students with both high self-concepts and high SAT scores are less economically oriented and perceive the demands of their curricula more realistically than other students. Although the major finding was contrary to expectations, the other findings were not. It appears reasonable to assume that students with both high self-concepts and high academic aptitude (as measured within the limits of the SAT) are more realistic in their evaluations.

Focusing again on the group, Heider (Mabel and Rosenfeld 1966) considered the relationship between self-confidence and group tension. As tension builds in groups, group members attempt to resolve whatever is producing the tension. Heider postulates that group members who are low in self-confidence are more likely to be influenced by situations in which there is tension. Studies reported by Heider support this notion and offer two explanations: (1) low self-confidence leads to a lower tolerance of tension and (2) greater tension is experienced by those with low self-confidence. To test which explanation was more reasonable, Heider asked individuals with assessed self-concepts to report on their felt discomfort in situations with varying amounts of imbalance (which generates tension). The poorer the self-concept, the greater the reported discomfort. Hence, individuals with little self-confidence and, consequently, poor self-concepts will be the first to attempt to rectify tension-filled situations, because such individuals experience more tension for a given situation than those with more self-confidence and better self-concepts.

The relationship between self-concept and group interaction has already been touched upon, but Griffit (1966) investigated the relationship between self-concept and interpersonal *attraction.* He conducted two experiments relating personality similarity, self-concept, and interpersonal attraction. Results indicated that similarity and interpersonal attraction are positively related. Perceived similarity to one's *ideal* self is also related to attraction. Individuals with similar personality characteristics will be attracted to each other, as will individuals with similar self-concepts; and attraction will lead to greater interaction.

If similarity increases interaction, it is reasonable to assume that homogeneous groups would be more effective than nonhomogeneous groups. Olivarri (1968) grouped high school students according to their self-concept: groups contained either all low self-concept members, all high self-concept members, or a mixture. Students in the homogeneous low self-concept groups indicated that they had higher self-esteem than low self-concept students in the heterogeneous settings. In homogeneous settings, low self-concept students could experience enough success to increase their own expectations; higher grades were given these students in their homogeneous settings. The opposite was true for the high self-concept students: performance was superior in the heterogeneous groups. The implications for group formation are clear: if the object of interaction is to increase each member's self-esteem, homogeneous groupings of low self-concept members are most effective; if the situation is a learning one, homogeneous groupings of low self-concept members are more effective for the low self-concept individuals than heterogeneous groupings; if the object is to help individuals with good self-concepts perform to their maximum, heterogeneous groupings are the most effective.

Kwal and Fleshler (1971) also worked with groups homogeneous in self-esteem. Four groups contained members all high in self-esteem, and four groups contained members all low in self-esteem. In the high self-esteem groups, members perceived each other as good contributors and leaders. These members were more satisfied with their discussions and found their groups more pleasant and cooperative than low self-esteem group members found theirs. According to Kwal and Fleshler, self-esteem and leadership are related. In the low self-esteem groups, the leadership was concentrated in the group member who initiated the discussion. Leadership in the high self-esteem groups was less concentrated: a great many group members performed leadership functions.

Confidence levels, which relate directly to self-concept, are also a function of group size, task complexity, and the correctness of the group decision. A recent study (Powers and Wright 1971) sought to clarify the relationships among these three variables. Comparing individuals alone with those in two-man or three-man groups, it was found that individuals working alone had the highest confidence level, individuals in the three-man groups had the next highest level of confidence. Regardless of the group size, a higher confidence level was displayed when the task was simple than when the task was complex. Finally, the level of confidence of members in all three sizes of groups was indicative of the group's ability to distinguish correct from incorrect decisions.

Interaction gives rise to and is in turn affected by self-concept. Understanding the relationships among the various variables affecting self-concept, such as group size, homogeneity or heterogeneity, task complexity, success and failure, and positive and negative evaluations, will help us make predictions of group effectiveness. In addition, such an understanding may allow for the creation of groups which should be the most effective for a given problem.

Poor Self-Concept

The group member with a good self-concept usually is an asset to the group. It is the member with a poor self-concept who needs consideration if he is to become a productive individual.

Self-concept is the major way an individual has of reflecting the good and bad feelings about himself. A high self-concept group member is usually highly productive, friendly, outgoing, and, in general, very effective. For a low self-concept member, the opposite is usually true. Most members, however, fall somewhere in between. Given enough time, it becomes clear even to the less perceptive group members how others feel about themselves.

A low self-concept group member is likely to be defensive. He may avoid interaction, avoid offering opinions, and, in general, function as an isolate. Attempts by other group members to cope with the problem of the low self-concept member are usually doomed to failure. This is because poor self-concepts, like good ones, are generally stable over time.

The following diary entries describe the interaction indicative of a poor self-concept group member.

February 1. . . . Jane is too quiet! I have a hunch she'll contribute very little. When it came to deciding the next meeting time and place, all she said was, "I don't have a car." And left it at that, waiting for someone to come to her rescue! No one did. . . .

February 15. . . . We decided on a seance. Some of us were skeptical, and a few enthusiastic, but Jane was nervous and uneasy.
. . . After the seance we rated each other and ourselves on how we thought the group perceived us, as either plus, minus, or zero if neutral. Jane was rated below the others (she also rated herself as a minus), and she took this rather badly. She definitely has a low self-concept, and the group's response to her didn't help her any. The meeting ended on that dubious note.

February 22. . . . Jane is still uptight. She told us that she came to this meeting expecting more of the negative reactions she re-

ceived at the last meeting. We all tried to give her positive strokes. We rated ourselves and each other again, and this time she came out okay. We all seem to be trying to help her. . . .

March 1. . . . Tonight we played the "Potato Game." We each used a potato to project our feelings and experiences to the other group members. We would introduce the potato and then tell a story about it.

We learned that Jane is (1) in possession of a really lousy self-concept, (2) feels everyone perceives her as a bad or useless person, (3) uses drugs, and (4) is really super lovely! She finds it hard to relate to people, and so has few if any friends. She avoids interacting and is only in the group because a course grade is riding on the final product. . . . I hope we can help her feel at ease.

Self-Concept: A Final Note

Who are you? Grove (Borden, Gregg, and Grove 1969) explains the complexity of this question:

Me is not a homogeneous block of wood carved from the same tree but a complex of remembered perceptions, cognitions, and bodily sensations from within, and recalled utterances and other sensory impressions from without—in short, a variety of nervous activity. Me is a morass of information filed away for future recall or eventual repression. Me is a million things at once and none of them separately, even though one's data-processing system generously permits one, on occasion, to select his best me from among the many existing combinations of data. The different me's one can detect are just partial selves called to any situation that demands a certain part of me be dominant, or brought into focus more than the other parts. . . . (p. 86)

Who are you? How do you know? What are the elements of your self-concept? What is your self-image? Can you make predictions for your *own* behavior in a particular group situation? If you were a flavor of ice cream, what flavor would you be? Why? What flavor would other members of your group be? What kind of car? Musical instrument? Color? What do these projections tell you about your relationships with the other members in your group? What do they tell you about who you are?

Bibliography

Backman, C., Secord, P., and Peirce, J. "Resistance to Change in the Self-Concept as a Function of Consensus among Significant Others." In *Problems in Social Psychology,* edited by Carl Backman and Paul Secord, pp. 462-67. New York: McGraw-Hill, 1966.

Borden, G. A., Gregg, R. B., and Grove, T. G. *Speech Behavior and Human Interaction.* Englewood Cliffs, New Jersey: Prentice-Hall, 1969.

Combs, A., and Snygg, D. *Individual Behavior.* Rev. ed. New York: Harper and Row, 1959.

Farkash, M. E. "Self-esteem, Authoritarianism, and Persuasibility." Yeshiva University, 1967. *Dissertation Abstracts* 28 (1967): 2120.

Fisher, S. *Body Experience in Fantasy and Behavior.* New York: Appleton-Century-Crofts, 1970.

Fisher, S., and Cleveland, S. E. *Body Image and Personality.* New York: Dover Publications, 1968.

Fontana, A. F. "The Effects of Acceptance and Rejection by Desired Membership Groups on Self-evaluation." University of Michigan, 1964. *Dissertation Abstracts* 25 (1964): 3675.

Galloway, C. G. "An Experimental Study of the Relation between Perceived Evaluation of Self by Others, Evaluation of Self, and of Others." University of California, Berkeley, 1966. *Dissertation Abstracts* 28 (1967): 122.

Gobel, A. S. "Self-perception and Leaderless Group Discussion." *Journal of Social Psychology* 40 (1954): 309-18.

Griffit, W. B. "Interpersonal Attraction as a Function of Self-concept and Personality Similarity-Dissimilarity." *Journal of Personality and Social Psychology* 5 (1966): 581-84.

————. "Personality Similarity Self-concept, and Positiveness of Personality Description, as Determinants of Interpersonal Attraction." University of Texas, 1967. *Dissertation Abstracts* 5 (1967): 1900-1901.

Harold, G. B. "Self-evaluation and the Evaluation of Choice Alternatives." *Journal of Personality* 32 (1964): 395-410.

Hass, H., and Maehr, M. "Two Experiments on the Concept of Self and the Reaction of Others." *Journal of Personality and Social Psychology* 1 (1965): 100-105.

Hechbaum, G. M. "The Relation between Group Members' Self-confidence and Their Reaction to Group Pressure to Uniformity." *American Sociological Review* 19 (1954): 678-87.

Hope, L. H., and Kerly, S. A. "The Relationship between Self-concept and Academic Aptitude of Entering Male Freshmen." *Psychology, a Journal of Human Behavior* 8 (1971): 43-47.

Jersild, A. T. *In Search of Self.* New York: Columbia University, Teachers College, 1969.

Jones, S. C. "Some Determinants of Interpersonal Evaluating Behavior." *Journal of Personality and Social Psychology* 3 (1966): 397-403.

Jones, S. C., and Ratner, C. "Commitment to Self-appraisal and Interpersonal Evaluations." *Journal of Personality and Social Psychology* 6 (1967): 442-47.

Jourard, S. M. *The Transparent Self.* New York: D. Van Nostrand, 1964.

Jourard, S. M., and Remy, R. "Perceived Parental Attitudes, the Self, and Security." *Journal of Consulting Psychology* 19 (1955): 364-66.

Kinslinger, H. J. "The Interest, Self-perception, and Life-History Correlates of Leadership." Purdue University, 1966. *Dissertation Abstracts* 27 (1967): 4155-56.

Krieger, L. H. "Individual or Group Success or Failure and Its Influence on the Evaluation of Self and Group." Rutgers University, 1966. *Dissertation Abstracts* 27 (1966): 1928.

Kwal, T., and Fleshler, H. "Self Concept and Leadership Behavior." Paper presented at the Speech Communication Association annual convention, San Francisco, December 1971.

Mabel, S., and Rosenfeld, H. M. "Relationship of Self-concept to the Experience of Imbalance in P-O-X Situations." *Human Relations* 19 (1966): 381-89.

Macbride, P. D., and Tuddenham, R. D. "The Influence of Self-confidence upon Resistance of Perceptual Judgments to Group Pressures." *Journal of Psychology* 60 (1965): 9-23.

Malamud, D. I., and Machover, S. "The Workshop in Self Understanding: Group Techniques in Self-confrontation." In *Group Therapy Today,* edited by H. M. Ruitenbeek, pp. 245-55. New York: Atherton Press, 1969.

Manneheim, B. F. "Reference Groups, Membership Groups, and the Self-image." *Sociometry* 29 (1966): 265-79.

Mead, G. H. *Mind, Self and Society.* Chicago: University of Chicago, 1934.

Olivarri, M. C. "Some Relations of Ability Grouping to Student Self-concept." University of California, Berkeley, 1967. *Dissertation Abstracts* 28 (1968): 2518-19.

Pfuetze, P. E. *The Social Self.* New York: Bookman Associates, 1954.

Powers, W. B., and Wright, D. W. "Individual Confidence Levels as a Function of Group Size, Task Complexity, and Correctness of Decision." Paper presented at the Internation Communication Association, Phoenix, April 1971.

Quen, J. F. "The Effect of Dissonance in Self-esteem on Susceptibility to Social Influence." University of Southern California, 1966. *Dissertation Abstracts* 27 (1967): 2618.

Reusch, J. "The Role of Communication in Therapeutic Transactions." *Journal of Communication* 13 (1963): 131-39.

Rogers, C. R. *On Becoming a Person.* Boston: Houghton Mifflin, 1961.

Sherwood, J. J. "Self-identity and Referent Others." *Sociometry* 28 (1965): 66-81.

Shontz, F. C. *Perceptual and Cognitive Aspects of Body Experience.* New York: Academic Press, 1969.

Stagner, R. *Psychology of Personality.* New York: McGraw-Hill, 1961.

Sullivan, H. S. *The Interpersonal Theory of Psychiatry.* New York: W. W. Norton, 1953.

Super, J. "Self and Other Semantic Concepts in Relation to Choice of a Vocation." *Journal of Applied Psychology* 51 (1967): 242-46.

Wapner, S., and Werner, H. eds. *The Body Percept.* New York: Random House, 1965.

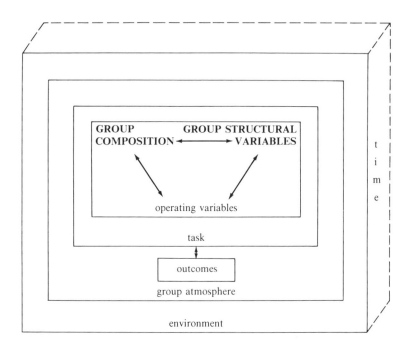

CHAPTER 8

PATTERNS:
COMMUNICATION AND ATTRACTION
NETWORKS

The patterns of interpersonal relations that exist in a given group constitute its structure. Role behavior and conformity behavior are two patterns which already have been discussed. This chapter will focus on two more patterns, those which result from the particular communication network a group uses and those patterns of preference which form among group members. The two are not independent; the communication network may result from the interpersonal relationships or vice versa. Regardless, group structure is one of the important variables affecting group performance.

Communication Networks

Experience 8-1. Form groups according to the diagrams on the following pages. Each group should solve the problem at the end of the diagrams.

Group 1: Group members 1, 2, 4, and 5 cannot speak to each other; they may only speak to member 3. Member 3 can speak to each of the other members, but only one at a time. Arrange yourselves so that while member 3 is speaking with one of the group members, the other members cannot hear the conversation.

Group 2: Group member 1 may speak to 3; 3 may speak to 1 and 5; 2 may speak to 4; 4 may speak to 2 and

5; 5 may speak to 3, 4, and 6; 6 may speak to 5 and 7; and 7 may speak only to 6.

Group 3: Group member 1 may speak to 2; 2 may speak to 1 and 3; 3 may speak to 2 and 4; 4 may speak to 3 and 5; and 5 may speak only to 4.

Group 4: Group members 1, 2, and 3 may speak to each other; 3 may speak to 4, and 4 may speak to 3; 5, 6, and 7 may speak to each other; 7 may speak to 4, and 4 may speak to 7.

Group 5: Group members 1, 2, 3, and 4 may speak to each other; 4 may speak to 5; 5 may speak to 4 and 6; and 6 may speak only to 5.

Group 6: Group members 1, 2, 3, 4, and 5 may speak to each other.

Group 1

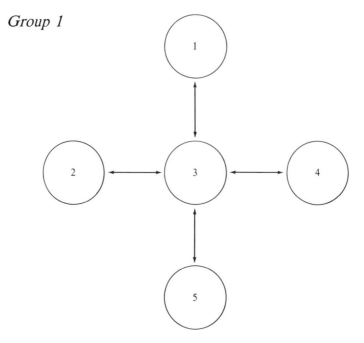

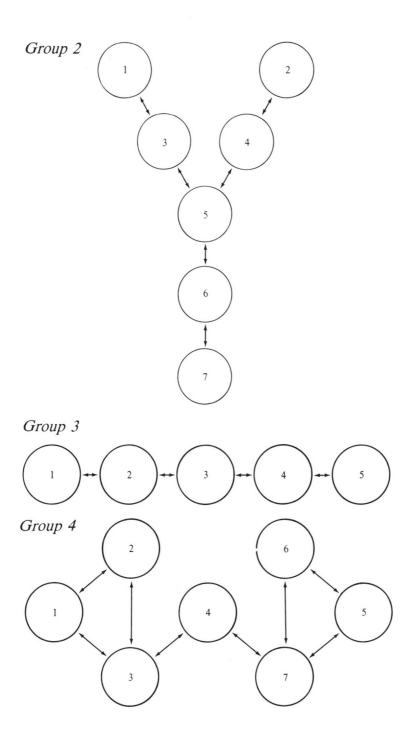

Group 2

Group 3

Group 4

Group 5

Group 6

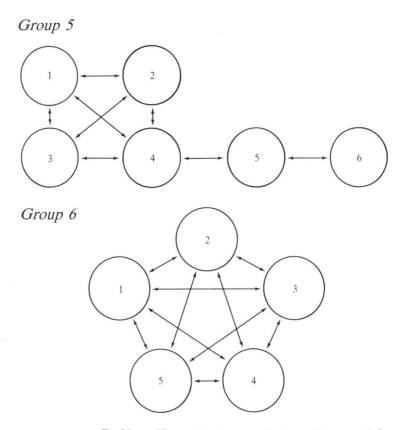

Problem: Have one person, who is not in any of the groups, read the problem aloud twice. Group members may not read the problem.

Freddie Fastbuck bought a horse, sold it for twice what he paid, then bought it back for two times what he sold it for, only to sell it again for one and a half times the original price. Did Freddie win or lose? Express the answer as a percentage of the original price of the horse.

The answer must be arrived at by consensus. Do not use voting or averaging to reach your answer.

If your group was not large enough to form each of the six structures, another problem is offered here so the task may be run again. Be sure everyone is in a different group from what he was for the first problem.

Problem: As before, have one person read the problem aloud twice; group members may not read the problem. Again, the answer must be reached by arriving at consensus within the group. Voting or averaging may not be used.

Freddie Fastbuck wanted to place a bet on a horse, but he fell short of the funds necessary to do so: he had one dollar, and he needed one dollar and twenty-five cents. So, Freddie took his dollar to a pawn shop and pawned it for seventy-five cents, then met a friend to whom he sold the ticket for fifty-cents. He took his one dollar and twenty-five cents and placed his bet. Who lost (disregarding whether the horse came in or not)?

Analysis: What happened in each of the different groups? Did the imposed communication network have any effect on the group? How did the communication patterns affect group performance and personal relationships?

Communication networks determine which communication channels are open or closed; therefore, networks affect the patterns of communication within a group. The effect of different communication networks on leadership was investigated by Leavitt (1951). He formed groups according to four different networks: the circle, wheel, chain, and *Y.*

Each group had to discover a common symbol shared by group members on cards provided them. When the task was completed, group members were asked who the leader was. In the majority of cases, the group member with the most central position was declared the leader. In the circle network, where there was no central position, no position was singled out more times than the others as the leadership position. Since Leavitt's study, other investigations have confirmed these results (Shaw 1954; Shaw and Rothchild 1956).

A member's position in the communication network has another important consequence. Leavitt found that central positions contribute more to member satisfaction than peripheral positions; the more central the position, the more satisfied the group member. In networks with no central positions, such as the circle, satisfaction was more evenly distributed among group members. How satisfied were you in terms of your position in the groups for the Freddie Fastbuck problems? The individual occupying position 6 in Group 5 should have felt highly frustrated. Once, while doing the Fastbuck problem, an indi-

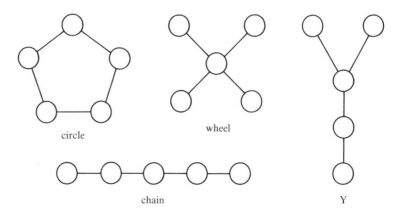

circle

wheel

chain

Y

vidual who occupied position 6 of Group 5 went so far as to throw over his chair, scream obscene insults at his group, and leave the class. He came back a week later but avoided the other five members of his group for another two weeks! He explained to the class that he knew that Freddie lost 150 percent on the original price, but given his position he could not find the means to convince the others. This outburst did much to confirm Leavitt's findings.

In order to assess the efficiency of different communication networks, Leavitt took several measures of performance for each network. Among these were the time it took to complete the task, the number of errors a group made, and the number of messages sent in solving the problem. His results indicated that the wheel pattern was more efficient than the Y and the Y was more efficient than the chain. The circle was the least efficient network. The type of message sent in the circle pattern may explain its inefficiency. The circle network sent more messages than any other network. Many of the messages were suggestions for how to organize. Members in other networks seemed able to adapt to their situation more easily and quickly.

Leavitt's conclusions concerning efficiency must be viewed in terms of the relatively easy symbol-identifying problem. This problem does not require more than one member to have all the necessary information or any real problem-solving ability. Investigations involving more complex problems than Leavitt's confirm the notion that problem complexity is an important variable which affects the efficiency of various communication networks.

In a survey of eighteen studies, Shaw (1964) summarized the relationship between problem complexity, efficiency, and centrality or decentrality of the network. A centralized network is one in which positions differ in the number of communication lines available to them. The wheel and chain networks are examples of centralized networks. In decentralized networks, positions do not vary according to available communication lines. The circle and comcon networks, the latter being a network in which every group member has equal access to all other members, are examples of decentralized networks. When the problem is a simple one, such as color identification, centralized networks send fewer messages, make fewer errors, and are faster than decentralized networks. When the problem is complex, decentralized networks are faster and make fewer errors, although centralized networks still send fewer messages. Regardless of the complexity of the problem, decentralized networks have higher member satisfaction.

Two concepts help to explain the different effects of various networks on group behavior. The concepts are *independence,* introduced by Leavitt (1951), and *saturation,* introduced by Gilchrist, Shaw, and Walker (1954). According to Leavitt, different networks affect the degree to which a given position is independent of the others. For example, in the wheel network, all the other positions are dependent on the central position. In the circle network, all the positions are equally independent. Thus, a decentralized network allows for greater independence of positions and higher member morale. In a centralized network, however, some positions are dependent on others. As a consequence, the degree of morale in the group differs from position to position. The degree to which a position in a given network is independent of the other positions determines the satisfaction of the member.

The concept of saturation refers to the number of requirements a position can handle before it is overloaded. A position has communication requirements, decision requirements, and information requirements. In the wheel network the occupant of the central position must communicate with all the other members as the line among them, and so the communication requirement is high. At the same time, this member must make most of the important decisions for the group, since he is in possession of the greatest amount of information; therefore, the decision requirement is also high. Finally, this member possesses the greatest amount of information, so the information requirement is high. The position becomes untenable at that point when it is said to be saturated or overloaded with requirements. When this happens, the position is rendered ineffective and the group's efficiency decreases. Because centralized networks are more prone to saturation than decentralized ones, especially if the task is complex, centralized networks are more effective than decentralized ones for simple problems: no saturation takes place, fewer messages are sent, and less time is required to solve the problem. For complex problems decentralized networks are more efficient, since there is no central position which can become saturated.

These results concerning the effects of communication networks are relevant only to short-lived groups. Guetzkow and Simon (1955) point out that a network's *operating structure,* the structure developed within a given network to meet the demands placed on it, allows for efficient operation regardless of the type of communication network in which the group is placed. Given enough time and opportunity to develop efficient operating structures, centralized and decentralized networks are equally efficient. Burgess (1968b) confirmed this conclusion. He found that the wheel and circle networks ultimately develop operating structures that make the two networks equally as efficient. The first 50 problems the groups had to perform revealed differences in efficiency, but after 900 problems, they performed similarly.

However, most of the groups in which we are members are short-lived. Classroom groups can be as short as ten minutes or as long as ten or fifteen weeks. But even fifteen weeks is a comparatively short time. The important point is that we usually do not find ourselves in groups having an imposed communication network. Without an imposed network a group will more than likely develop a network which is the most efficient for its problem and composition.

The number of people involved in a discussion is one of the variables which helps determine the kind of communication network formed or the relative efficiency of one imposed. As the number of members increases arithmetically, the number of possible lines of communication increases geometrically. For example, in the three-person group there are three possible interpersonal relationships; in the five-person group there are ten; and, in the six-person group there are fifteen. When the number of possible interpersonal relations increases, the opportunity for each individual to communicate with the others decreases. This may result in decreased effectiveness and, finally, lower morale (Schellenberg 1959).

If a group is so large that members feel frustrated in their attempts to influence other members, two types of operating structures are likely to form, *clique-groups* and/or a new *hierarchical network.* Clique-groups are subgroups of individuals within a larger group who communicate almost exclusively with each other and satisfy the need for effective interaction. Because members of clique-groups can influence each other, they often ignore influencing the larger group. When this happens, they may be engaging in what are sometimes called side conversations. Since side conversations impede the group's ability to achieve consensus, clique-groups, in the long run, may be detrimental to group functions. Occasionally, isolated clique-groups will split away from the larger group and establish independent groups. These new groups are usually hostile to the original group, and this hostility sets the stage for intergroup conflict.

A hierarchical network results when subgroups form which interact with each other on a limited basis. For example, a group might consist of two viable subgroups, each containing several members of different statuses. A communication link between these subgroups is formed by the two members with the highest status. The overall effect is something like a pyramid. As the size of each sub-group increases, there is an increased probability for the communication link to be formed by men near but not at the top of the hierarchy in each subgroup.

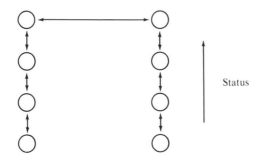

Status

A hierarchical network may also be detrimental to proper group functioning for it is an indication of a serious split in the group—a split with limited chance for reconciliation because of the decrease in contact among members. As the goals of the two subgroups move farther apart, the chance for group cooperation decreases. As with clique-groups, hierarchical networks may result in the formation of two distinct groups. A hierarchical network may involve several viable subgroups, with the potential for a variety of splits.

When considering the effects of different communication settings, differences in the number of interactants and the types of communication network employed, the following variables may provide a basis for analyzing potential group efficiency. What opportunity does a member have to (1) interact, (2) gain information about the others, (3) allow others to gain information about himself, (4) control the importance of group membership, (5) control the amount of communication, and (6) manipulate the environment? As the opportunities for each of these increase, the relative efficiency of the group increases.

Sociometry

Experience 8-2. If you had to choose, whom would you choose for each of the following? (Consider the entire class excluding yourself as the population from which to choose.)

1. For a boss: _____
2. To work with in solving a problem (rank order):

   _____

   _____

   _____

3. To be marooned with on a small, tropical island:

   _____

4. To escort your boyfriend/girlfriend across Europe for a summer: _____
5. To ask for help if you were having some personal problem: _____
6. *Not* to work with in solving a problem (rank order):

   _____

   _____

   _____

7. Most intelligent: _____
8. As a date: _____
9. To kick out of the life-raft for safety reasons:

   _____

10. To discuss a new idea with: _____
11. To invite to a party: _____

    _____

    _____

12. *Not* to invite to a party: _____

    _____

    _____

Sociometry, "the study of the patterns of interrelations between people, and the process of their measurement in respect to membership in the group" (Jennings 1959, p. 11), has a history dating back to 1934 when Moreno and Jenning's book, *Who Shall Survive?*, was published.

According to Moreno, human preferential systems cannot be explained or examined by direct observational techniques. It is, nevertheless, important to know and understand preferences, because they direct interpersonal behavior. The sociometric questionnaire, such as the one at the beginning of this section, is designed to find out the actual choices individuals make regarding the people with whom they come into contact.

Information Provided by Sociometric Analysis

The sociometric questionnaire determines the degree to which individuals in the group are accepted or rejected, and the basis for that acceptance or rejection. For example, questions 11 and 12 on the questionnaire are designed to elicit information concerning which individuals are socially accepted or rejected. Question 8 is also related to social acceptance, but is of a more personal nature, since the number of people involved is smaller (two) than that found at a party. Questions 2 and 6 are designed to elicit information concerning which individuals are accepted or rejected on a work or problem-solving basis. Question 1 is also related to work acceptance, but in connection with the super-subordinate relationship. Questions 3 and 9 seek information about general acceptance and rejection. The person with whom we might want to be marooned would have to be accepted both socially and as a worker, but depending on our own preferences, one or the other attribute might be more important. Questions 4 and 5 may be related to different kinds of trust. The person with whom I would trust my girlfriend is not necessarily the same person with whom I would trust personal confidences. Question 7 is only one of many that could be asked relating to different status hierarchies which might exist in a group. Question 10 may or may not be specifically work related. An individual could be picked for social reasons, i.e., because he is open and uncritical, or for work reasons, i.e., because he is the most capable to offer advice.

To make full use of the questionnaire, questions such as number 10 must be examined in connection with others. If the person with whom you would like to discuss a new idea is the same as the person with whom you would like to work solving a problem, this indicates something about your own orientation to the group. If the person you choose to discuss a new idea with is the same as the person you would like to invite to a party, we have a different piece of information about you.

The sociometric questionnaire also helps determine the relationships among individuals in the group. Individuals may be accepted or rejected on several dimensions, including the acceptance-rejection dimension. Individuals who are both highly accepted and highly rejected by other members of the group are usually dynamic and controversial, often task leaders. If a member is highly accepted and unrejected by other members of the group, he is a well-liked person with a great deal of appeal, usually a socio-emotional leader. Members who are unaccepted and highly rejected are antagonistic to the group and usually unsupportive of group activities. The unaccepted and unrejected member is usually a nondescript, inconspicuous, and often withdrawn group member.

Besides revealing the general relationship of a group member to the entire group, the sociometric questionnaire also provides more specific information dealing with relationships among group members, and these relationships to the group in general. For example, two members who accept each other on both a work and social basis have a different relationship in the group than members who reject each other on both dimensions. These relationships are reciprocal, that is, whatever one member prefers, the other member prefers, e.g., I accept you on a social basis, and you accept me on a social basis. Relationships which are not reciprocal may have considerable impact on socio-emotional and task development. The sociometric questionnaire provides the investigator with such detailed information on the nature of the relationships: the basis of relationships, as well as whether or not they are reciprocal.

Third, the sociometric questionnaire helps determine the structure of the group. The degree to which individuals are accepted and rejected, as well as the relationships that exist among individuals, determines to a great extent what the structure of the group will be. If a subgroup of three individuals accepts each other but rejects the others, and if the others also reject the subgroup, we have evidence to suggest that the structure for this group might be different from one in which all members are accepted. Furthermore, we can predict with some certainty the nature of the communication network that will operate within this structure.

Sociometric questionnaires also provide us with information concerning other aspects of group structure, namely, other roles and the amount and direction of interaction. As already discussed, individuals who are both highly accepted and highly rejected are most likely to be task leaders, whereas those who are highly accepted and unrejected are most likely to be socio-emotional leaders. When the task leader rejects the socio-emotional leader on both a work and social basis, the group is in trouble. Without the support of the socio-emotional leader, the task leader will be less effective and more highly rejected.

Other roles that can be diagnosed are those of the isolate and self-centered members. The isolate is neither accepted nor rejected by the other members of a group. The number of isolates in a group affects the amount of interaction, and the group's concentration on the task. The self-centered member usually is highly rejected. He may generate a great deal more antagonism and many more negative acts than other members, thus his effect on group interaction is primarily detrimental.

Sociometric analysis also provides us with information to make predictions concerning the amount and direction of the interaction. Isolates rarely speak; consequently, the more isolates in a group, the lower the rate of interaction. On the other hand, dynamic, controversial members speak a great deal; therefore, we would expect a greater rate of interaction when these members are present. The direction of interaction, or who speaks to whom, may be predicted by an analysis of the patterns of acceptances and rejections. Mutual acceptance, mutual rejection, and lack of a reciprocal relationship will each differentially affect interaction. With nonreciprocal relationships, interaction is likely to be one-way. Again, these patterns help define group structure.

Developing a Sociometric Test

A number of formats may be used to develop a sociometric questionnaire. The one at the beginning of this section is only an example. Regardless of the format selected, application of the following five general rules will help insure an adequate testing instrument:

1. Select situations which provide a real opportunity for interaction. Information derived from an artificial situation or one which is structured to minimize interaction will be meaningless. Asking an individual to select someone he would prefer to be with in a therapy group, where interaction would necessarily be great, is more meaningful than asking him to select someone to type his term paper, where there may be no interaction at all.

2. Select situations where there are a variety of possible types of interaction. Individual preferences differ according to the circumstances in which individuals are placed. Selecting someone to be part

of a crowd, as many parties turn out to be, is easier and certainly less crucial than selecting someone to form a dyad (pair), as on a date. But information concerning both is necessary to understand the individual's preferences. Along with varieties in *levels* of interaction (certainly the level of individual interaction at a party is different than on a date), variety in the *types* of interaction should be given. Both work and social relationships should be sampled on the questionnaire, as well as levels of interaction for each. Asking someone with whom he prefers to work on a problem may result in a different answer than asking him to select someone with whom he can discuss a new idea; although both situations ostensibly relate, they differ in level and type of interaction. A full analysis of the interrelationships in a group requires responses to different types of situations.

3. Require a limited number of responses to questions. Most of the questions on the sociometric questionnaire at the beginning of this section require only one response, a few call for three. It is often difficult for individuals to provide more than three responses to any given question. As the number of responses required increases, the quality of the distinctions made decreases proportionately.

4. State questions in the conditional ("should," "would") tense. It is difficult for individuals to accept and reject others. Accepting one individual implies the rejection of others. To help ease the tension that this might create, questions should be stated in the conditional tense. Under this condition, individuals are more likely to be honest, and honesty is crucial if the analysis is to be meaningful and accurate.

5. Avoid negative questions. As already mentioned, people do not like to make negative judgments of others. Negative questions are likely to make respondents uneasy, which in turn might make them respond less than honestly. Negative questions may also cause some resentment; often they are not even responded to. How many people in your group left out answers to questions 6 and 12 on the sociometric questionnaire?

When administering the questionnaire, instruct subjects to answer as if the answers will be used for re-organization of the group. Honesty must be stressed, since less than honest answers decrease the utility of the results. Finally, in doing an analysis, it is important to remember that the responses are applicable to the group at the testing time, and at that time only.

Tabulating and Presenting the Information

Borgotta (1951) recommends a two-fold table on which the names of persons are listed both horizontally and vertically. Individual choices are placed in the resulting boxes, e.g., a "1" in a box might indicate that individual A chose individual B as "a boss." Such a table reveals mutual choices and allows for the summation of the number of choices made and received by each person. One drawback to the use of this table, though, is that it fails to point out clusters of relationships, which leads to another technique for tabulating the information, the sociogram. See figure 8-1 for an example of a two-fold table. In the example, the numbers refer to the questions on the sociometric questionnaire in this chapter. The entries in the Mary-John boxes indicate that Mary chose John for a boss (question 1), and John chose Mary as someone with whom to be marooned (question 3). Bob chose Sue as most intelligent (question 7), and Sue chose John as most intelligent (question 7).

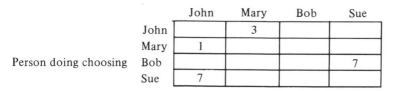

Person selected

	John	Mary	Bob	Sue
John		3		
Mary	1			
Bob				7
Sue	7			

Person doing choosing

Figure 8-1:   *An example of a two-fold table*

A sociogram is a diagrammatic representation of the interrelationships in a group. There are a number of types of sociograms: the one chosen depends upon the number of individuals involved and the information to be displayed. Generally, each person is represented by a circle, unless a differentiation is to be made on the basis of sex (males may be represented by triangles, and females by circles). As a general rule, isolates are placed at the outside of the immediate diagram. Relationships are represented with lines: double lines can indicate mutual choices, or single or double arrows can be used to represent one- or two-way choices.

Two of the more usual diagram techniques are given below:

1. *Star Sociogram:* In this sociogram the most chosen person is placed in the center of the diagram with the others around him. Lines and arrows are used to represent choices. From the diagram it is evident that only two reciprocal relationships exist in this group (a-g, g-d), and that only two members of the group chose two members (*a* chose *b* and *g,* and *g* chose *a* and *d*).

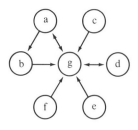

2. *Target Sociogram:* In this sociogram individuals are classified according to a number of variables and then are placed within the
diagram to depict these variables. The target refers to the number of
choices an individual receives; again, the most chosen member is at
the center of the target. This diagram provides more information than
the star sociogram. Whereas on the star diagram we knew only that
a selected *b* and *g,* on this diagram we know that *a* and *b* are both
young females, and that *g* is a young male. Because of their position
in the target, we can tell at a glance that *c,* an older male, *d* and *e,*
younger males, *a,* a younger female, and *f,* an older female, received
no choices. On the other hand, *b,* a younger female, received one
choice. We can tell that *g,* at the center of the target, received six
choices.

A variety of other diagramming techniques are available, but we
will consider only one other and that only in part. In addition to

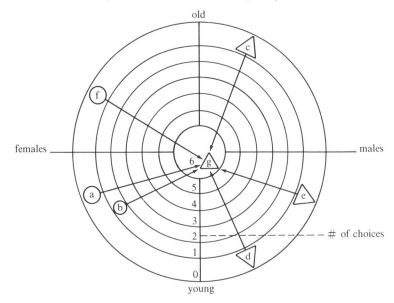

diagramming acceptances, rejections may be graphically portrayed. Jennings (1950, pp. 189-95) developed the following method:

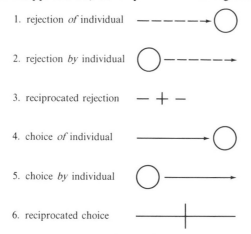

1. rejection *of* individual
2. rejection *by* individual
3. reciprocated rejection
4. choice *of* individual
5. choice *by* individual
6. reciprocated choice

The best method for learning sociometric analysis is to use it. Analyze the information gathered by the sociometric questionnaire at the beginning of this chapter. Start with the two-fold table technique and progress to the others. The type of sociogram you decide to use in the future will probably reflect your interests, as well as the size of the group.

In what ways can the results of your analysis be used to make your group more efficient? Given your analysis of the larger group, do you think you can form smaller groups which will vary in productivity? What is the basis for your predictions? Does the sociometric questionnaire tell you anything about your relationships in and to the group? How stable are the judgments individuals make on sociometric questionnaires? How quickly do groups change, and can that change be measured on sociometric questionnaires?

Generate some specific use to which you can apply sociometric technique, then develop and use a sociometric instrument. What does your data tell you? How useful, in practice, is sociometry?

Bibliography

Bavelas, A. "A Mathematical Model for Group Structure." *Applied Anthropology* 7 (1948): 16-30.

———. "Communication Patterns in Task-oriented Groups." *Journal of the Acoustical Society of America* 22 (1950): 725-30.

Borgotta, E. F. "A Diagnostic Note on the Construction of Sociograms and Action Diagrams." *Group Psychotherapy* 3 (1951): 300-308.

Burgess, R. L. "Communication Networks: An Experimental Re-evaluation." *Journal of Experimental Social Psychology* 4 (1968a): 324-37.

————. "An Experimental and Mathematical Analysis of Group Behavior within Restricted Networks." *Journal of Experimental Social Psychology* 4 (1968b): 338-49.

Cohen, A. M. "Changing Small Group Communication Networks." *Journal of Communication* 11 (1961): 116-24, 128.

Davis, J. H., and Hornseth, J. "Discussion Patterns and Word Problems." *Sociometry* 30 (1967): 91-103.

Gilchrist, J. C., Shaw, M. E., and Walker, L. C. "Some Effects of Unequal Distribution of Information in a Wheel Group Structure." *Journal of Abnormal and Social Psychology* 49 (1954): 554-56.

Glanzer, M., and Glaser, R. "Techniques for the Study of Group Structure and Behavior: II. Empirical Studies of the Effects of Structure in Small Groups." *Psychological Bulletin* 58 (1961): 1-27.

Guetzkow, H., and Dill, W. R. "Factors in the Organizational Development of Task-oriented Groups." *Sociometry* 20 (1957): 175-204.

Guetzkow, H., and Simon, H. A. "The Impact of Certain Communication Nets upon Organization and Performance in Task-oriented Groups." *Management Science* 1 (1955): 233-50.

Heise, G. A., and Miller, G. A. "Problem Solving by Small Groups Using Various Communication Nets." *Journal of Abnormal and Social Psychology* 46 (1951): 327-35.

Hirota, K. "Group Problem Solving and Communication." *Japanese Journal of Psychology* 24 (1953): 176-77.

Hollander, E. P., and Webb, W. B. "Leadership, Followership, and Friendship: An Analysis of Peer Nominations." *Journal of Abnormal and Social Psychology* 50 (1955): 163-67.

Jennings, H. H. "Individual Differences in the Social Atom." *Sociometry* 4 (1941): 269-70.

————. "Leadership and Sociometric Choice." *Sociometry* 10 (1947): 32-49.

————. *Leadership and Isolation.* New York: Longmans, Green, 1950.

————. "Sociometric Structure in Personality and Group Formation." In *Group Relations at the Crossroads,* edited by M. Sherif and M. O. Wilson, pp. 332-65. New York: Harper, 1953.

————. *Sociometry in Group Relations: A Guide Work for Teachers.* 2d ed. Washington, D.C.: American Council on Education, 1959.

Lawson, E. D. "Change in Communication Nets, Performance, and Morale." *Human Relations* 18 (1965): 139-47.

Leavitt, H. J. "Some Effects of Certain Communication Patterns on Group Performance." *Journal of Abnormal and Social Psychology* 46 (1951): 38-50.

Lundberg, G. A., and Style, M. "Social Attraction Patterns in a Village." *Sociometry* 1 (1938): 375-419.

Moreno, J. L. "Foundations of Sociometry, an Introduction." *Sociometry* 4 (1941): 15-35.

———. "Sociometry and Cultural Order." *Sociometry* 6 (1943): 299-344.

———. *Who Shall Survive?* New York: Beacon House, 1953.

Mulder, M. "Communication Structure, Decision Structure and Group Performance." *Sociometry* 23 (1960): 1-14.

Schein, E. H. "The Development of Organization in Small Problem-solving Groups." Final Report, Sloan Project No. 134, Massachusetts Institute of Technology, 1958.

Schellenberg, J. A. "Group Size as a Factor in Success of Academic Discussion Groups." *Journal of Educational Psychology* 33 (1959): 73-79.

Shaw, M. E. "Some Effects of Unequal Distribution of Information upon Group Performance in Various Communication Nets." *Journal of Abnormal and Social Psychology* 49 (1954): 547-53.

———. "Communication Networks." In *Advances in Experimental Social Psychology,* edited by L. Berkowitz, 1: 111-47. New York: Academic Press, 1964.

Shaw, M. E., and Rothchild, G. H. "Some Effects of Prolonged Experience in Communication Nets." *Journal of Applied Psychology* 40 (1956): 281-86.

Tagiuri, R. "Relational Analysis: An Extension of Sociometric Method with Emphasis upon Social Perception." *Sociometry* 15 (1952): 91-104.

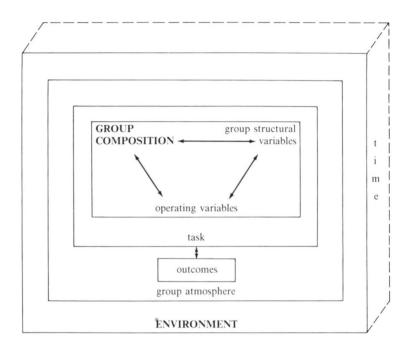

CHAPTER 9

NONVERBAL COMMUNICATION
IN THE SMALL GROUP

You cannot *not* communicate. You are always communicating something to other people, even when you are not speaking. The way you
place your hands, the position of your body, your facial expression,
your tone of voice, the way you touch, the clothes you wear, and
where you position yourself communicate something to others. The
shape of the room, the color of the walls, the type and size of the
chairs, the temperature, time, and day communicate something to you
and thereby affect your behavior in the small group.

Research in the area of nonverbal communication rarely focuses
on the impact of nonverbal communication on small group interaction. Yet, the implications of research findings are relevant to the
small group setting for several reasons. First, individuals working in
groups have a great deal at stake: they value group membership, good
interpersonal relationships, and effective task completion. Because of
the value of successful interaction, group members seek cues to increase the probability of their effectiveness. Nonverbal cues, if interpreted correctly, provide one means.

Second, nonverbal communication is the means whereby group
members project their feelings and attitudes. Therefore, nonverbal
communication is closely related to a group's socio-emotional development. The greater a group's awareness to nonverbal cues, the greater
the sensitivity to implicit meanings in gestures, vocal intonations, and
various postures, the greater the probability of smooth and effective
socio-emotional development. The effect is cumulative: effective socio-
emotional development helps task development.

Finally, the small group, functioning as a microcosm for the
larger society, makes it easier to focus upon the effects of verbal and

183

nonverbal communication. Interaction in a small group appears concentrated, so the causes and effects may be more apparent than on the societal level.

How all the various nonverbal cues relate to one another is difficult to determine. Which cues are attended to and which provide the most meaningful information depends upon a number of variables. For example, if the group task is highly cognitive in nature, vocal cues become of prime importance since group members are focusing their attention on the ideas expressed. If the task is a more affective one, cues other than vocal ones gain in importance.

Let's collect some data.

Experience 9-1. Several members of the class must volunteer to become *interlopers*. They will be required to join a group of three or more strangers and to change the topic of conversation to one predetermined by the class. First, the class should decide on a topic(s) (it does not have to be the same for each interloper). Then, class members should split up and go to an area where a number of people are engaged in conversation, not simply sharing some space. The student union building on most college campuses usually is a good place. *Do not* enter the building in such a way that it is obvious you are a group and that you are going to perpetrate some madness on unsuspecting individuals. Note: the interloper *cannot* tell the group why he has "joined" them.

After the interlopers have completed their task with at least one and, hopefully, several groups, return to the classroom and analyze the interaction. This exercise should provide an opportunity to compare verbal (for those who were close enough and could hear what went on) and nonverbal behavior. Be sure to discuss how the interloper became part of the group; what effect he had on the group; what the interaction was like; who the leader was, and why; what roles were played; what the topic of conversation was when the interloper sat down, and how it was changed; what nonverbal communication was important, and why; what the relationship was between the verbal and nonverbal behavior; and what the immediate reaction was in the group *after* the interloper left.

A last note is necessary. Although nothing violent has yet occurred during this exercise, I always offer the follow-

ing: *If you do not wish to be beaten to death by a small, angry group of students, know when to cut out. The teacher will probably avoid coming to your aid. Good luck.*

Experience 9-2. Place a broomstick on the floor. Ask six volunteers to come to the front of the room and position themselves around the broomstick. *The six volunteers may not talk with each other at any time.* Each volunteer must keep both his hands on the broomstick at all times and may do whatever he wishes. Without talking, the task is to decide when the exercise is completed.

Experience 9-3. Form pairs. It is imperative that you choose someone whom you do not know *at all.* It may be necessary to get members from other classes or to combine two classes. Do not speak to the other person—simply sit opposite him/her and observe. After a few minutes, write your answers to the following questions:

  1. What is his/her age?
  2. What is his/her religion?
  3. On a continuum from *extreme left-wing* to *extreme right-wing,* where does this person fall politically?
  4. *Do not speak yet!*
  5. In a phrase, how does this person deal with other people? (For example, shy? extroverted?)
  6. What did he/she put as an answer for #5 for you?
  7. Where does he/she come from?
  8. What did he/she put as an answer for #7 for you?
  9. What is his/her grade point average?
  10. What is his/her I.Q.?
  11. What is his/her socio-economic level?
  12. How many brothers and sisters does he/she have?

Now, talk to each other about something, but avoid talking about the answers to these questions. After a few minutes look over your answers. Change any you think are incorrect. Then, exchange papers and discuss your answers. Which ones did you change, and why? On what basis did you answer each of the questions? What cues did you receive from the environment? For example, how might your being enrolled at Harvard affect your answers to questions 10 and 11? What effect did your original perceptions have on your reactions to your partner? For example, if you perceived that his/her I.Q. was 150, did this affect your later perceptions and evaluations of him? What role do first impressions play in directing our interpersonal behavior?

These three exercises should have indicated that there are differences between verbal and nonverbal communication. They neither provide the same kinds of information, nor do they seem to operate in a similar fashion, e.g., verbal communication has a discrete beginning and end, whereas nonverbal communication seems to flow continuously. What kind of information is best suited to nonverbal communication? Is the information consistent across different contexts, or would a new context change the meaning implicit in the nonverbal communication?

The basic element of the verbal code is the word. Sounds and letters have discrete beginnings and ends; analysis is often easy. With nonverbal communication, there is no discrete beginning or end to a message; rather, messages seem to come from the context in pulses instead of beginnings and endings. Consider the facial gestures that take place in the small group setting: these gestures provide continuous feedback for group members.

Because of the nature of the nonverbal stimuli, attempts to systematically describe the area have yielded ambiguous results. Three approaches to the study of nonverbal communication have helped to define the object of study. The *transcription* approach, developed by Birdwhistell (1970) and Hall (1963), attempts to identify individual units of behavior and codify them. The complexity of the Birdwhistell system is testimony to the difficulty of this approach which, from the outset, seems contrary to one basic feature of the nonverbal code, that is, it is made up of continuous, not discrete, parts.

The *external variable* approach devised by Ekman and Friesen (1968) appears to be more reasonable. The meaning of nonverbal behavior is a complex function of (a) the behavior exhibited and (b) a given context. A broad classification schema helps pinpoint the object of study, e.g., facial expressions or body movements, and then the behaviors are observed and measured. Meaning is abstracted from the data.

Third, the *contextual* approach designed by Scheflen (1964) attempts to describe the rules and structure of the nonverbal language code. Units of behavior have meaning because they occur in patterns under similar contexts. A behavioral unit contains specific parts, organized in a certain way, and fitted into a larger system of behavior. This approach recognizes the continuous nature of the stimuli under investigation.

Verbal and nonverbal codes differ in how they are learned. Whereas the verbal code is consciously acquired, the nonverbal code usually is learned in a more intuitive fashion. Words and sounds are arbitrary symbols, and each culture has to teach its young exactly what a particular symbol represents. This makes verbal language intellectual and, therefore, suitable for transmitting information in a reasonably sophisticated manner. Nonverbal behavior is less intellectual and more spontaneous than verbal behavior. Because of the basic differences between the two codes, each serves a different purpose. The nonverbal language code is best for expressing emotions and attitudes, noncognitive information. Therefore, nonverbal communication is more suitable than verbal communication for establishing interpersonal rapport.

Although the two language systems have been contrasted for purposes of clarification, it is obvious that they work together. When we express ourselves verbally, we are, simultaneously, expressing ourselves nonverbally. Our tone of voice, our facial gestures, and all the other nonverbal behaviors we perform, compliment, supplement, and provide a context for our verbal behavior. At times the two may be incongruent, we may say one thing with our words and express the opposite with our gestures. For instance, hardly a day goes by that we do not say yes to someone while screwing up our eyebrows. The two languages are incongruent: one says yes, the other says no. This, of course, raises problems. Which code do you read when you receive conflicting information?

For purposes of analysis, nonverbal communication may be broken down into several areas. These areas are interdependent and interactive, that is, they often produce effects that cannot be predicted by examining each area (apparel, facial expression, posture, vocal cues, territoriality, personal space, environment, and body rhythms) separately. When we first join a group, we immediately form impressions of the other members. We most likely base our judgments on physical characteristics and apparel. We are attracted by what we consider well-formed and pretty, and repelled by what we consider malformed and ugly. Beyond this, our first impressions are formed by the clothes and jewelry worn by other members of the group. Then we observe facial gestures and posture, and listen to the other members speak—their vocal nonverbal cues (for example, pitch, variety, and volume) provide us with some of the best data available on which to base our judgments. After a while we notice that each person seats himself a certain way and in a certain place. Finally, we take notice of the environment and how it affects the interaction.

Apparel

Clothes and jewelry often serve as symbols of status in our society. As a consequence, we choose what we wear carefully, since our clothes "tell" something about ourselves.

A number of significant relationships exist between the dress an individual selects and various personality measures. Aiken (1963), studying undergraduate women students, correlated responses to questions concerning dress likes and dislikes to several personality measures. The questions were divided into five topics: decoration in dress, comfort in dress, interest in dress, conformity in dress, and economy in dress. Aiken found that a correlation exists between women who like decoration in dress and such traits as conformity, sociability, and nonintellectualism. Comfort in dress correlated with controlled extroversion. Interest in dress correlated with social conscientiousness, as well as uncomplicatedness. Conformity in dress correlated with conformity (in general) and submissiveness. Lastly, economy in dress correlated with intelligence and efficiency. The Aiken study was conducted in 1963. It may be that the changes in style and attitudes toward clothing would yield different results today. Regardless, clothing is taken as an indication of emotional states, certain personality characteristics, and other personal qualitites. Because clothes are consciously selected, they offer a fairly accurate statement of the individual wearing them.

Apparel not only affects our judgments of others, but often influences our own behavior directly. Lefkowitz, Blake, and Mouton (1955) found that pedestrians were more likely to follow a well-dressed individual (shined shoes, white shirt, tie, and freshly pressed suit) violating a pedestrian "wait" signal than a poorly dressed one (worn shoes, soiled, patched pants, and blue denim shirt).

If you have been keeping a group process diary, look back at your first entries. Can you think back and determine the effect of apparel on your first impressions? Is there a relationship between apparel and the roles adopted by the various members? Do some members consistently dress more formally or casually than others? Do they differ in terms of their roles in the group?

Facial Expression

Experience 9-4. Make three drawings: one of a glum face, one of a smiling face, and one of a frowning face. Have a number of people agree that the drawings do indeed represent the conditions named.

Present the drawings in all possible pairs to individuals who have not seen them. For example, present the smiling face with the glum face to one person, and the smiling face with the frowning face to another. Get as many people to view each combination as possible. While they are viewing, ask them how they would describe the faces. Catalogue the responses under six headings (for each possible pair).

The experiment you just conducted is similar to one conducted by Cline (1956), who tested the hypothesis that "the perception of social interactions corresponds to the pattern of expressive properties between the interactors, and that this pattern is present as an extended stimulus and yields an organized experience of a social event" (p. 157). In other words, what we see is a function of surrounding stimuli, as well as the specific stimuli on which we focus. We see things as patterned. Cline found that a *paired* face was responded to differently than when it was alone. For instance, the *glum* face with the *smiling* face was seen as defeated or embarrassed, angry, jealous, unhappy, or dismayed, while the *glum* face with the *frowning* face was seen as aloof, independent, self-sufficient, or cool. For each pair, observers tended to integrate the properites of the two faces into a social situation with its own properties.

Osgood (1966), Shapiro (1968), and Shapiro, Foster, and Powell (1968) found that observers make relatively accurate judgments of the emotions expressed by various facial expressions. The judgments, though, are subject to stereotyping (Secord 1958). Secord, Bevan, and Katz (1956) found that Caucasian judges rated pictures of Negroes lower on traits such as alertness, honest face, air of responsibility, and intelligent look, and higher for lazy, superstitious, untidy, and immoral. What is interesting about this study is that there was no difference in the degree of personality stereotyping of Negro photographs varying widely in physiognomic "negroidness." Individuals tend to focus on a few unique characteristics, and then assign the whole range of stereotypes.

Secord (1958) found that cultural factors play a role in how an individual learns to respond to facial expressions. The culture dictates which features are to be attended to and which ignored. The general American culture teaches individuals to attend to slight variations in facial cues in order to attribute thoughts or sentiments to a speaker, whereas Navajos seldom make such attributions from facial cues, but instead depend upon explicit statements.

Pupil size has also been investigated as a source of information about the person observed. Hess (1965) found that pupil size related to the interest value of the stimuli, as well as the emotional state of the subject. Pupil dilation accompanied observation of a picture that was deemed interesting or stimulating, such as a pin-up or a picture of a mother and child. Another interesting finding was that men liked women with larger pupils. Consequently, an aspect of facial expression to which we respond, but are often unaware, is pupil size.

Facial expressions, including pupil size, are context bound, and often idosyncratic. Culture and the surrounding stimuli help determine how we interpret these cues. Isolating any one cue from its total context will result in misleading conclusions; on the other hand, an awareness of the specific factors which make up the whole of any situation is likely to facilitate an accurate reading of individuals.

Posture

How we stand and sit, the way we organize our bodies, may reveal something about how we feel. Davis (1958) observed elementary school children and hypothesized psychological divergencies from postural variations. Two basic signs of tension were noted: static and kinetic (moving). Static signs of tension were characterized by sitting in a chair with legs wrapped tightly around the chair, clasping hands tightly, clenching fists, and holding the head rigidly to one side. Kinetic signs of tension were continually moving feet or hands, twisting the head from side to side, and running about the room. Although Davis observed elementary school children, the conclusions are applicable to groups composed of older individuals. Individuals who engage in a great deal of extraneous activity, such as foot movements and constant changing of postural position, *appear* anxious or tense, whether they are or not. The *perception* of their tension may disrupt group activity, deflecting conversation to tangential matters, such as personal problems and their possible resolution.

The presence or absence of chairs can affect interaction significantly. Without chairs, group members sit closer, touch more, and assume relaxed postures. Members who refuse to give up their chairs may be refusing to become intimate with the group.

Mehrabian and Friar (1969) focused on *projected* postural arrangements of individuals. Subjects were asked to assume the posture they would use if addressing a friend, a person of higher status, male or female, and a person they did not like. Researchers noted such things as eye contact, distance between the subject and the imagined person, head orientation, leg orientation, shoulder orientation, arm and leg openness, and the degree of limb relaxation. Results indicate that the most important variables for communicating positive attitude are a small backward lean of the torso, close distance, and great eye contact. Interacting with persons of higher status is accompanied by more eye contact and less sideways lean than interaction with persons of lower status.

Select a group meeting and focus on the postural messages of other members. Make inferences about their psychological states. Can you detect tension in the group? What adjustments do other members make to changes in postural cues?

Vocal Cues

Experience 9-5. The scene: the movie has just ended, and the couple gets into the car. They drive for a while and then pull off the road into a dark, quiet, secluded area. As expected, "the make" is about to be chanced.

Request volunteers to act out this scene, speaking no other words than "onions taste good in the morning." *Only* these words may be used. Anything to be communicated must be transmitted with these words. After the role playing, discuss what happened. Who was passive, and who aggressive? How did they get their meanings across? What vocal changes connoted what meanings? How did the vocal variations and body movements work together to convey meaning?

The paralinguistic dimension of language, the vocal features which accompany our words and sentences, including pitch, clarity, breathiness, articulation, rhythm, resonance, and tempo, are more likely to convey information about the speaker than the literal message.

The paralinguistic dimension offers a variety of interpretable cues to listeners. Studies conducted since the early 1930s have produced fairly consistent results: listeners tend to agree on the characteristics they ascribe to speakers based on the paralinguistic code of their speech (Addington 1968). In a summary article by Ernest Kramer (1963), the following conclusions were posited. (1) *Physical characteristics* that can be judged from the voice include speaker's age, height, overall appearance, Kretschmerian body type, and whether the speaker has a particular form of brain damage. (2) *Aptitudes and interests* that can be judged from the voice include the speaker's intelligence, dominant values, and vocation. (3) *Personality traits* that can be judged from the voice include whether the speaker is a dominant person, whether he is extroverted or introverted, and his degree of sociability. (4) Concerning the *personality as a whole,* listeners are able to match voices with personality sketches of several speakers, and can sort normal speakers from those with hypertension. (5) The final area concerns judgments dealing with an individual's *adjustment and psychopathology.*

More recent studies confirm Kramer's conclusions and expand the realm in which listeners make accurate judgments. Nerbonne (1967) studied the performance of listeners identifying the following characteristics: ethnic group, education, and dialect region, as well as those variables enumerated in Kramer's summary. Nerbonne concluded that listeners correctly differentiate Negro from Caucasian speakers, speakers with less than a high school education, a high school education, and college graduates, and speakers from the Eastern, Southern, and General American dialect regions.

Anisfeld, Bogo, and Lambert (1962) compared the stereotypic personality characteristics attributed to speakers speaking American English with and without a Jewish accent. They conclude, "The accented guises were comparatively devalued on height, good looks, and leadership for both gentile and Jewish subjects and when the accented guise was perceived as being either Jewish or non-Jewish. The gentile subjects did not consider the accented guise as more favorable on any trait while the Jewish subjects [did]" (p. 230).

Ruesh and Preistwood (Starkweather 1961) concluded that anxiety can be transmitted by sound alone and that some vocal aspects of anxiety were common enough to be detected immediately. Davitz and Davitz (1961) identified certain voice qualities with different emotional states. Active feelings were associated with loud voice, high pitch, blaring timbre, and fast rate. Passive feelings were associated with quiet voice, low pitch, resonant timbre, and slow rate.

Variations in the expression of emotion have been linked to force differences, differences in the rate of expiration, speech rates, breathing rates, and differences in the duration of phrases. Listeners recognize the intended emotion of speakers with better than chance accuracy. However, when speakers and listeners were of the same socio-economic background, judgments were more accurate. This infers that the expression of emotion is, in part, a cultural product.

Status

Status is an important mediating variable. Ascriptions of high or low status affect credibility ratings, attitude change, and judgments of speaker background which relate to status, such as the level of education attained. Two studies indicate that accurate judgments of status are possibly based on vocal cues alone.

Harms (1961) presented subjects with a 40 to 60 second sample of speech and asked subjects to judge each speaker's status and credibility. Both speakers and subjects were objectively classified as being of either high, middle, or low status, using the Hollingshead *Two Factor Index of Status Position* (which considers education and occupation). Harms concluded that subjects, regardless of their own status, could differentiate among speakers according to status, and that these distinctions are in accordance with the Hollingshead measure. Also, speaker status and credibility are positively correlated regardless of listener status. Exactly which dimension of the paralinguistic code is used as the basis for ascribing status is not known.

Ellis (1967) attempted to isolate the variables used by listeners as the basis for ascribing a certain level of status to a speaker. He concluded that status may be ascribed from cues given in single words (eliminating variables such as vocabulary, grammatical usage, and fluency), and that even under conditions of faking vocal qualities, listeners can still identify primary social status.

Credibility and Attitude Change

Perhaps two of the most important areas in speech communication are credibility and attitude change. As already discussed, the Harms study (1961) considered judgments of status and credibility based on vocal cues. Concerning credibility, Harms concluded that regardless of their own status, listeners found perceived high status speakers more credible than perceived low status speakers.

Recent studies by Miller and Hewgill (1964), Addington (1971), and Pearce and Conklin (1971) attempted to discover how various aspects of the paralinguistic code affect ratings of source credibility: the effects of nonfluencies; the effects of speaking rate, pitch variety, voice quality, and articulation; and the effects of "conversational" and "dynamic" delivery styles. Sereno and Hawkins (1967), Bowers (1965), Pearce (1971), and Pearce and Brommel (1971) considered the effects of nonfluencies and different delivery styles on credibility in relation to attitude change.

The following variables were found to be associated with decreases in speaker credibility: increases in the number of nonfluencies (vocalized pauses, such as "uh," and repetitions); decreases in pitch; increases in nasality or denasality; increases in tenseness; and increases in throatiness. Those factors which had either no effect or an inconsistent effect on credibility were: increases or decreases in speaking rate; and increases in pitch. Delivery style had no effect on the perceived competence of the speaker, although it did affect other perceptions. A "conversational" delivery style was perceived as more trustworthy than a "dynamic" one.

The relationship between vocal cues, credibility, and attitude change is a complex one. Generally, variations in vocal cues produce variations in credibility ratings, but not attitude change, unless high or low credibility is established with an introduction (which is not always available in the small group setting) and a dynamic delivery is used. Although credibility has been classed as a major factor in attitude change, it is interesting that variations in vocal cues, which produce variations in credibility, do not produce variations in attitude change. It may be that *changes in attitudes are affected by a dimension or combination of dimensions of credibility which are unaffected by variations in vocal cues.* (See Hovland, Janis, and Kelley [1953]; Weiss and Fine [1955, 1956].)

Conclusion

Questions may be raised concerning the accuracy of listeners' judgments. Raymond Hunt and Tip Kan Lin (1967) conducted a study concerned with the accuracy of judgments of personal attributes from speech. Their findings provide evidence of accurate judgment and also some evidence of individual performance consistency across samples of speech expressive of dissimilar personalities; they also found that accuracy was greater for affective attributes than for behavioral-physical ones. They conclude,

> The most noteworthy findings to emerge from this research are those that support the idea that stable cues to personality are carried by general voice "qualities" *independently of the lexical content* of speech. The fact that listeners could judge personality accurately from speech samples, but that passage content had no effect on accuracy suggests either that speech content tends to be no more than redundant with voice quality or simply irrelevant to the judgmental task. (p. 453)

A more basic question which must be answered about listener judgment and agreement concerns the validity of the assigned personality characteristics. Ernest Kramer (1964) concluded that interjudge agreement concerning assigned personality characteristics to unseen speakers is not without validity. However, the role of seeking correlations with external criteria, e.g., objective personality measures, has not been fully understood. An objective personality measure, like *any* measure including one provided by a *single* judge, taps only part of the construct being measured. Judgments from aural cues may be prompted by another part or aspect of the same construct untapped by objective measures. The fact that judges agree with one another may be taken to represent only concurrent validity.

Territoriality

Experience 9-6. Do this exercise in the library. Either as a group, or when you are alone, try the following: wait until someone gets up from his seat at the library, then sit down and move the person's books and coat to another place. When the person comes back, watch his reaction as inconspicuously as you can.

Experience 9-7. A group of nine-year-olds have built a tree fort in the empty lot on their street. For about a month they have been meeting in the tree fort after school. One day, upon arriving at the fort, they find that a rival gang from another street has taken it over. Have four volunteers role-play the fort-builders. Another four should play the intruders.

Experience 9-8. Look around the room. Note where each person in the class is sitting. How often does each person occupy either the seat he is in or the seats close around him?

If you went so far as to "steal" someone's seat in the library, you probably noticed that when he returned, you were either the object of some verbal/nonverbal deprecation or that you became subject to an argument based on territorial rights. You may have argued that the seat does not belong to anyone, that it is available for all the students. The angry reply may have been that the books and coat should have indicated to you that the seat was, indeed, occupied. You may have countered that all the seats are the same, after all, and that the whole argument is silly. The nonverbal messages you encountered may have forced a retreat.

The tree fort became a *cause celebré.* The group of nine-year-olds returning to their tree fort probably wasted no time in talking. Icy stares and a show of teeth are the usual outcomes when the defense of territory is at stake. The odds are that the builders won. But the question which remains is an important one. What was at stake? Was it simply the chair in the library? Was it simply the fort? Or was it a great deal more?

What do you do when you walk into a classroom after the first few weeks of class and someone is in "your" seat? Immediately aware that something is "wrong," you probably stand in front of your seat and stare at its new occupant. You look slightly idiotic, and you certainly, by now, feel that way. Now what? You cannot stand there all period. One of two things occurs to you: either ask the person to move or find another seat. But how can you ask him to move when there is no *real* reason? Frustrated, you find another seat, either close to your original territory or far enough away so you can establish a new territory.

Territoriality is characterized by two features. First, there is the assumption of proprietary rights toward a geographical area and, second, there is the recognition that there is no legal basis for the proprietary rights. The library seat is yours because you were there first. The classroom seat is yours because you have been occupying it for the greatest length of time. Proprietary rights with the tree fort are "stronger" because the four boys built the fort with their own tools, materials, and labor. The investment is greater than time. The fight, if one were to occur, is likely to be more physical. By the same token, a fight is less likely to occur at all; the claim to the territory is stronger.

The notion of territoriality has been examined in animals more extensively than in humans (Ardrey 1966, 1970; Hall 1969; Mowat 1963; Henderson 1952). Hall defines territoriality as "behavior by which an organism characteristically lays claim to an area and defends it against members of its own species." The net result of this behavior is that territoriality regulates the species density in a given area and provides a framework for coordinating the activities of the group.

Territoriality may be as much an aspect of human behavior as it is of other animals (see Alland [1972] for an opposing view). The entire concept of territoriality first became clear to one student when, she reported, "It wasn't until two weeks ago at dinner when one of the neighborhood dogs graciously left a sampling on our front lawn and my aggressive father arose from the table and ran out screaming, 'That's my bush!' as if he intended to use it next, that I knew . . . the concept of territoriality" (Ullrich 1971, p. 1). Studies of isolated pairs (Altman and Haythorn 1967) and old age homes (Lipman 1968) also indicated that territoriality is a human characteristic. Several researchers have focused on territorial behavior in humans. Whyte (1949), reporting on the social structure which exists in restaurants, found a clear relationship between status and territory. Each worker had his own territory and invasions caused disruptions.

The relationship between territoriality and dominance has been subject to little systematic investigation with humans. De Long (1970) hypothesized that in a seminar situation, a direct relationship would exist between seating position and rank within the student hierarchy. Members closer to each other in rank would also be closer spatially. After the fifth meeting, the teacher withdrew as the authority figure. At the end of the eleventh and twenty-third meetings, the group ranked its membership for demonstrated leadership ability, quantity and quality of participation, aggressiveness, relaxation, positive and negative attitudes, and friendliness. Over the first eleven meetings, there was no clear relationship between dominance and territoriality. The next group of eleven meetings supported De Long's hypothesis.

A territorial analysis of a classroom is quite easy and often very revealing. Where does the professor sit? Who sits around him? Who has access to chalk, the lights, the door, the window shades? Spatial position and role are closely related. The person nearest the window usually assumes the responsibility of opening and closing it, while the person nearest the chalkboard usually fetches chalk or erases. What other examples of position and role relationships can you think of?

Experience 9-9. Have a volunteer place himself in a central position in the room. The other members of the class should now position themselves around him in such a way that their distance from him indicates some aspect of their relationship. For example, a person may stand far away, indicating a negative feeling, or close up, indicating a positive feeling. A person standing close may feel the volunteer in the center to be a powerful member of the class and may desire to share that power. Do we unconsciously do what in this exercise we did consciously?

Territoriality in humans is more complex than in other animals. We claim territory and define it for a variety of reasons, some conscious, some unconscious. By the same token, how we defend our territory varies. Animal species have fewer choices; they defend first by threatening sounds, then by physical aggression. Humans, on the other hand, have many alternatives. Sommer (1969) describes the numerous ways that individuals maintain territory. For example, books may be left on a seat, someone may be asked to "save my place," "occupied" signs may be left, and so on.

Personal Space

Whereas territory remains stationary, personal space is carried around with you. Personal space is the space that you place between yourself and others, the invisible boundaries which become apparent only when they are crossed.

Our personal space varies according to the situation and the persons with whom we are interacting. Comfortable and intimate situations call for a smaller personal space than situations which are uncomfortable or threatening. The closer we feel to a person psychologically, the closer we will stand physically. If the relationship becomes less friendly, the physical distance will increase (Willis 1966; Little 1965; Justice 1969).

The average distance in a nonthreatening situation with strangers is approximately two feet. This, of course, varies from culture to culture (Hall 1959) and from subculture to subculture. For example, Jones and Aiello (1972) found that blacks in the first grade stand closer to each other than do whites in the first grade. Adding this finding to those of a previous study (Jones 1971), the authors concluded that "lower-class blacks maintain a closer interaction distance than middle-class whites in the first grade" (Jones and Aiello 1972, p. 12).

Sommer (1962), studying pairs and groups, found that two people prefer to sit across from one another, at a slight angle, rather than side-by-side, but, if the distance across is too great, they will prefer to sit side-by-side. A comfortable distance for conversation for people sitting across from each other is five and a half feet between heads (three and a half feet between couches). Sommer (1959) also found that women sit closer to both men and women than do men. Finally, people will arrange themselves around a *corner* of a table to facilitate discussion.

Personal space in animals is related to flight distance and fight distance. Flight distance refers to the distance an animal will allow an intruder to approach before it flees. Fight distance refers to the distance an animal will allow an intruder before he attacks him. The relationship between personal space and self-protection is also apparent in humans.

Dosey and Meisels (1969) presented subjects with three situations in either stress or nonstress conditions. In the first, subjects were instructed to walk toward each other; in the second, subjects were instructed to trace a silhouette representing themselves in a room with a printed silhouette of the opposite sex; and, in the third situation, subjects entered a room in which the experimenter was seated and were told to be seated—they could choose either a near or far seat. In the stress condition, subjects were told that the purpose of the experiment was to determine their physical attractiveness, sex appeal, and feelings about initiating relationships with strangers. In the nonstress condition, subjects were told that the purpose of the experiment was to study the "orienting reflex," a natural reaction in all people. In all three situations, there was a significant difference between the stress and nonstress conditions. In general, personal space was greater in the stress than nonstress conditions.

Our personal space determines the degree of contact that we have with other people. In a study by Bardeen (1971), subjects interacted with a confederate on either a tactile, verbal, or visual level. For the tactile mode (blindfolded without conversation), the subjects described the confederate as trustful and sensitive. For the verbal mode (blindfolded without touching), the subjects described the confederate as distant and noncommunicative. For the visual mode (no talking or touching), the subjects described the confederate as artificial, arrogant, and cold. Although Bardeen was not interested in personal space, note the implications of his findings for the area. The tactile condition provided the most complete circumstances for a violation of personal space. The confederate was described as trustful. In the verbal condition there was no invasion of personal space. Since the circumstance was an impersonal one (in that there was no physical contact or eye contact, which are intimate), the confederate was described as distant. Compare this to the first condition in which the source of contact was intimate and in which personal space was violated. The third condition, visual, also constituted an invasion of personal space, but not to the degree as in the first condition. Eye contact is an intimate form of communication, and so an invasion of personal space occurred, but not enough information was provided to sanction the invasion. Subjects could maintain enough distance to label the confederate as arrogant.

Environment

Experience 9-10. **Arrange to meet with your group in different locations. Select large rooms, small rooms, a member's apartment, and an area with which no member is familiar. Meet in attractive rooms, and unattractive rooms; vary the meeting times. Record the effects of different times and places. Note when the group seemed to be most and least productive. Note when tension was highest. Did the time or place have any influence on the group?**

March 15. We met in the Conference Room of the Speech building to accommodate Martha and Joanie, who live on campus and have no cars, and Chuck, who lives near campus and has, unfortunately, only a broken car. No one was happy over the prospect of meeting in a classroom.

Janice picked me up to get some beer, which we all drank during the meeting. But! between drinking on campus (a no-no), and having our meeting in a classroom, things never got off the ground. There's something oppressive about a classroom when it's dark outside and classes are, for the most part, over for the day. RULE: no more meetings on campus.

Environmental surroundings have a direct influence on group behavior. Maslow and Mintz (1956) studied the effects of different room decorations on subjects' ratings of pictures of faces on dimensions of "energy" and "well-being." Subjects were placed in a beautiful room—two large windows with drapes, beige walls, indirect overhead lighting, and attractive furnishings; an ugly room—two half-windows, battleship gray walls, overhead bulb with a dirty lampshade, and furnishings to give the impression of a dirty storeroom; or an average room—a professor's office with three windows with shades, battleship gray walls, indirect overhead lighting, and somewhat attractive furnishings. Subjects in the beautiful room gave significantly higher ratings to the faces in the pictures than the subjects in either of the other rooms. The ratings of subjects in the average room were closer to those of the subjects in the ugly room than those of the subjects in the beautiful room.

In a follow-up study, Mintz (1956) attempted to determine if the effects of being in a beautiful or ugly room were long-term. Whereas in the first study subjects were in the experimental rooms for approximately ten minutes, this second study required that each subject be in the room a total of eight hours, four one-hour sessions, and two two-hour sessions.

Observational notes showed that in the [ugly] room the examiners had such reactions as monotony, fatigue, headache, sleep, discontent, irritability, hostility, and avoidance of the room; while in the [beautiful] room they had feelings of comfort, pleasure, enjoyment, importance, energy, and a desire to continue their activities. It is concluded that visual-esthetic surroundings . . . can affect significantly the persons exposed to them. These effects are not limited either to laboratory situations or to initial adjustments, but can be found under naturalistic circumstances of considerable duration. (p. 466)

The size of a particular room and the furniture arrangement also affect interaction. Hare and Bales (1963) found that the way chairs are placed in a room determines the type and amount of interaction. In a circle, individuals talk to those opposite them, rather than to those sitting on either side. At a rectangular table, the individuals who sit at the corners contribute least to the discussion, and the central and head positions appear to be dominant. Whether the position is the major factor in determining the amount of member participation, or whether members who normally contribute a certain amount select the position which seems to best suit them, is difficult to assess. Most likely, it is a combination of the two.

Sommer (1962) found that room size affects the distance that individuals sit from each other. The relationship is an inverse one: as the size of the room increases, the distance between individuals decreases. Sommer also determined that in a private home, as opposed to a large public room, eight feet is a comfortable distance for conducting conversations.

The environment may also influence the amount of contact between groups and, therefore, influence intergroup relations. Deutsch and Collins (1951) studied conditions which favor friendly outcomes of intergroup relations. They hypothesized that proximity and friendliness are inversely related, that is, the closer the two groups, the greater the friendliness. Two housing projects were used for the study. In one, families were assigned to apartments without regard to race; in the other, families were segregated with regard to race. In the interracial housing project, there were many more instances of friendly contact between members of different races. Also, there were more favorable attitudes toward blacks and Chinese, as well as toward living in an interracial housing project.

Body Rhythms

Do you sometimes refer to yourself as a "day" or "night" person? If so, then you are already acquainted with certain body rhythms. Our bodies have certain biological rhythms which affect our capacity to perceive, respond, and perform according to outside stimuli. These rhythms are referred to as *circadian,* i.e., rhythms synchronized with environmental cycles. For example, our sleep cycle is synchronized with the day and night cycle.

Lane (1971) reviews some of the effects of circadian rhythms on our communicative behavior, and the specific implications they have for interpersonal relations. "A recent experiment demonstrated that an individual can become synchronized with the activities of a social group and if removed desynchronized, as revealed in changes in the concentration of sodium, potassium, and calcium in the urine, and variations in body temperature" (p. 20). Although the specific cause-and-effect relationships have yet to be discovered, "the identification of social activity and daily routine as synchronizers means that formation of opinion, as it involves the individual's association with his social groups, depends to some extent on a biological synchronization between individuals, and between individuals and their environments" (Lane 1971, p. 20).

Luce (1971) provides us with a method for determining our own body rhythms, consisting of questions such as, "At what hour do you rise?" "When do you prefer to make love?" and "At what time during the day are you happiest?" By answering these and other questions, you may be able to chart your own body cycles and, therefore, determine the "best" and "worst" times for you to be interacting with your groups. For instance, your sleep schedule synchronizes other internal rhythms. Changes in your sleep patterns may adversely affect your ability to work well with others. In general, it is best to synchronize sleep patterns with activity patterns, timing it so sleep precedes a period of great activity.

Experience 9-11. Cut out five triangles all the same size, then cut each into three pieces, with no two triangles being cut the same way. (This makes enough material for one group with five members.) Form a group with five members and place the shuffled pile of pieces of triangles in the center of the group. Without the use of any direct means of communication, such as talking and facial gestures, the group must reassemble the five triangles. No member of the group is allowed to *take* a piece of a triangle from another, but *only* from the center pile. Group members may *give* a piece they hold to another member.

A good place to try this exercise is the library.

Bibliography

Addington, D. "The Relationship of Selected Vocal Characteristics to Personality Perception." *Speech Monographs* 35 (1968): 492.

_____. "The Effect of Vocal Variations on Ratings of Source Credibility." *Speech Monographs* 38 (1971): 242-47.

Aiken, L. "Relationships of Dress to Selected Measures of Personality in Undergraduate Women." *Journal of Social Psychology* 59 (1963): 119-28.

Alland, A. *The Human Imperative.* New York: Columbia University, 1972.

Altman, I., and Haythorn, W. W. "The Ecology of Isolated Groups." *Behavioral Science* 12 (1967): 169-82.

Anisfeld, M., Bogo, N., and Lambert, W. E. "Evaluational Reactions to Accented English Speech." *Journal of Abnormal and Social Psychology* 65 (1962): 223-31.

Ardrey, R. *The Territorial Imperative.* New York: Atheneum, 1966.

──────. *The Social Contract.* New York: Atheneum, 1970.

Bardeen, J. P. "Interpersonal Perception through the Tactile, Verbal, and Visual Modes." Paper presented at the International Communication Association annual convention, Phoenix, Arizona, April 1971.

Birdwhistell, R. *Kinesics and Context: Essays on Body Motion Communication.* Philadelphia: University of Pennsylvania, 1970.

Bowers, J. W. "The Influence of Delivery on Attitudes Towards Concepts and Speakers." *Speech Monographs* 32 (1965): 154-58.

Cline, M. G. "The Influence of Social Context on the Perception of Faces." *Journal of Personality* 25 (1956): 142-58.

Davis, E. A. *The Elementary School Child and His Posture Patterns.* New York: Appleton-Century-Crofts, 1958.

Davitz, J. R., and Davitz, L. J. "Nonverbal Vocal Communication of Feeling." *Journal of Communication* 11 (1961): 81-86.

De Long, A. J. "Dominance—Territorial Relations in a Small Group." *Environment and Behavior* 2 (1970): 170-91.

Deutsch, M., and Collins, M. E. *Interracial Housing: A Psychological Evaluation of a Social Experiment.* Minneapolis: University of Minnesota Press, 1951.

Dosey, M., and Meisels, M. "Personal Space and Self Protection." *Journal of Personality and Social Psychology* 11 (1969): 93-97.

Eisenson, J., Sourther, S., and Fisher, J. "The Affective Value of English Speech Sounds." *Quarterly Journal of Speech* 26 (1940): 589-94.

Ekman, P. "Communication through Nonverbal Behavior: A Source of Information about an Interpersonal Relationship." In *Affect, Cognition, and Personality: Empirical Studies,* edited by S. S. Tomkins and C. E. Izzard, pp. 390-442. New York: Springer, 1965.

Ekman, P., and Friesen, W. "Nonverbal Behavior in Psychotherapy Research." In *Research in Psychotherapy,* edited by J. Shlien, 3: 179-216. Washington, D.C.: American Psychological Association, 1968.

Ellis, D. S. "Speech and Social Status in America." *Social Forces* 14 (1967): 431-37.

Fay, P., and Middleton, W. "The Ability to Judge Truth-telling or Lying from the Voice as Transmitted over a Public Address System." *Journal of General Psychology* 24 (1941): 211-15.

Forston, R. F., and Larson, C. "The Dynamics of Space: An Experimental Study in Proxemic Behavior among Latin Americans and North Americans." *Journal of Communication* 18 (1968): 109-16.

Goffman, E. *Presentation of Self in Everyday Life.* New York: Doubleday, 1959.

_____. *Asylums—Essays on the Social Situation of Mental Patients and Other Inmates.* New York: Doubleday, 1961.

_____. *Behavior in Public Places.* New York: Free Press, 1963.

Hall, E. T. *The Silent Language.* Greenwich, Connecticut: Fawcett, 1959.

_____. "A System for the Notation of Proxemic Behavior." *American Anthropologist* 65 (1963): 1003-26.

_____. *The Hidden Dimension.* New York: Doubleday, 1966.

Hare, A., and Bales, R. F. "Seating Position and Small Group Interaction." *Sociometry* 26 (1963): 480-86.

Harms, L. S. "Listener Judgments of Status Cues in Content Free Speech." *Quarterly Journal of Speech* 47 (1961): 164-68.

Harrison, R. "Nonverbal Communication: Explorations into Time, Space, Action, and Object." In *Dimensions in Communication,* edited by J. Campbell and H. Hepler, pp. 158-74. Belmont, California: Wadsworth, 1965.

_____. "Nonverbal Approaches." In *Communications Handbook,* edited by I. deSola Pool, W. Schramm, N. Maccoby, and E. Parker. Chicago: Rand McNally, 1972.

Henderson, J. Y. *Circus Doctor.* New York: Bantam, 1952.

Hess, E. H. "Attitude and Pupil Size." *Scientific American* 212 (1965): 46-54.

Hovland, C., Janis, I., and Kelley, H. *Communication and Persuasion.* New Haven: Yale University, 1953.

Hunt, R., and Kan Lin, T. "Accuracy and Judgments of Personal Attributes from Speech." *Journal of Personality and Social Psychology* 6 (1967): 450-53.

Jones, S. E. "A Comparative Proxemics Analysis of Dyadic Interaction in Selected Subcultures of New York City." *Journal of Social Psychology* 84 (1971): 35-44.

Jones, S. E., and Aiello, J. R. "The Acquisition of Proxemic Norms of Behavior: A Study of Lower-Class Black and Middle-Class White Children at Three Grade Levels." Unpublished paper, 1972.

Justice, M. T. *Field Dependency, Intimacy of Topic and Interaction Distance.* Dissertation, University of Florida, Gainesville 1969.

Kramer, E. "Judgment of Personal Characteristics and Emotions from Nonverbal Properties of Speech." *Psychological Bulletin* 60 (1963): 408-20.

_____. "Personality Stereotypes in Voice: A Reconsideration of the Data." *Journal of Social Psychology* 62 (1964): 247-51.

Knapp, M. L. *Nonverbal Communication in Human Interaction.* New York: Holt, Rinehart and Winston, 1972.

Lane, L. L. "Communicative Behavior and Biological Rhythms." *Speech Teacher* 20 (1971): 16-20.

Lefkowitz, M., Blake, R., and Mouton, J. "Status Factors in Pedestrian Violation of Traffic Signals." *Journal of Abnormal and Social Psychology* 51 (1955): 704-6.

Leventhal, H., and Sharp, E. "Facial Expressions as Indicators of Distress." In *Affect, Cognition, and Personality: Empirical Studies,* edited by S. S. Tomkins and C. E. Izzard, pp. 296-318. New York: Springer, 1965.

Lipman, A. "Building Design and Social Interaction." *The Architects Journal* 147 (1968): 23-30.

Little, K. B. "Personal Space." *Journal of Experimental Social Psychology* 1 (1965): 237-47.

Luce, G. B. "Understanding Body Time in the Twenty-four Hour City." *New York,* November 15, 1971, pp. 38-43.

Luft, J. "On Nonverbal Interaction." *Journal of Psychology* 63 (1966): 261-68.

Maslow, A. H., and Mintz, N. L. "Effects of Esthetic Surroundings: Initial Effects of These Esthetic Conditions upon Perceiving 'Energy' and 'Well-being' in Faces." *Journal of Psychology* 41 (1956): 247-54.

McKeachie, W. "Lipstick as a Determiner of First Impressions of Personality: An Experiment for the General Psychology Course." *Journal of Social Psychology* 36 (1952): 241-44.

Mehrabian, A. "Orientation Behaviors and Nonverbal Attitude Communication." *Journal of Communication* 17 (1967): 324-32.

———. "Communication without Words." *Psychology Today* 2 (1968): 53-55.

——— *Silent Messages.* Belmont, California: Wadsworth, 1972.

Mehrabian, A., and Friar, J. T. "Encoding of Attitudes by a Seated Communicator via Posture and Positional Cues." *Journal of Consulting and Clinical Psychology* 33 (1969): 330-36.

Miller, G., and Hewgill, M. "The Effect of Variations in Nonfluency on Audience Ratings of Source Credibility." *Quarterly Journal of Speech* 50 (1964): 36-41.

Mintz, N. L. "Effects of Esthetic Surroundings: II. Prolonged and Repeated Experience in a 'Beautiful' and an 'Ugly' Room." *The Journal of Psychology* 41 (1956): 459-66.

Moult, R. "Experimental Measurement of Clothing as a Factor in the Social Ratings of Selected American Males." *American Sociological Review* 19 (1954): 324-28.

Mowat, F. *Never Cry Wolf.* New York: Dell, 1963.

Nerbonne, G. P. *The Identification of Speaker Characteristics on the Basis of Aural Cues.* Dissertation, Michigan State University, 1967.

Osgood, C. E. "Dimensionality of the Semantic Space for Communication via Facial Expressions." *Scandinavian Journal of Psychology* 7 (1966): 1-30.

Pearce, W. B. "The Effect of Vocal Cues on Credibility and Attitude Change." *Western Speech* 34 (1971): 176-84.

Pearce, W. B., and Brommel, B. "Vocalic Communication in Persuasion." Unpublished manuscript, 1971.

Pearce, W. B., and Conklin, R. "Nonverbal Vocalic Communication and Perceptions of a Speaker." *Speech Monographs* 38 (1971): 235-41.

Scheflen, A. E. "The Significance of Posture in Communication Systems." *Psychiatry* 27 (1964): 316-31.

————. "Quasi-courtship Behavior in Psychotherapy." *Psychiatry* 28 (1965): 245-57.

Secord, P. "Facial Features and Inference Processes in Interpersonal Perception." In *Person Perception and Interpersonal Behavior,* edited by R. Tagiuri and L. Petrullo, pp. 300-316. Stanford: University of California, 1958.

Secord, P., Bevan, W., and Katz, B. "The Negro Stereotype and Perceptual Accentuation." *Journal of Abnormal and Social Psychology* 53 (1956): 78-83.

Sereno, K., and Hawkins, G. "The Effects of Variations in Speaking Nonfluency upon Audience Ratings of Attitude toward the Speech Topic and Speakers' Credibility." *Speech Monographs* 34 (1967): 58-64.

Shapiro, J. G. "Responsibility to Facial and Linguistic Cues." *Journal of Communication* 18 (1968): 11-17.

Shapiro, J. G., Foster, C. P., and Powell, T. "Facial and Bodily Cues of Genuineness, Empathy, and Warmth." *Journal of Clinical Psychology* 24 (1968): 233-36.

Sommer, R. "Studies in Personal Space." *Sociometry* 22 (1959): 247-60.

————. "The Distance for Comfortable Conversation: A Further Study." *Sociometry* 25 (1962): 111-16.

————. "Small Group Ecology." *Psychological Bulletin* 67 (1967): 145-58.

————. *Personal Space.* Englewood Cliffs, New Jersey: Prentice-Hall, 1969.

Starkweather, J. "Vocal Communication of Personality and Human Feelings." *Journal of Communication* 11 (1961): 63-72.

Steinzor, B. "The Spacial Factor in Face to Face Discussion Groups." *Journal of Abnormal and Social Psychology* 45 (1950): 552-55.

Thorndike, E. "Euphony and Cacaphony of the English Words and Sounds." *Quarterly Journal of Speech* 30 (1944): 201-7.

Ullrich, D. A. "Territoriality: A Review and Experiment." Unpublished term paper, 1971.

Weiss, W., and Fine, B. J. "Opinion Change as a Function of Some Intra-Personal Attributes of the Communicatees." *Journal of Abnormal and Social Psychology* 51 (1955): 246-53.

————. "The Effect of Induced Aggressiveness on Opinion Change." *Journal of Abnormal and Social Psychology* 52 (1956): 109-14.

White, A. "The Patient Sits Down." *Psychosomatic Medicine* 15 (1953): 256-57.

Whyte, W. F. "The Social Structure of the Restaurant." *American Journal of Sociology* 54 (1949): 302-8.

Willis, F. N. "Initial Speaking Distance as a Function of the Speaker's Relationship." *Psychonomic Science* 5 (1966): 221-22.

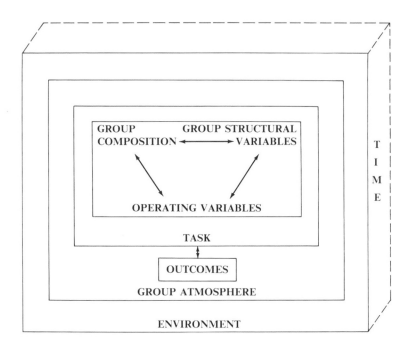

CHAPTER 10

CONFLICTS, BREAKDOWNS, AND THEIR RESOLUTION

Conflict and communication breakdowns, which result in misunderstanding, hostility, and aggression, are the rule in small group interaction, not the exception. Conflict occurs over task and socio-emotional matters. The conflict phase in group development may have a discernable beginning and end, but group conflict does not. It is omnipresent and consumes an enormous amount of group time and energy. Although it is simple to state that conflict and communication breakdowns are part of the essence of group interaction, it is not easy to define conflict causes and situations, describe the results of conflict, or develop methods for dealing with it.

July 7.   HOLY ———! AND HOLY CONFLICT! Well, ladies and gentlemen, it finally happened; here it is the third meeting and what we have is a real honest-to-goodness conflict. Not one of your implicit ones, but a real open hostile one.

The scene: At 6:00 Margaret, Elsa, and I showed up. Gary told us before that he would be late, so there was no problem. Carol and Roy said nothing about being late, so we wondered where they were. At any rate, we discussed what we did at the last meeting, about having divided up the topic. All fine and good. Roy and Carol showed up at about 6:30. I think that they immediately sensed that we were annoyed with their being late. Carol asked what we had done so far, and I filled her in. Roy became upset. He claimed that he had no idea that the topic had been divided up. He implied (obviously!) that I was railroading the group into doing what I wanted to see done. But, did this anger me? Me? YOU BET!! The others came to my defense: yes, the topic was divided the week before. Wasn't he listening? Now, Roy started a side conversation with Carol. He then tried to joke (sarcastically). But it was late, and no one responded.

No member tried to ease the situation. The only suggestion was that we meet in subgroups to work on specific problems with the presentation. This was in response to Roy's claim that a meeting in a few days with all of us would be a waste. He may have been trying to avoid more conflict.

July 16.   The hostility is still evident! Perhaps Roy's caustic comment, half-heartedly pronounced, is close to the truth: this group contains six high-powered people each of whom, in one way or another, insists on getting his or her way. This may not be that obvious, but it sure as hell comes close. Also, a norm has developed which seems to bear this out: no one is trying to lead the group! How's that for a norm! It seems that whenever someone tries to direct the group the others make short work of his suggestions. Funny.

The problem with Roy is not getting any better. No matter what was said he would say something to the effect that he did not understand what was going on, nor did he like what was happening in the group. No one will say anything to him because we all empathize with his taking his comprehensive examinations. This puts all the other members in a strange position: we'll accept his desire to put less into the group (because of his exams), but that makes it harder to deal with his criticisms.

On top of this it seems that I have antagonized virtually every member of the group. I'm too task oriented. I find it hard to function in a group that doesn't have a great deal of task leadership. Relations with Roy are singularly strained. Outside of meetings I avoid discussing the group with him.

Elsa has quit arguing, although she is obviously tense. Margaret and I still attempt to lead (dirty word!), and we are still yelled at for it.

Our next meeting is July 21. I'm going to try to avoid antagonizing anyone by interacting on a more limited basis. If it can be demonstrated to me that what needs to be done will *be done within the time allotted, then I'll be happy to assume a more passive role. IT'S JUST THAT GROUPS ARE SO DAMNED SLOW!*

July 21.   Roy is annoyed with something in the universe. No one questions him about it. We don't want to know if it's about the group.

Margaret ran this meeting without any trouble. I think this was more a function of time than anything else. This was our final meeting before the class presentation. There was no conflict during this meeting: I kept as quiet as possible, Roy did likewise, and Margaret ran the show. A great deal was accomplished.

July 28.   The presentation is tonight. We worked together quickly and with a great deal of humor. The end was in sight, and we were confident that our product was excellent. Elsa joked about needing an extra minute (to take her clothes off—so as to generate interest!). We were high and enjoying it. Interpersonal problems seemed to be a thing of the past.

A last general observation: we worked hard and long, and in the end, we worked well. We were challenged from within and SURVIVED. This made us stronger. We developed an internal system that allowed us to finally cope with the interpersonal problems. It was important for us to work well together, and we finally did.

Searching for Root Causes: May's *Love and Will**

Rollo May (1969), in his book *Love and Will,* provides insight into the root causes of conflict. The problem is greater than a lack of time, a difficult task, or the inability of different personalities to work together. The problem is the *present time.*

We live in an age that May describes as schizoid, a world in which we are out of touch with one another and ourselves, a world characterized by apathy, by lack of clear self-identity, by lack of caring, and by lack of ability to become emotionally involved. Within

---

*Many of the ideas in this section are taken from R. Berko (1971).

this framework, old beliefs are being thrown over and new beliefs are taking shape, but new beliefs are hard to come by, therefore producing frustration and anger. We live in a world with a highly sophisticated system of communication, including the ability to transmit messages from distant planets, but *personal* communication is difficult and rare. In such a world, feelings of purposelessness, worthlessness, meaninglessness, and unimportance are common. The world is sterile, and "the essence of sterility is futility, aimlessness, purposelessness, lack of zest in life" (p. 213). "When inward life dries up, when feeling decreases and apathy increases, when one cannot affect or even genuinely touch another person, violence flares up" (p. 30).

One of the causes of this schizoid condition is the tendency to see ourselves as impotent. To perform an act, to affect some portion of your own life and the lives of others, is to accept responsibility, and to accept responsibility is a burden. Patients follow doctors' orders; workmen follow foremen's directions; students follow teachers' instructions. Decisions, in an age characterized by an over-awareness of consequences, are *too* important to make. But, ultimately, we have no control over the really important decisions. So, there is a paradox: *"Our curious predicament is that the same processes which make modern man so powerful—the magnificent development of atomic and other kinds of technical energy—are the very processes which render us powerless"* (pp. 186-87). The result: Man makes significant acts, but men do not.

Other paradoxes or inconsistencies which give rise to conflicts and contribute to the schizoid man are: love–aggression, prohibition–attraction, and hate–love. Love and aggression are intimately related. We expect more from those we love and, when our expectations are not fulfilled, we agress against them. The same person is the object of seemingly conflicting behavior: our love *and* our aggression.

Sources of attraction lead to conflict. "It is the very badness of the act that gives it its vertiginous fascination. Remove the prohibition, and the attraction stops" (p. 150). The role of playboy may cease to be interesting when it is no longer the object of scorn. This role seems to be attractive only so long as it is prohibited by the group.

Another inconsistency is the love–hate dichotomy. Some individuals feel that hate is bad, and should be eliminated from their feelings. Hate feelings, thoughts of negation, must be hidden, for they are wrong. But hate is as human an emotion as love. The inability to recognize that both emotions are healthy restricts an individual's ability to communicate honestly and leads to feelings of guilt and inner turmoil.

The solution for the problems May uncovers lies in interpersonal relationships. *Caring* may be the key to and the core of healthy interpersonal relationships, for caring is synonymous with involvement, and involvement leads to decisions. The schizoid world lacks care, yet care is necessary to seal the rifts between people, to insure that they touch and are, in turn, touched. A recent advertisement reads, "To communicate is the beginning of understanding." Communication, related to "commune" implies both the experience of communion and community with our fellow man.

Conflict Situations

Levinger (1957) maintains that there are three basic cases of conflict situations. The first case he labels *plus–plus* and is defined as conflict between two equally attractive objectives. The second case, *minus–minus,* is defined as conflict between two equally disdainful choices. The third case, *plus–minus,* is defined as conflict arising when there are both positive and negative valences in one region.

Maslow (1966b) defines four types of conflict situations. The first, *sheer choice,* exists when no information is available on which to base a choice, so the choice made is directed by chance. A rat at a choice point in a maze is an example of a sheer conflict situation.

The second type of conflict situation is characterized by *multiple means* and exists when there is more than one way to achieve a desired end and the alternatives are equally attractive. For example, a woman choosing between two dresses to wear to the movies is in a very low level of conflict, given the consequences. A different situation exists when a woman must choose between two marriage proposals. She may love both men, but the consequences of choosing one or the other are great.

The third type of conflict situation involves *multiple goals.* In the second exercise in this chapter, two goals are set up for each individual: (1) to be a member of the winning team and (2) to accumulate the greatest amount of money. These goals may be complementary or mutually exclusive.

The fourth conflict situation, *catastrophic conflict,* occurs when there are no choice alternatives. An individual about to be executed probably suffers from catastrophic conflict; there are no choice alternatives, and the situation is one of pure threat.

Combining Maslow's and Levinger's approaches, conflicts may be seen in terms of the choices offered in a given situation, the viability of those choices, external pressures forcing coping decisions, and internal forces related to affect and desire.

A final distinction among types of conflicts concerns manifest versus underlying conflicts. Up to this point, conflicts have been viewed as relatively undisguised phenomena, but this view is simplistic. Deutsch (1969a) defines *manifest* conflict as the stated reason for conflict, and *underlying* conflict as the deeper cause for the conflict. For example, in groups where a leader has been deposed, conflicts between individuals continue long after the initial conflict seems to have been resolved. The manifest conflict during later meetings may be tied to different viewpoints concerning particular suggestions; the underlying conflict, though, is rooted in the initial interaction.

The probability of solving manifest conflict is high. Changing the circumstances usually will suffice. For instance, a disputed suggestion can be either accepted or rejected, a time and place to meet can be decided upon. However, if an underlying conflict prompted the manifest conflict, then solving the latter will be little more than a "stop-gap" measure. Without determining the underlying conflicts, the probability of continued conflicts is high. Separating manifest from underlying conflict, and dealing with each one separately, is difficult but necessary if conflict resolution is to be effective.

Before discussing some specific causes and effects of conflicts and breakdowns in the small group setting, let us generate some conflict of our own to observe and analyze.

Experience 10-1. Draw a tic-tac-toe board on the chalkboard and label each of the squares 1 through 9. Assign each of nine members in the class to a single square. The nine individuals have to decide who will be X and who will be O. The object of the game is for each individual to be a member of the winning team. Each member of the class should contribute a small amount of money to a winner's pot. The winning team in the tic-tac-toe game may do with the money *as it pleases.*

Experience 10-2. Arrange a time and place where the class can meet for a period of several hours and play a game of chess. Divide the class into two groups, a white team and a black team. Each team is to distribute the parts among its members. If there are too few people in each group to fill each position, eliminate some of the positions. Be sure that the teams have an equal number of players.

Each king receives $1500 in play money to run his army, bribe whom he can, pay off loans, etc. Queens receive $500; bishops receive $300; knights receive $200; rooks receive $100; and pawns receive $50 each. If a player is captured by the opposing team, he must give half his money to the foreign king; he may retain the other half. A fifteen-minute time limit is to be observed for each move. Work out a system of rewards for the winning team and the individual who finishes the game with the greatest amount of money.

Experience 10-3. Divide the class into four groups. Place the following information on the chalkboard in clear view of each group.

$$R = \text{Red}, \ G = \text{Green}$$

RRRR, R = +50
RRRG, R = −100, G = +300
RRGG, R = −150, G = +150
RGGG, R = +300, G = −100
GGGG, G = −50

The object of the game is for each team to score as many points as it can. This is all the information needed. Before beginning, decide on a prize for the winning team. Each team is given three minutes to choose a color, either red or green. Have an independent class member score the game using the following procedure: If each team chooses red, then each receives 50 points; if three teams choose red, and one chooses green, then of the three teams (red), each receives *minus* 100 points and the fourth team (green) receives *plus* 300 points, etc. The procedure is repeated ten times.

The points are tabulated on the following table. On trial 3 a representative from each of the four groups is allowed to confer with the other representatives for five minutes. On trial 5 the number of points added or subtracted is multiplied by five. On trial 7 another conference, of seven minutes, is allowed. On trial 10 the number of points added or subtracted is multiplied by ten.

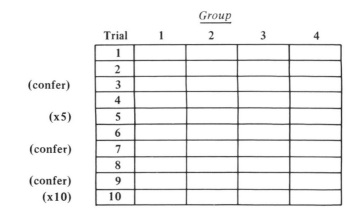

	Trial	1	2	3	4
	1				
	2				
(confer)	3				
	4				
(x5)	5				
	6				
(confer)	7				
	8				
(confer)	9				
(x10)	10				

Sources of Trouble

Impersonal Sources

A wide variety of impersonal sources of trouble plague small group interaction. The following list contains only those which seem to reoccur most often.

1. *Time.* All groups work within a time limit; this time limit may or may not allow for the group to develop properly. The greater the pressure for a quick decision, the greater the probability that conflicts will arise. However, when groups are under such pressure, conflicts tend to be internalized rather than manifest; thus group progress is usually not impeded. Time may also be thought of in terms of meeting time. When to meet, how long, and how often are practical problems which every group must solve. The degree to which group members can work smoothly and efficiently to solve the practical problems raised by time considerations determines the degree to which they can avoid major conflicts.

April 1.   The pressures of a deadline may make a group more cohesive and willing to cooperate in order to accomplish the goal, but in our group it produced a great amount of tension. As the deadline grows closer, everyone gets more anxious. Personal differences are maximized, and cooperation is impossible. Chuck and Laing refuse to give up their idea for the project, yet they still refuse to allow any of the other members to help. They refuse to support alternative suggestions.

2. *Energy.* Individuals working in a group usually have a great number of other responsibilities, including other classes, homework, and employment. The degree to which members are able to devote their energy to the group, and the degree to which the amounts devoted by each member tend toward equality, determines the degree to which the group task may be handled adequately. When some members contribute more than others, problems will arise.

3. *Physical problems.* Problems in this area concern where to meet, how to secure the necessary equipment, and how to adapt the group meetings and presentation (if one is required) to the physical surroundings available. Most physical problems cannot be "handled," they must be worked around. The earlier groups recognize these problems and take steps to alleviate them, the fewer conflicts and last minute hassles they will experience. Solutions to problems in this area may be creative, and may help the group perform exceptionally well. For example, one group in an oral interpretation class, seeking an area in which to present a final reading, decided that a classroom would not provide the proper atmosphere. They read their cuttings in a stairwell, with the members of the class seated on the stairs. Their solution to the problem was excellent; it enhanced their presentation greatly.

4. *Task.* Tasks vary in level of complexity, difficulty, amount of information required, and the degree to which the solution is easily verified. Each one of these characteristics affects the probability of an adequate solution, and so affects frustration. For a more complete discussion, see chapter 4.

5. *Understanding the problem.* During the initial stages of group development, the group must orient itself to the task: it must define the problem which confronts it and attempt to determine its causes and consequences. Lack of a clear understanding of the problem is a *potential* source of conflict. When group members wrongly assume that a clear understanding of the problem exists, time and energy must be devoted to clearing up misconceptions and conflict which already may have led to open hostility among group members.

6. *Information.* The information necessary to understand or solve a particular problem may not be available to the group. In such cases, conclusions are tenuous, and there is a lack of stability in the group. This may lead to frustration resulting in hostility, or the group insecurity may produce dysfunctional flight behavior.

7. *Facilities.* Resources may be scarce, resulting in competition among members of the same group, or between members of different groups. For instance, reading material for different class groups usu-

ally overlaps, resulting in a conflict over which group should get the material first, and how long it should keep it before giving it to the other groups. This form of competition between groups usually leads to conflict.

8. *Method of operation.* Once a group has determined what its task is, it has to develop the means by which to achieve it. If the means are inadequate, the group will waste time and become frustrated. An efficient, effective method of operation helps reduce internal conflicts and develops confidence in the group.

9. *Criteria for evaluation.* Once a problem is defined to the group's satisfaction and the group agrees on the possible causes and consequences of the problem, it must develop a system whereby it can evaluate whether a decision or solution is right or wrong, or good or bad, for the group. Premature choice making, that is, considering decisions and solutions *before* a means to test them has been established, is another source of conflict. For example, in the third exercise at the beginning of this chapter, one group may have decided on red or green without having developed a method whereby it could test its decision. Any attempt to test the group's decision would have indicated that only through negotiation could any reasonable prediction be made concerning the winning or losing of points.

10. *Roles.* In order for a group to be an effective problem-solving unit, a wide range of roles must be enacted. A source of conflict within a group may be a lack of individual decision-making skills, which can lead to either role fixation, where an individual enacts only one role, or a situation in which only a few roles are enacted. Individuals differ not only in their abilities but also in their desires to assume particular roles. Conflicts arise as individuals feel pressured into assuming roles for which they believe they are not suited. Therefore, the particular individuals comprising the group will affect the range of roles enacted and, ultimately, the group's ability to solve its task.

May 10.   A final evaluation. . . .

> *The roles our group members assumed were not conducive to the task. Although we all played task and maintenance roles, we also indulged in self-centered roles. It would seem that with Janice elaborating on ideas and setting the standards by which we could work, Jane functioning as an effective information and opinion seeker, as well as a follower, Joan encouraging, supporting, and elaborating on the ideas presented, Laing also encouraging and supporting some ideas, Norah operating as gate-keeper and initiator,*

and Chuck functioning as an initiator and standard-setter,
that we had a good and wide variety of roles helping the
group function. But! Several self-centered roles kept us from
ever becoming a group.

Janice and Jane were deserters. Janice deserted the
group in a physical way—she missed a great many meetings.
Jane deserted the group mentally—she was neutral on virtu-
ally every point brought up for discussion. Chuck enacted
the role of blocker. He initiated an idea for the project, and
then refused to listen to or consider any other idea. He did
not want any help either, insisting he would work on his
project alone. Laing played behavioral rapist, someone who
manipulates others and does not assume the responsibility
for the consequences of his actions. He adopted modes of
behavior simply to see the results, without thinking through
the consequences.

11. *Cliques.* When a few group members agree on some particular end or means for the group that is not endorsed by the other
members, they often will form a clique. If the clique forces its will on
the group, or refuses to open itself to other points of view, or cooperate
with the larger group, it will be detrimental to group functioning.

12. *Observations, inferences, and judgments.* Distinguishing
between observations, inferences, and judgments is necessary to avoid
certain conflicts. Observations describe phenomena which may be
observed by others, and do not involve value judgments of what is
observed. Inferences relate known or observed events to unknown
events. Because no empirical validation exists for inferences, they are
likely to be sources of conflict in the group. The more inferences are
tied to reality, the less likely they are to cause conflicts. Judgments
describe phenomena and express the degree to which the phenomena
described are acceptable to the person making the judgment. Whereas
an observation is either true or false, an inference probable or improbable, a judgment is either believed or not believed.

Personal Sources

Impersonal sources usually generate problems that can be solved once
they are recognized. Even if a problem stemming from an impersonal
source is not easily solved, it may cease to disrupt the group once it
has been recognized as insolvable.

Personal sources of trouble are not as easily solved. Unlike impersonal sources of conflict, it is much harder to define personal

sources of problems. One reason is that they are not of a binary nature, i.e., either "off" or "on." Personality clashes may occur in waves, first strong, then weak, but rarely do they have definite beginning and end points. For these and other reasons, most of the writing done on conflict resolution has focused on the strategies necessary to overcome personal sources of conflict.

1. *Belonging.* At some time during the group interaction, each member asks himself, "Do I want to belong to this group?" The answer depends upon whether the group is perceived as fulfilling the member's needs and whether the group is perceived as essential in fulfilling those needs. Knowledge of each member's CL and CL$_{alt}$ will help predict whether the member will choose to belong to the group or not.

2. *Involvement.* Belonging to a group does not imply involvement. A member may contribute little or nothing, or serve neither as a disruptive nor a helping force. A member may express token membership or total involvement, depending on his concerns and priorities. Involvement considers such dimensions as identity, objectivity, individuality, and the relation of these factors to the group.

3. *Control.* Each group member wishes to exercise a certain amount of control over both his own actions and the actions of the other members. On the other hand, he also wishes to have others direct his and the group's actions. The degree to which members are able and willing to assume responsibility may be a source of conflict. Members must establish a stable system of power relationships in order to avoid conflicts over leadership and control.

4. *Affection.* Affection may be viewed from two perspectives, although the two are intertwined. First, there is affection relating to in-group feelings. Do group members appear to like or dislike each other or are they indifferent? Are they friends, or simply a group of strangers bound together by an assigned task? From another perspective, affection may be thought of as the amount of interaction having to do with closeness and affection that a given member wants. Individuals differ according to the amount of closeness they need or desire; these differences are a common source of trouble.

5. *Roles.* The ability to enact a particular role may be an impersonal source of problems, but roles are also associated with personal sources. One common source of trouble concerns the difference between how the actor conceives the role and how others conceive the role. Other sources of trouble are individual members' desires to perform certain roles in certain ways. For instance, a member may feel that relieving tension is more important than asking for needed clarifi-

cation, or a member who has performed leadership functions during prior meetings is forced to assume the same role even though he simply does not desire to do so.

6. *Task.* Task difficulty, complexity, and information requirements are potential impersonal sources of trouble. Personal sources of conflict involving the task are affective in nature, and are not easily solved. Tasks vary according to how personal or impersonal they are perceived to be by each member. Individuals respond differentially to problems which they consider to be personal: some individuals avoid personal problems, while others seek them out. Tasks also vary according to how exciting or pleasing they are perceived to be by each member. It is difficult to become involved with a task perceived as dull or unpleasant.

7. *Rewards.* Rewards may be either intrinsic or extrinsic. Intrinsic rewards are associated with working with individuals who are liked or admired, or solving a difficult task. Rewards may also be thought of in terms of more objective criteria. Will group success result in financial benefits to the group or a high grade on the project?

Which rewards are most desirable is usually a matter of individual preference. The first experience at the beginning of this chapter designated money as the reward. How many members of the tic-tac-toe game seemed to be motivated by the money, how many by the desire to win? The second experiment did not designate a particular reward. What did the class decide? How much trouble was there in deciding? Did the decision for the second experiment, which was long, complex, and difficult, differ from the decision for the third experiment, which was shorter, less complex, and less difficult? What effect does the task have on the rewards necessary to motivate a high level of interaction?

8. *Personality.* A variety of personalities exist in any group. The degree to which these personalities work together, and the degree to which any one is disruptive, affects interaction. Individuals with low self-images, for example, normally appear insecure and rigid. Sadistic individuals may disrupt the group process to satisfy their own needs. Individuals with a high need for control will undoubtedly be the source of power conflicts, whereas those with a high need for affections may cause socio-emotional conflicts. Closed-minded individuals may be unable to differentiate among various means in achieving a particular goal. Regardless of the particular composition of your group, it is necessary to be aware of the fact that different personality make-ups perceive the same stimuli differently and react differently to

them. How complementary different personalities are determines the
kinds and degrees of problems in the group.

*October 3.   Seems I got caught up in eating fried chicken and was
fifteen minutes late. I guess it really didn't matter because
nothing important had been said. Tony, Louise, and Dave
were the only other people there. They really didn't have
anything specific to talk about, since the audio tapes they
ordered hadn't arrived yet. So, we planned when we would
meet to put the project together.*

*Every now and then our discussion got side-tracked
and focused upon our personal lives. Marriage no less! I was
astounded to find out that Tony had been married for only
four months, and that he had known his wife for only four
months before that.*

*About then Judy appeared. She apparently needed
counseling more than Dave or I, so most of Tony's attention
focused on her. Throughout the entire project, of which this
evening was only an example, Judy focused much of her
attention on Tony. I thought this was rather interesting,
because in another class, Judy had a somewhat similar relationship with another fellow. He too was extremely good-
looking, friendly, and married.*

*Dave became depressed about our exploration into in-
terpersonal relationships and kept trying to redirect the conversation to a nonpersonal, more academic topic. Tony
wanted to continue with the topic of marriage. Dave, frustrated, left. Our group was social this evening, and Dave
functioned best when the group was task oriented. Soon
after this occurrence Dave stopped coming to the meetings.*

*I'm glad Ellen didn't come. I would have felt more
inhibited about talking this way if she were here. Louise
seems like the good mother, and Ellen like the skeptical
mother to me. Louise said a lot of things to us that I'm sure
she must have thought twice about before saying. Afterwards, she declared herself the mother, and Tony the father
of this conversation: Judy and I were the children. She has
done this before. Wonder why she feels she has to view
herself as the watchful mother?*

9. *Self-interests.* The line between behavior directed at satisfying self-interest or group interest may be difficult to define. How
similar self-interests and group interests are determines whether goal

conflicts will occur. Each individual has personal needs and goals which direct his behavior. Personal goals may cause a member to work *through* the group to satisfy self-interests. For example, an individual desiring to meet other people may join a group to satisfy this personal goal, in which case the group goal becomes of secondary importance. The ultimate success of any group may well depend on how well individual and group goals or interests are integrated.

10. *Subgroups.* Whereas a clique is formed on the basis of common task interests or procedures, subgroups are formed on the basis of mutual social or emotional interests or goals. How much a subgroup avoids task behaviors and forces its presence on other group members, determines the extent to which it is a disruptive force.

11. *External loyalties.* We all aspire to and are members of many groups and associations. These multiple associations keep us from entering a particular group and becoming totally committed to it. Because they constitute a large part of our identity, we cannot simply dismiss them—to do so would be a denial of self. On the other hand, these associations may keep us from adhering to certain norms in the new group, from being committed to its goals, or even from getting emotionally close to the membership. Because our other groups satisfy enough of our needs, new groups are at best stimulating —at worst an annoyance.

Some Effects of Conflict

Any source of trouble in a group can lead to conflict, which in turn can lead to aggression, hostility, and, possibly, a complete breakdown in a group's ability to function smoothly and effectively. Within-group conflict is usually disruptive and must be dealt with if the group is to function.

Intergroup conflict, unlike intragroup conflict, is often beneficial to the groups involved. While intragroup conflict usually tears a group apart, decreases its task activity, and produces a negative attitude toward the group's product, intergroup conflict brings group members together, increases the group's task activity, and causes members to positively evaluate their product.

Intergroup conflict strengthens intragroup bonds (North, Koch, and Zinnes 1960) because it offers a vent for dissatisfactions and can help crystalize a group's goals and attitudes. On a broader scale, intergroup conflict may force unrelated groups to form coalitions to resolve an issue. In this case, members of the two groups bring divergent points of view to the task, therefore stimulating the development of new and better solutions. For example, a professor may require that two groups generate test items for a course on small group dynamics: one group wishes to focus the test on theory, the other wishes to focus on practical implications. The two groups cooperate and develop a fifty minute test. A conflict in values may result, but as long as both groups work toward the common goal, the final product is likely to be better than the single tests each group might have developed independently.

Before discussing the last effect of intergroup conflict, do the following exercise.

Experience 10-4. Divide the class into groups with four to six members. Each group member is to generate several improbable headlines, such as NATIONAL RIFLE ASSOCIATION BACKS GUN REGULATION LEGISLATION. Then each group must select one of the headlines generated and develop a pantomime for the rest of the class. The object is to present the pantomimed headline in such a way that the other groups can guess what it is. No signs, pictures, or drawings may be used. You may, if needed, use nonverbal vocal sounds, such as humming, coughing, and screaming.

Discuss each of the pantomimes. Which group did the best job? Defend your own pantomime for the rest of the class.

Bass (1963) found that allied groups commonly over-appraise each other, whereas enemy groups commonly under-appraise each other. Using supervisors and engineers from a refinery, Bass established four groups, Red, Black, Yellow, and Green. The first two groups and the last two groups were to join forces and draw up a plan for judging, collecting evidence about, and grading all of the groups. Regardless of the fact that the Yellow-Green plan was objectively superior, the rankings of the four groups were based on group membership. Before defeat or success a member ranked his own group first, his ally second, and the other groups third and fourth. After defeat, the effects were decreased, but after success, they were increased. Bass concluded that our evaluations of other groups are based on subjective criteria, and only partly on observed performance.

Few sources of objective criteria are available for evaluating the results of exercise four. What effect did the lack of objective criteria have on your discussion? What defense did a group offer if it was consistently evaluated poorly by other groups? Did the groups perceive that they were in competition? How do you know? What were the behavioral manifestations of the conflict? What happens to verbal and nonverbal communication in a group with intergroup conflict? What happens to its leadership?

Little research has been done to answer these questions, although one study by Harmon (1971) considered groups in a crisis situation. A crisis situation is characterized by "urgency, time pressure, threat to the integrity of a group, and a need for immediate action" (p. 267). Except for the time element, groups in conflict and groups in crisis have common aspects. Harmon's study may help point out areas for the fruitful investigation of groups in conflict.

Observing a group attempting to cope with a cardiac seizure followed by death, Harmon generated several hypotheses. The first hypothesis concerns the quantity of communication: during a crisis the quantity of verbal communication decreases. This may be the case with groups in conflict when interaction is directed toward a well-defined goal. Increased intragroup cohesion may result in a decrease in the quantity of communication.

The second hypothesis, derived from Bales, considered the group's equilibrium: during a crisis there is a disequilibrium between task and social processes. As with groups with intergroup conflict, during crisis the task is the most important group function. The emphasis on task efficiency may result in a disequilibrium of acts, with more acts related to task, and fewer related to socio-emotional matters, being performed.

The third hypothesis dealt with leadership: during a crisis leadership becomes autocratic. Applying this to groups in conflict, it appears reasonable to assume that as the stress caused by the conflict increases, the style of leadership is more likely to tend toward autocratic. This, again, has to do with the emphasis on task accomplishment; autocratic leaders are more efficient in terms of time.

The fourth hypothesis also dealt with leadership: leadership will change as the kind and degree of needed expertise changes. Although an autocratic leader may be the most efficient in terms of time, he may not provide the best solutions. Shifts in leadership, while maintaining the autocratic style, provide efficiency both in terms of time and solutions.

While doing the three exercises at the beginning of this chapter, did you notice any changes in communicative behavior from prior exercises where there was no direct conflict? Generate a list of plausible hypotheses relating phase development, role behavior, conformity behavior, group structure, and leadership to the conflict situation. Is it necessary to generate theory specifically related to groups in conflict or do the theories presented in chapters 2 and 3 suffice? What changes, if any, are necessary?

Avoiding Conflicts

February 18. We gossiped a lot, kidded each other, tried to think, and gossiped some more. Paul and I both suffer from verbal diarrhea. We speak like we think. Is this a New York syndrome? Barrage them with words and they can't interrupt until the idea is worked out. This is not premeditated, mind you. It just seems to work this way.

The ideas came flying out from me. It was good, if a little mad. I would like to be less oppressive and learn to LISTEN. Eve is so quiet. It must be hard for her to compete with the over-talkers. I'll have to watch myself. Try and LISTEN, Elizabeth (I tell myself over and over again).

We are all capable of having good ideas. Everyone must get into the act. WE ARE A GROUP, and we'll stand or fall that way. We will all work together on the task we choose because we all WANT to. Our conflicts make us cohesive by clarifying our task and insuring that we know that we are altogether.

Although it may be impossible to avoid all conflicts related to group functioning, Hall (1971) makes the following suggestions.

1. *Avoid arguing for your own judgments.* It is possible for one member to bring group activity to a standstill by refusing to acknowledge that the group is composed of a number of individuals, each of whom is entitled to his own private judgments. It is necessary to know when to *listen* to others and avoid pressing your own judgment, solution, or decision. Hearing and understanding the other members' inputs is essential if the group is to function effectively.

2. *Avoid perceiving interaction as a zero-sum game.* A zero-sum game is one in which the sum of the rewards and losses equals zero; someone must win, and someone must lose. When disagreement is conceived in zero-sum fashion, there are no alternatives for open interaction. Each member will perceive that he has no choices in order

to win. Interaction must be viewed as a non-zero-sum game, that is, each member of the group must judge any decision, solution, or judgment in terms of the amount of benefit the group will derive from it. The solution may not suit all members, but it should not be untenable for any. With this perspective on interaction, problems may avoid becoming conflicts as the group moves easily and quickly through the exploration of a variety of alternatives.

3. *Avoid changing your mind simply to avoid conflict and promote harmony.* Groups develop slowly, with subsequent development resting firmly on prior development. Agreement which is not firmly based on objective and logical grounds may cause future problems. Ideas develop from earlier ones, and a premature agreement may not cause trouble until later when a group has expended a great deal of time and energy in building a "bad" idea. As the group retraces its steps and discovers the root cause, hostility and aggression increase.

4. *Avoid conflict-reducing techniques.* Conflict-reducing techniques such as voting and averaging may cause the same trouble as premature or undesired agreement. A decision reached by voting is likely to result in the formation of cliques which may be detrimental to further task operations.

5. *Avoid viewing differences of opinion as detrimental.* One advantage in using groups for problem solving is that a wide variety of opinions and viewpoints are brought together to generate a solution. Differences of opinion should be encouraged and explored, not avoided. As long as differences of opinion are not viewed as a zero-sum game, resolved with premature agreement or some conflict-reducing technique, differences of opinion should prove beneficial to the group.

Conflict Resolution

When conflict cannot be avoided, the first step toward resolving it is to clarify its source. The manifest reasons for the conflict may be easy to reveal, but the underlying causes may pose a greater problem. Nevertheless, finding a solution to the problem is like looking for a needle in the proverbial haystack, if you do not know the problem's causes. Once the cause has been isolated, the solutions may be directed toward either the individual or the group.

There are several solutions that focus on the individual (Levinger 1957). First, the individual may choose to tolerate the conflict. This is appropriate when the conflict is perceived as trivial (it may not be worth the effort to resolve it) or when an attempt at conflict resolution may cause more problems than the original conflict. For example, in groups where there is hostility among the members, identifying and discussing the cause of the hostility may increase it by making it the focus of attention. An individual also may change his perception of the conflict and thereby eliminate it. A power struggle which threatens a group's existence may be redefined as an effective group procedure for determining leadership. Finally, an individual may resolve the conflict by simply engaging in irrelevant activities.

Group conflicts which are not easily resolved even when the causes have been determined may be resolved by bargaining. Bargaining attempts to maximize the gain to all parties involved. In order for the "bargained" solution to be the best one, game theory enumerates the qualities it must possess (Steinfatt and Miller 1971). "First, the solution cannot depend on personal characteristics of the players, such as bargaining ability, but must remain constant, if the roles and abilities of the two players are reversed" (p. 7). Second, the solution must lie somewhere within the range of possible and acceptable solutions. Third, additions or deletions of points in the range of possible solutions should have no effect on the remaining solutions. This requirement insures that the alternatives are independent of irrelevant factors. Fourth, any change in the utility of the outcomes for one party should have no effect on the solution, provided the same change is applied to the other party's outcomes.

Given that these requirements do not allow for personality differences, differences in bargaining abilities, and other personal characteristics, they are stringent. Because the bargaining process is hardly as rational as the requirements demand, the usual solution arrived at through bargaining is rarely satisfactory to all parties. Individuals will try to maximize their own rewards at the expense of their opponents, and seldom strive to satisfy the four requirements that game theory establishes as necessary to insure an adequate solution. Experience 10-3 provided the opportunity for bargaining on trials three, seven, and nine. What happened? Did the group representatives cooperate to maximize the points for all the groups, or did they oppose one another and accomplish little? Describe the characteristics of the group representatives, the task, and the time limit in terms of their effects on the bargaining process.

The use of a third party or arbitrator poses many of the same problems as bargaining. In arbitration, the parties must agree to abide by the arbitrator's decision. This raises a new problem, i.e., finding a third party trusted by all parties in the conflict. In addition, the solutions provided by the arbitrator may be short range in nature. For example, when union-management contracts are settled through arbitration, the negotiation for the next contract, one or two years later, appears to be just as involved and conflict-ridden.

Very often, bargaining or arbitration solutions are compromises. Compromise provides for the development of new dissatisfactions or the revival of old ones. Where conflict is continuous, *integration* may prove to be an adequate solution (North, Koch, and Zinnes 1960). Through integration, new alternatives are posed, including the opportunity for a new basis for cooperative effort and the formation of a new organization.

Integration may be achieved by clearly analyzing the sources of dissatisfaction leading to conflict in an effort to discover areas of common interest, then re-evaluating each of the positions in light of the other's position. Re-evaluation should lead to re-organization which provides the opposing forces a place for both their goals. Although this form of conflict resolution has been examined mostly in terms of int*er*group conflict, it may also be applicable to int*ra*group conflict.

A final solution to conflict, which is not really a form of resolution but is effective in ending the conflict, is to disband the group. Individuals may terminate conflict by leaving the group. Similarly, if enough members refuse to resolve the conflict and leave the group, they will have effectively avoided the conflict.

Communication and Conflict Resolution

There is no clear effect of communication on conflict resolution. Deutsch (1961) found that the outcome of a game was unaffected by allowing subjects to communicate with notes. In a subsequent study using oral instead of written communication, Deutsch and Krauss (1962) came to substantially the same conclusion. Both studies revealed, however, that the ability of one player to enforce threats against another player did affect the results.

Conflicting evidence is presented by Terhune (1968), who found that the opportunity to communicate (via written messages) increased the number of cooperative choices made. Terhune, though, did not use the same game that Deutsch, and Deutsch and Krauss used. This may account for the differences in their results.

In a recent study by Bliese (1971), "communication was defined as the opportunity for unrestricted face-to-face oral communication" (p. 6). The other studies did not define communication as broadly; in those studies communication usually consisted of simply passing notes through a screen or listening to voices over a loudspeaker. Bliese drew four conclusions:

1. There was no evidence to indicate that the opportunity to communicate made any difference in the ability of the dyads to reach the maximum joint payoff.

2. The split of the joint payoff was significantly more even in the communication condition than in the no communication condition.

3. Significantly fewer failures to strike a bargain occurred in the communication than in the no communication condition.

4. The opportunity to communicate was associated with a more favorable attitude toward the opponent and the game than the no communication condition. (Bliese 1971, p. 14)

In regard to the fourth conclusion, Bliese found that opponents who communicated thought "their opponents were more similar to themselves . . . were more likeable . . . [and] were more cooperative" (p. 14). They also found it easier to reach a decision.

The ability to communicate has either a facilitative effect on conflict resolution, or no effect at all. It is unreasonable to conclude, given the few studies that have been done, that the effect may be a detrimental one. Causes of conflict are normally very complex, and solutions are usually difficult to find. Each group is, in a sense, a unique entity, with its various personalities working together on certain tasks within prescribed limits. The specific causes of conflict are usually unique, so, also, are the solutions.

Bibliography

Adams, J. "Inequity in Social Exchange." In *Advances in Experimental and Social Psychology,* edited by L. Berkowitz, 2:267-99. New York: Academic Press, 1965.

Bandura, A., Ross, D., and Ross, S. "Transmission of Aggression through Imitation of Aggression Models." *Journal of Abnormal and Social Psychology* 63 (1961): 575-82.

Bass, B. M., and Dunteman, G. "Biases in the Evaluation of One's Own Group, Its Allies and Opponents." *Journal of Conflict Resolution* 7 (1963): 16-20.

Berko, R. M. "The Implications of Rollo May's *Love and Will* for the Study of Communication." Unpublished paper, 1971.

Berkowitz, L. "Some Factors Affecting the Reduction of Overt Hostility." *Journal of Abnormal and Social Psychology* 60 (1960): 14-22.

_____. *Aggression: A Social Psychological Analysis.* New York: McGraw-Hill, 1962.

_____. "Aggressive Cues in Aggressive Behavior and Hostility Catharsis." *Psychological Review* 71 (1964): 104-22.

Bliese, N. W. "The Effect of Communication Vs. No Communication in Two Types of Games of Strategy." Paper presented at the Speech Communication Association annual convention, San Francisco 1971.

Buss, A. H. *The Psychology of Aggression.* New York: John Wiley, 1961.

_____. "Physical Aggression in Relation to Different Frustrations." *Journal of Abnormal and Social Psychology* 67 (1963): 1-7.

Coser, L. *The Functions of Social Conflict.* New York: Free Press, 1968.

Daniels, V. "Communication, Incentive, and Structural Variables in Interpersonal Exchange and Negotiation." *Journal of Experimental Social Psychology* 3 (1967): 47-74.

Dollard, J., Doob, L., Miller, N., Mower, O., and Sears, R. *Frustration and Aggression.* New Haven: Yale University, 1939.

Deutsch, M. "A Theory of Cooperation and Competition." *Human Relations* 2 (1949): 129-52.

_____. "Trust and Suspicion." *Journal of Conflict Resolution* 2 (1958): 265-79.

_____. "The Face of Bargaining." *Operations Research* 9 (1961): 886-98.

_____. "Conflicts: Productive and Destructive." *Journal of Social Issues* 25 (1969a): 7-42.

_____. "Socially Relevant Science: Reflections on Some Studies of Interpersonal Conflict." *American Psychologist* 24 (1969b): 1076-92.

Deutsch, M., and Krauss, R. M. "The Effect of Threat on Interpersonal Bargaining." *Journal of Abnormal and Social Psychology* 61 (1960): 181-89.

_____. "Studies of Interpersonal Bargaining." *Journal of Conflict Resolution* 6 (1962): 52-76.

Deutsch, M., Epstein, Y., Canavan, D., and Gumpert, P. "Strategies of Inducing Cooperation: An Experimental Study." *Journal of Conflict Resolution* 11 (1967): 345-60.

Feshback, S. "The Stimulating Versus Cathartic Effects of a Vicarious Aggressive Activity." *Journal of Abnormal and Social Psychology* 63 (1961): 381-85.

French, J., and Raven, B. "The Bases of Social Power." In *Studies in Social Power,* edited by D. Cartwright, pp. 150-67. Ann Arbor: University of Michigan, 1959.

Hall, J. "Decisions, Decisions, Decisions." *Psychology Today* 5 (1971): 51-54, 86, 88.

Haney, R. D. "The Role of Encoding and Decoding Aggressive Messages on Subsequent Hostility." Paper presented at the Speech Communication Association annual convention, San Francisco 1971.

Harmon, S. J. "Crisis: Group Response to Emergency." *Journal of Communication* 21 (1971): 266-72.

Harsanyi, J. C. "Bargaining in Ignorance of the Opponent's Utility Function." *Journal of Conflict Resolution* 6 (1962): 29-38.

Horney, K. *Our Inner Conflicts.* New York: Norton, 1945.

Krauss, R. M., and Deutsch, M. "Communication in Interpersonal Bargaining." *Journal of Personality and Social Psychology* 4 (1966): 572-77.

Lane, I. M., and Messé, L. A. "Differential Inputs as a Determinant in the Selection of a Distributor of Rewards." *Psychonomic Science* 22 (1971): 228-29.

Levinger, G. "Kirt Lewin's Approach to Conflict and Its Resolution." *Journal of Conflict Resolution* 1 (1957): 329-40.

Loomis, J. L. "Communication, the Development of Trust and Cooperative Behavior." *Human Relations* 12 (1959): 305-15.

Maslow, A. H. "A Comparative Approach to the Problem of Destructiveness." In *Man and International Relations,* edited by J. K. Zawodny, pp. 156-61. San Francisco: Chandler, 1966a.

———. "Conflict, Frustration, and the Theory of Threat." In *Man and International Relations,* edited by J. K. Zawodny, pp. 166-69. San Francisco: Chandler, 1966b.

May, R. *Love and Will.* New York: W. W. Norton, 1969.

Miller, N. E. "The Frustration-Aggression Hypothesis." *Psychological Review* 48 (1941): 337-42.

Nash, J. F. "The Bargaining Problem." *Econometrica* 18 (1950): 155-62.

North, R. C., Koch, H. E., and Zinnes, D. A. "The Integrative Functions of Conflict." *Journal of Conflict Resolution* 4 (1960): 355-74.

Oskamp, S., and Perlman, D. "Factors Affecting Cooperation in the Prisoner's Dilemma Game." *Journal of Conflict Resolution* 9 (1965): 359-74.

Pepitone, A., and Reichling, G. "Group Cohesiveness and the Expression of Hostility." *Human Relations* 3 (1955): 327-37.

Rapoport, A. *Two-Person Game Theory.* Ann Arbor: University of Michigan, 1966.

————. "Conflict Resolution in Light of Game Theory and Beyond." In *The Structure of Conflict,* edited by P. Swingle, pp. 1-44. New York: Academic Press, 1970.

Rapoport, A., and Chammah, A. M. *Prisoner's Dilemma: A Study in Conflict and Cooperation.* Ann Arbor: University of Michigan, 1965.

Raven, B., and Kruglanski, A. "Conflict and Power." In *The Structure of Conflict,* edited by P. Swingle, pp. 69-110. New York: Academic Press, 1970.

Scheff, T. J. "A Theory of Social Coordination: Application to Mixed-Motive Games." *Sociometry* 30 (1967): 215-34.

Steinfatt, T. M., and Miller, G. R. "Suggested Paradigms for Research in Conflict Resolution." Paper presented at the Speech Communication Association annual convention, San Francisco 1971.

Terhune, K. W. "Motives, Situation, and Interpersonal Conflict within Prisoner's Dilemma." *Journal of Personality and Social Psychology* 8 (1968): 8.

Thibaut, J. W., and Coules, J. "The Role of Communication in the Reduction of Interpersonal Hostility." *Journal of Abnormal and Social Psychology* 47 (1952): 770-77.

Vinacke, W. E. "Variables in Experimental Games: Toward a Field Theory." *Psychological Bulletin* 71 (1969): 293-318.

Vinacke, W. E., and Arkoff, A. "An Experimental Study of Coalitions in the Triad." *American Sociological Review* 22 (1957): 406-14.

CONCLUSION

Analyzing group interaction, which entails breaking it down into its component parts and studying each part separately, is a sterile task unless it is followed by synthesis. Synthesis entails reassembling the parts, a process that allows us to grasp the whole phenomenon. The synthesizing process is crucial to a study of small group interaction because the parts of that interaction, including the operating variables, group composition, the task and group structure, are all interdependent; changes in one component produce changes in the others.

Small group behavior is extremely complex and, therefore, difficult to study. However, it is important to study because the consequences of interacting in the small group setting are so great.

> *The fragility of human interaction cannot be overstated. We cannot afford to underestimate both the destructive and therapeutic powers of the small group. Through group interaction we may become strong and productive human beings, or we may be crushed and relegated to the scrap heap of society. Participation in small groups calls forth from us our basic animal behavior and the most sophisticated of human activities, the capacity to communicate.* (Phillips and Erickson 1970, p. 218)

Bibliography

Phillips, G. M., and Erickson, E. C. *Interpersonal Dynamics in the Small Group.* New York: Random House, 1970.

NAME INDEX

SUBJECT INDEX

245

Roles, types of, 113-15; maintenance, 114-15; self-centered, 115; task, 114

Satisfaction, 8-9
Saturation, 169
Schizoid world, 213, 214
Seating arrangments, 199
Secrets, 109-110
Selective perception, 32
Self-centered roles, 115
Self-concept, origins of, 143-58; and aptitude, 153-54; and evaluation of others, 150; and homogeneous/heterogeneous grouping, 154-55; and influence, 152-53; and interaction, 155; and interpersonal attraction, 154; and past experience, 150; and reference groups, 151; communication and, 146, 151; definition, 149; generalized other, 147-48; "I," 147-48; "me," 147-48, 149; society and, 147
Significant symbol, 146
Social system, primary elements, 22-23
Socio-emotional development, 183
Socio-emotional leader, 125-27
Sociometry, 172-79; defined, 173; questionnaire, 175-79; star

sociogram, 177-78; target sociogram, 178; two-fold table, 176-77; uses, 174-75
Speaking rate, 194
Status, 20, 188, 193; and conformity, 71; and risk, 86; social, 20; subjective, 20
Stereotyping, racial, 189, 190, 192
Subgroups, 225
Symbolic Interactionist Theory, 151

Tactile communication, 199, 200
Task, 8, 20, 52-53, 81-83, 219, 223; and conformity, 73-74; and leadership, 134-35, 125-27; complexity and network efficiency, 168-69; functions, 21; group versus individual, 88-92; roles, 114
Tension, static and kinetic, 190
Territoriality, 196, 197
The War of the Worlds, 71
Transcription approach, 186

Vocal cues, 183, 184, 187, 191

Wheel network, 165-69

Y network, 165-69

Zero-sum game, 228, 229